Q & A SERIES
LAND LAW

FOURTH EDITION

Martin Dixon

University Senior Lecturer
Fellow in Law, Queens' College
University of Cambridge

Cavendish
Publishing
Limited

London • Sydney

Fourth edition first published in Great Britain 2002 by Cavendish Publishing Limited, The Glass House, Wharton Street, London WC1X 9PX, United Kingdom.

Telephone: +44 (0)20 7278 8000   Facsimile: +44 (0)20 7278 8080

Email: info@cavendishpublishing.com

Website: www.cavendishpublishing.com

© Dixon, M   2002

First edition   1993
Second edition   1995
Third edition   1999
Fourth edition   2002

British Library Cataloguing in Publication Data

Dixon, Martin
Land law – 4th ed – (the Cavendish Q & A series)
1 Land tenure – law and legislation – England
2 Land tenure – law and legislation – Wales
I Title
346.4'2'043

ISBN 1 85941 627 6

Printed and bound in Great Britain

INTRODUCTION

Land law holds a certain fascination for the student: usually one of dread. There is no point denying that it is a difficult subject and students face conceptual and practical problems of a kind not found in other branches of the law, none of which is helped by a phalanx of statutory provisions overlaying ancient principles of common law. Furthermore, an examination in land law cannot be treated as a series of separate questions, nicely compartmentalised. Anyone who attempts to understand land law is this manner is in for a rude awakening as the subject can be viewed only as an integrated whole. What the student learns in their first week of study may well be relevant in a question set on work they cover in their last week.

However, it is also true that land law has a structure: it does not (or rarely) run about on a frolic of its own. Understand the principles and how they relate to each other, and most students will see the land law jigsaw fall into place. The new edition of this book is designed to help students find that structure and to answer the practical problems raised by land law. The questions are presented in a logical order – the order that gives the student a slowly developing but clear picture of the subject as a whole. Of course, the answers can be taken on their own for what they are: an aid to revision and examination performance. However, this book can also be used as a teaching aid.

There are a number of new questions in this edition, and many have been updated by the addition of recent case law. I have also been able to incorporate the provisions of the Land Registration Act 2002. Although this revolutionary statute is not yet in force (anticipated in part in mid-2003), it will come to revolutionise the way we think about modern land law. Its effect will be as far reaching as the property legislation of 1925.

Martin Dixon
February 2002

CONTENTS

TABLE OF CASES

Tables of Statutes

CHAPTER 1

REGISTERED LAND

Introduction

Land lawyers in England and Wales fall into two broad groups. First, there are those who believe that the 1925 property legislation and, specifically, the 1925 Land Registration Act, established a new machinery for controlling the creation and transfer of land but did not radically alter the nature of property law. Thus, some textbooks will explain in detail the nature of, say, co-ownership or easements and add a section at the end of each chapter on the implications of 'registered land'. Others take the view that the system of registered conveyancing has produced fundamental changes in the nature of the rights and interests falling within the concept of 'land law'. Thus, on this view, a detailed understanding of the *mechanics* of registered land is necessary before a student can fully appreciate substantive property concepts such as easements or mortgages. There is, of course, merit in both views but even without the powerful theoretical arguments that could be used, there are practical advantages for the student in following the second approach. Since 1 December 1990, all of England and Wales is designated as an area of compulsory registration of title and it is now estimated that over 85% of all currently registrable titles are registered. In the fullness of time, therefore, unregistered conveyancing will all but disappear from the legal landscape. Moreover, and more importantly for students, examiners set problem questions which require the student to explain how easements or leases, or whatever, operate in registered land and no amount of pre-1925 property law will solve these puzzles. There is, for example, no point in discussing the doctrine of notice in registered land when it is entirely irrelevant. Even more importantly, the Land Registration Act 2002 has now received Royal Assent. It is not yet in force, as this will occur in stages in the next few years, with some provisions being activated by mid-2003. This new Act operates on the fundamental twin assumptions that registered land is intrinsically different from land of unregistered title and that unregistered conveyancing will fast disappear from the legal landscape. In due course, it will change the way we deal with registered land and it has already changed the way we think about it.

If a plot of land is described as 'registered', this means that 'title' to it (that is, ownership) is to be found recorded at the relevant District Land Registry. In contrast, 'unregistered land' is land to which title is not registered but is established by the title deeds of the particular property. Whether title is registered or not depends simply on whether there have been any dealings with the land such as to give rise to the opportunity to register or whether the 'owner' has applied for voluntary registration. As such, there is no magic about land being registered: it is simply a way of saying that the title is recorded and that dealings with the land fall within the procedures established by the Land Registration Acts. When answering questions in an examination, one of the first things to establish is whether the land is registered and normally you will be told. If you are not told, it is not important as there is no way that you can deduce whether title is registered from the facts of a problem, unless there is some obvious clue, such as 'X is the *registered* proprietor of ...'. After all, whether there has been registration of title does not depend on the quality of the land but whether an event has occurred which triggers registration of title.

Checklist

Broadly speaking, the system of registered land falls into four sections, the first three of which are more important for the purposes of an examination. The student should be familiar with these basic issues before tackling examination questions:

- *Registered titles*: what Gray and Gray (*Elements of Land Law*) call 'major interests'. These are the leasehold or the freehold and they are substantively registered in their own right with a title number. Most questions in land law examinations require no more than a passing knowledge of the mechanics of registering or transferring titles. Of much more interest and complexity are the rules relating to the transfer and creation of interests *in* the land such as easements, covenants, etc, and short term leases (that is, those which cannot be registered as titles, currently being for 21 years or less, but changing to leases for seven years or less under the Land Registration Act 2002. Registered titles continue under the 2002 Act).

- *Overriding interests*: these are interests in the land which will bind a new purchaser of the land automatically. They do not have to be registered anywhere to take effect against a third party. They currently are defined in s 70(1)(a)–(m) of the Land Registration Act 1925 as supplemented by the Land Registration Rules. In substance, most are inherently proprietary (that is, *capable* of binding third parties) but some are legal and some are equitable. No student should attempt a land law paper without a thorough understanding of overriding interests. This category will remain under the Land Registration Act 2002, although it will be reduced in scope and renamed 'interests that override' within Scheds 1 and 3 of the LRA 2002.

- *Minor interests*: these are those interests, nearly all of which are equitable, that have to be registered in order to bind a purchaser of registered land. If they are not registered, they are generally not binding against a purchaser irrespective of the question of notice. In essence, this class comprises all rights and interests in land not falling in the other categories. It remains as a concept under the LRA 2002, although not formally called 'minor interests'.

- *Registrable charges*: these are essentially mortgages. They, too, must be registered to take effect as legal mortgages (otherwise they may be equitable) and are considered in the chapter on mortgages. They remain under the LRA 2002.

Question 1

What were the objectives of the Land Registration Act 1925? Have they been achieved?

Answer plan

Pre-1925 problems:
- the mechanics of land registration – titles;
  - o overriding interests;
  - o minor interests;
- mirror principle;
- insurance principle;

- curtain principle;
- some problems:
  - o undiscoverable but binding interests;
  - o protecting the purchaser or the occupier;
  - o certainty or justice.

Answer

The 1925 property legislation, and the 1925 Land Registration Act in particular, inaugurated a fundamental change in the structure of land law in England and Wales. Prior to then, the mechanics of conveyancing were hindered by formalism and with danger for all but the most conscientious purchasers. Likewise, the operation of the equitable doctrine of notice meant not only that holders of equitable rights could have their rights destroyed through chance or caprice – because a purchaser might have no 'notice' of them – but also that purchasers of property might find their land burdened by legal rights of which they had no knowledge and which they could not have discovered even by the most diligent of inquiries. Similarly, the reliance on title deeds to prove ownership of land was both cumbersome and, for the purchaser, an expensive way to prove title, especially given the multitude of legal and equitable estates that could exist. The net result was a choking of the property market and at a time when the free movement of capital was essential for economic development. In conjunction with the Law of Property Act 1925 and the Settled Land Act 1925, the Land Registration Act (LRA) 1925 sought to simplify and codify. It aimed to bring certainty where there was obscurity and to bring equity where there was often inequality.

The basic tenet of the LRA 1925 was that title to land (that is, effective ownership) should be recorded in a register and guaranteed by the State. Registration of title would replace deeds of title and the register would reflect the totality of land ownership throughout the entire country. The original timetable called for full registration of all land within 30 years and it is a matter of some regret that only on 1 December 1990 did all of England and Wales become a compulsory registration area. It will be a while longer before near universal registration of title is achieved, but at least over 85% of all titles are now registered. However, in addition to establishing a mechanism for registering ownership, the 1925 Land Registration Act also established three other mechanisms for protecting rights in the land (that is, those usually owned by some other person). If correctly used, these procedures will ensure that rights in land are not destroyed by a transfer of a registered title to a third party. First, there are registrable charges, usually mortgages, which must be registered before they can be regarded as legal mortgages – s 26(1) of the LRA 1925. Once registered, these bind subsequent purchasers of the mortgaged land unless, of course, the mortgage is paid off (as most will be on sale, by the proceeds of that sale). If not registered, such mortgages take effect as equitable interests only and will be void against a purchaser unless protected by the land registration system in some other way.

Secondly, there are overriding interests. These are interests, statutorily defined in s 70(1) of the LRA 1925, that take effect against a purchaser automatically; that is, they require no registration and the doctrine of notice is irrelevant – ss 20 and 23 of the LRA 1925. It is immaterial whether such interests are legal or equitable, so long as they fall within one of the defined classes defined in s 70(1) of the LRA 1925. The logic behind the automatic effect of such interests is that they comprise such rights as *should* be obvious to a purchaser on physical inspection of the property or the title documents (for example, legal easements – s 70(1)(a)), or are such that they benefit the community as a whole without seriously restricting a purchaser's enjoyment of the land (for example, liability in respect of embankments, sea and river walls – s 70(1)(d)). Whether this logic is still persuasive remains to be seen.

Thirdly, there are minor interests. This category essentially comprises all other interests that may subsist in or over land (s 3(xv) of the LRA 1925). In order to bind a purchaser, such interests, whether legal or equitable (in practice, nearly all are equitable), must be protected by entry on the register, either by way of a notice, caution, inhibition or restriction. Actual notice of the right (or lack of it) is irrelevant – s 59(6) of the Land Registration Act: the minor interest is binding if registered, void against a purchaser for value if not (ss 20 and 23 of the LRA 1925).

This reclassification of land law rights (proprietary rights) obviously places much more emphasis on statutory definition than it does on the legal or equitable quality of a right. Likewise, in registered land, it is clear that the doctrine of notice – particularly whether the purchaser knows of the existence of a right or interest – is irrelevant. Such a radical shift was designed to relieve the conveyancing logjam as well as to bring certainty and stability for persons with interests in land owned by another. In this connection, it is often said that the LRA 1925 was premised on three principles: the mirror principle; the curtain principle; and the insurance principle. The mirror principle suggests that the register should be a mirror of all the proprietary rights – both estates and interests – that exist in any given piece of land. Thus, the register should amount to a comprehensive picture of the land for any prospective purchaser. Obviously, however, this is not the case with the 1925 Act. The inclusion of overriding interests denies the mirror principle. In itself, this is not a cause of serious criticism. Overriding interests were not an accident. They were deliberately created by the legislature and given automatic effect precisely because they should be obvious to any prospective purchaser. The problem is, however, that social and judicial developments have enlarged the opportunity for the existence of overriding interests with the result that a purchaser cannot always determine whether such interests exist by inspection of the land or title documents. The most obvious example is the right of equitable co-ownership, stemming from *Pettitt v Pettitt*, whose effect under s 70(1)(g) on an unwary purchaser was first fully appreciated in *Williams and Glyn's Bank v Boland* (see also the 'hidden' occupation in *Malory v Cheshire Homes* (2002)). Another is the equitable estoppel easement said to fall within s 70(1)(a) in *Celsteel v Alton*, and a recent example is *Ferrishurst Ltd v Wallcite Ltd* (1998) where the plaintiff's overriding interest in respect of the property (an option to purchase the land) was undiscoverable because his 'actual occupation' (see s 70(1)(g) of the LRA 1925) extended only to part of that property. This difficulty concerning overriding interests is one reason why the Law Commission recommended a reduction in their scope and effect (Law Comm 271) and this has now been implemented in Scheds 1 and 3 of the LRA 2002.

The curtain principle is, perhaps, the most ambitious motive behind the 1925 Act. The aim is to keep certain types of equitable interests off the register completely. Such equitable rights, being those taking effect behind a trust, will not bind a purchaser on sale of the land because of overreaching. In essence, a purchaser will not be concerned with such equitable rights – they are behind the curtain – so long as purchase money is paid to two trustees: s 2 of the Law of Property Act 1925. The equitable interests then take effect in that purchase money, so that, instead of having a right (or share) in land, the equitable owner has a right in money. Such a system works well when the statutory requirement of two trustees exists. However, the direct result of *Pettitt* and *Bull v Bull* is that, on many occasions, there will be just one trustee of land and so overreaching will not be possible. In such circumstances, a purchaser must look behind the curtain to determine whether any equitable interests exist and then must negotiate with the equitable owners as required. As *Boland* shows, if the curtain is not raised, the purchaser can easily be bound by such equitable interests. This problem clearly involves balancing the protection of the purchaser and protection for the occupier of land and it arose largely due to social and judicial changes (viz, the rise of the equitable co-owner through the *Pettitt* rules). Cases such as *Abbey National Building Society v Cann, Woolwich Building Society v Dickman* and *Birmingham Midshires Mortgage Services Ltd v Sabherwal (Sudesh)* illustrate that the full implications of this delicate balancing act are still being worked out.

Finally, there is the insurance principle or, rather, the idea that, once title is registered, the State guarantees the authenticity and effectiveness of that title against the world: ss 19, 20 and 69 of the LRA 1925. Obviously, such a system cannot be absolute in its effect and there are provisions for rectification of the register in cases where registration has produced hardship or inequity: s 82 of the LRA 1925. The potential wide ranging discretion given to the court under this section once caused some concern in the Law Commission (Report No 158) (see, for example, *Argyle Building Society v Hammond*) as it could be used to undermine significantly the sanctity of registered title. This fear has not been realised in practice and, in any event, the Court of Appeal in *Norwich and Peterborough BS v Steed* (1992) has made it clear that the court's power to order rectification is not 'at large' but can be exercised only within the confines of s 82 of the LRA (confirmed in *Horrill v Cooper* (2000)). A second limb of the 'insurance principle' is to be found in s 83 of the LRA 1925 (as amended by s 2 of the LRA 1997) which stipulates the circumstances in which a person suffering loss by reason of the operation of the registration system can receive an indemnity (money compensation). Although it is not always the case that compensation will reflect the real loss to the person injured (for example, he may have preferred to use the right denied rather than receive its value), these provisions (especially after their amendment in 1997) support strongly the effectiveness of the land registration system.

On a general level then, the LRA 1925 has been a success. It introduced certainty, fairness and relative simplicity to a system of conveyancing that was completely unsuited to the modern age. Of course, there were and still are problems of detail and the question of undiscoverable overriding interests has produced an overhaul of the law in the Land Registration Act 2002. This new Act goes a long way to meet these concerns. Indeed, the Land Registration Act 2002 goes much further than a mere tinkering with the system, though whether its system of 'electronic conveyancing' becomes a reality in the near future is less certain. Currently, there is a tension between the purchaser of land and the occupier of it, but generally speaking the provisions on overreaching can deal with this if the statutory mechanisms are observed. It is no fault of the LRA 1925 that the incidence of single trustee co-ownership (*Pettitt*) has increased. This does produce problems but the way to tackle this is to establish clear rules on *when* joint ownership of property can arise rather than to alter the machinery which merely regulates it. Fortunately, decisions such as *Lloyds Bank v Rosset* and *Cann* are proving that this is possible.

Notes

This is a standard question on the scheme of the 1925 registration system. The basic answer to the question will be known to most students but, correspondingly, it can be quite difficult to score highly with such well worn material. Examiners will be looking for originality and criticism and to this end a thorough understanding of the Land Registration Act 2002 and the reasons for its enactment is invaluable.

Question 2

In 1991, Abigail sold her large farm, title to which is registered, to Bernadette. At the time of purchase, Bernadette's solicitor made an official search of the register and obtained a clear certificate. Unfortunately, the search was carried out by an inexperienced clerk and failed to reveal a restrictive covenant correctly registered against the land for the benefit of the adjoining farm owned by Roger. The covenant stipulated that no trade or business other than farming may be carried on the land. When walking over the farm on the day after she has been registered with title, Bernadette discovers that Zeus, a new age squatter, has established a home in a derelict farm cottage. Next door, Bernadette finds Lydia who claims to have been paying rent to Abigail for the last four years under an agreement that she could live in the cottage for 10 years. Lydia produces a written record of the agreement typed on a plain piece of white paper.

Bernadette comes to you for advice as she wants to build an out-of-town supermarket on part of the site and, in any event, wants possession of the cottages.

Answer plan

The following should be discussed:
- effect of registration as owner:
  - overriding interests;
  - minor interests;
- primacy of register over search certificate;
- rectification and indemnity.

Answer

When Bernadette is registered as proprietor of the farm, the estate in the land is transferred to her statutorily under s 19 of the Land Registration Act (LRA) 1925. However, under s 20 of the LRA 1925, a registered owner takes the land subject to any minor interests appearing on the register and any overriding interests, despite apparent comments to the contrary in *Malory v Cheshire Homes* (2002). It is necessary, therefore, to establish whether Bernadette's registered title is subject to any adverse interests which may prohibit her proposed development. Secondly, if Bernadette's title is so encumbered, there arises the question of rectification or indemnity.

(a) The restrictive covenant

Bernadette will be unable to build the proposed supermarket if she is bound by the restrictive covenant. Assuming that all the conditions for its enforceability required by the law of freehold covenants are established (see Chapter 8), the issue turns on whether the restrictive covenant has been properly protected within the system of registered land: in other words, whether it has been protected as a minor interest, usually by way of notice: s 20(1) of the LRA 1925.

When Bernadette requested a search from the Land Registry, she received a clear search certificate. However, it is clear from *Parkash v Irani Finance Ltd* (1970) that it is the *register* itself that is conclusive, irrespective of any statements made on an official certificate or by an officer of the Registry. In our case, therefore, Bernadette is bound by the restrictive covenant because it has been properly registered, and this is so even though she is entirely blameless. Of course, Bernadette can make an application to the Lands Tribunal under s 84 of the Law of Property Act 1925 to have the restrictive covenant discharged if she wishes to proceed with her proposed development, but as a matter of property law it is binding on her.

It is possible that Bernadette will be eligible for a statutory indemnity under s 83(2) of the LRA 1925 (as amended by s 2 of the LRA 1997) if it can be established that she suffered loss because 'an error or omission has occurred *in the register*'. As it is not certain that this is possible (that is, because the error was not in the register itself), she should be advised to sue the Land Registry in negligence (*Minister of Housing and Local Government v Sharp* (1970)).

(b) The squatter

Zeus appears to be in the process of trying to establish a right to the land under the law of adverse possession. Again, whether Bernadette is bound depends on the application of the relevant provisions of the LRA 1925. In the case of adverse possessors, it is clear that they may have an overriding interest against a new proprietor under s 70(1)(f) of the LRA 1925, being a person having 'rights acquired or in the course of being acquired under the

Limitation Acts'. Thus, so long as Zeus was in the process of acquiring his rights on the day when Bernadette was registered with the title to the farm (*Abbey National BS v Cann* (1991); *Barclays Bank v Zaroovabli* (1997)), he has an overriding interest binding on her. Of course, if Zeus has not been in adverse possession of the cottage for the full limitation period (currently 12 years), Bernadette may take proceedings to have him removed: after all, if 12 years has not been completed, it is only the 'process' of acquiring rights that is binding and that process can be stopped under the normal mechanisms for ousting adverse possessors, such as an action for possession. There is a greater problem, however, if Zeus has completed 12 years adverse possession; in other words, if Bernadette's title is statute barred. In such circumstances, the 'statute bar' is binding on Bernadette under s 70(1)(f) and Zeus can apply to the Land Registry to be registered as proprietor of the land under s 75(2) of the LRA 1925. A successful application results in a 'parliamentary conveyance' of the title to Zeus (*Central London Commercial Estates Ltd v Kato Kagku* (1998)).

Assuming then that Zeus has completed 12 years adverse possession, the crucial question is, can the register be rectified in favour of him? Normally, the register will not be rectified against a proprietor in possession, and this is clearly Bernadette (*London Borough of Hounslow v Hare* (1992); *Kingsalton Ltd v Thames Water Developments* (2001)). However, even a proprietor in possession may have the register rectified against them to give effect to an overriding interest (s 82(3); *Malory v Cheshire Homes* (2002)). Thus, if Zeus has completed 12 years adverse possession, he can have the register rectified in his favour (because it amounts to an overriding interest) and Bernadette will be deprived of title to the cottage. This apparently makes a mockery of the principle that the State guarantees a registered title; so, is Bernadette entitled to an indemnity on the ground that she has suffered loss? Under s 83(1) of the LRA 1925 (as amended), any person suffering loss 'by reason of any rectification of the register' is entitled to an indemnity. Unfortunately, according to *Re Chowood's Registered Land*, where rectification is ordered to give effect to an overriding interest, the former proprietor does not suffer loss 'by reason of any rectification': rather, the loss arises from a pre-existing overriding interest which the register has merely acknowledged. The opportunity to reverse this rather technical construction of s 83(1) was not taken when other amendments were made by s 2 of the LRA 1997. It would invalidate Bernadette's claim to an indemnity. It is just possible that Bernadette might be able to sue the person who sold the land to her (Abigail) for breach of contract (that is, for not disclosing a matter materially affecting the land) but this will depend crucially on the terms of the contract and the events leading to its completion.

(c) The lease

Lydia is in occupation of the second farm cottage under some form of lease given to her by Abigail. Is this lease binding on Bernadette? Clearly, the lease claimed by Lydia is of less than 21 years duration (in fact, it is 10), so there is no question that it should have been substantively registered in its own right – it is not currently within s 8(1)(a) of the LRA 1925. So, the lease can only be binding on Bernadette if it is a protected minor interest or an overriding interest.

If this is a legal lease, then it constitutes an overriding interest under s 70(1)(k) of the LRA 1925. However, the lease is not made by deed – it is *written* but not in a deed – so the only circumstance in which it could be legal lease is if it amounts to a legal periodic tenancy where the period is three years or less – see ss 52(1) and 54(2) of the Law of Property Act (and Chapter 5). The question makes no reference to the period for which Lydia pays rent, we are told only that she has been in occupation for four years and expects to be free to occupy for another six. In such circumstances, the implication is against a legal periodic tenancy. It is worth noting, however, that, even if this were a legal periodic tenancy, binding as an overriding interest, there is nothing to prevent Bernadette from terminating it according to its own terms – that is, the giving of notice of one period.

It is more likely that the lease is equitable. There is written evidence of it and it is probably capable of specific performance (see s 2 of the Law of Property (Miscellaneous Provisions) Act 1989 and *Walsh v Lonsdale* (1882)). Equitable leases can be protected as minor interests, by making an entry on the register, but Lydia has not done this. However, this lease – assuming it is equitable – is still binding on Bernadette for its intended duration (10 years from grant by Abigail) because Lydia falls within s 70(1)(g) of the LRA 1925, being a person with a proprietary interest (the lease) in actual occupation at the time the property was transferred (*Abbey National BS v Cann* (1991)).

To conclude, then, there is every possibility that Bernadette must allow Lydia to occupy one cottage until her lease expires in six years time, assuming, of course, that, in the meantime, Lydia does not breach the terms of the lease and continues to pay rent to her new landlord. Although Zeus's rights as an adverse possessor are binding on Bernadette, she can evict him under normal process if 12 years have not elapsed. Should 12 years have expired, Zeus can apply to have the register rectified in his favour and Bernadette has no indemnity. She is also bound by the restrictive covenant even though it was not disclosed on the search certificate. Bernadette's real hope for substantive remedies lies in tort against the Land Registry and possibly in contract against Lydia.

Question 3

Oswald, a diplomat, owns a large detached house, divided into two self-contained flats, title to which is registered in his sole name. In anticipation of an overseas posting, Oswald advertised for a tenant of the upper flat and entered into negotiations with Terrance. Unfortunately, they could not agree terms but, on payment of a deposit, Terrance was allowed to occupy the flat while their solicitors negotiated an acceptable lease. Meanwhile, Oswald agreed in writing to sell the bottom flat to his daughter Connie should he be posted abroad. Hearing of Oswald's possible departure, Eric, his neighbour asked whether he could use Oswald's drive for easier access to his large double garage. Oswald readily agreed provided that Eric pay for resurfacing of the drive. Eric employs contractors and the drive is completely resurfaced. On hearing of his overseas posting, Oswald realises that he needs to raise some capital. Penny, his mistress, is willing to buy the property at much more than his daughter could ever afford. Realising that Connie has not registered her interest, he sells the entire property to Penny by registered disposition. Penny wishes to re-convert the house and asks Terrance to leave. She also erects a fence preventing Eric from using her drive. Connie hears of the sale and seeks to enforce her right to buy the bottom flat against Penny.

Advise the parties.

Answer plan

The following should be discussed:
- effect of registration as owner:
  o overriding interests;
  o minor interests;
- formalities of leases;
- conditions for proprietary estoppel;
- *Midland Bank Trust Co v Green.*

Answer

As the new registered proprietor of the land, Penny will be bound only by those overriding interests subsisting at the date of registration of her new title (that is, those in s 70(1)(a)–(f) and (h)–(m)) of the LRA 1925) and those subsisting at the date of transfer of the title (that is, that in s 70(1)(g) of the LRA 1925; *Abbey National BS v Cann; Barclays Bank v Zaroovabli* (1997)), as well as any registered minor interests (s 20(1) of the LRA 1925). In addition, there is the possibility that she could be bound by proprietary interests that are not protected in the proper fashion if there has been some fraud or bad faith associated with her purchase (see, for example, *Lyus v Prowsa Developments* (1982) and *Lloyd v Dugdale* (2001)).

(a) Terrance

The essential question here is whether Terrance has any estate or interest in the land and, if so, whether it has been protected against a third party purchaser under the appropriate mechanism of the LRA 1925. In order for a right to be binding on a purchaser, it must be *capable* of being binding; that is, it must be proprietary. In this case, there is the possibility that Terrance has a lease and, of course, this is a proprietary interest. For example, Terrance has paid some money and he appears to have gone into occupation in pursuance of it. Indeed, his lease in these circumstances would be a legal periodic tenancy of three years or less and binding (until terminated by appropriate notice) as an overriding interest under s 70(1)(k). (There is no possibility of an equitable tenancy because there is no written document within the formality requirements of s 2 of the Law of Property (Miscellaneous Provisions) Act 1989.) However, there is also the possibility that Terrance does not have a lease at all. He has, in fact, gone into occupation pending the negotiation of a lease in the knowledge that no agreement has been concluded with the landlord. Following *Javad v Aqil* (1991), there will be no lease if there was no intention to create legal relations, as seems likely while negotiations are still proceeding. Terrance will, therefore, be a 'tenant at will' which (contrary to its name) confers no estate or interest in the land, being a mere licence. If this is the case, there is no proprietary right capable of being a minor or an overriding interest and so Terrance must depart the flat at Penny's will. (See *Ashburn Anstalt v Arnold* and *Lloyd v Dugdale* (2001).)

(b) Eric

In the case of Eric, the position is not so clear. From his point of view, he will be claiming, first, that the right to use the drive amounted to an easement (right of way), and, secondly, that this easement is binding on Penny. First, does the easement exist? It is axiomatic that a right of way can amount to an easement but, in this case, there is the question of whether it has been properly created. Clearly, there is no deed nor even a written record of the agreement between Oswald and Eric: the easement is not legal and cannot be equitable within the *Walsh v Lonsdale* principle. However, it may be that Eric can claim the creation of an easement in his favour under the law of proprietary estoppel, as explained generally in *Taylor Fashions Ltd v Liverpool Victoria Trustees* (1981) and in respect of easements in particular, in *Ives v High* (1967). In this case, there appears to have been an assurance – by Oswald to Eric that he could use the drive – which was relied upon by Eric to his detriment. How else is it possible to explain Eric's expenditure on the driveway? This may well mean that Eric has the benefit of an easement, albeit an easement that must be equitable because of the informal manner in which it was created. If this is true, Eric has a right which is capable of binding Penny and will do so if it is either registered as a minor interest or amounts to an overriding interest (see the analysis in *Bhullar v McCardle* (2001)). Clearly, there is no registration in this case. However, following *Celsteel v Alton* and *Thatcher v Douglas*, an equitable easement which is openly enjoyed with the land may well fall within s 70(1)(a) of the Land Registration Act. In other words, estoppel easements may be overriding interests because, even though they are equitable and apparently excluded by the wording of sub-para (a), they are not *required* to be protected by notice on the register. Despite the fact that the clear purpose of the LRA 1925 was to make equitable easements subject to a requirement of registration, Eric can rely on *Celsteel* to enforce his easement against Penny as an overriding interest if the easement is 'openly exercised and enjoyed' (see Land Registration Rule 258). The position will be different under the LRA 2002 as equitable easements will no longer qualify as overriding interests: see para 3 of Scheds 1 and 3.

(c) Connie

By his written agreement with his daughter, Oswald has granted Connie some right in connection with the flat. What is the nature of that right? At first sight, it appears that Connie's right could be a 'right of pre-emption' – a right of first refusal to the land should the owner decide to sell. If this were the case, Penny may be able to ignore Connie's claim because, following *Pritchard v Briggs*, rights of pre-emption are not proprietary rights capable of binding third parties. (They appear to become proprietary when exercised.) That decision has, however, been subject to considerable criticism and the position will change under the LRA 2002 (see also *Dear v Reeves* (2000)). For the time being, it would be better for Penny to argue an alternative reason why she is able to ignore Connie's claim.

The better view is that Oswald has granted Connie an option to purchase the flat. The essence of an option is that the grantee (Connie) has an enforceable right to purchase the property at a moment of their choosing providing that any conditions in the option are fulfilled (see, for example, *Ferrishurst Ltd v Wallcite Ltd* (1998)). Here, the fact that the option is conditional upon the overseas posting does not alter its character because, if Oswald is posted, Connie has an enforceable right to buy at her choosing. Oswald has no choice if the condition is fulfilled (if he is posted) and he has no control over whether the condition will be fulfilled (see *Haslemere Estates Ltd v Baker* (1982) in support of this view). Assuming this to be an option, it is clear that it is a proprietary right, capable of binding third parties. Yet, once again, in order to be actually binding, the proprietary right must be protected in the proper manner under the LRA 1925. There is no prospect of the option being an overriding interest as it does not fall within any of the statutory definitions (for example, Connie is not in actual occupation under s 70(1)(g)). Hence, it can only be a minor interest. In this case, however, the option has not been protected by entry on the register and is, therefore, void against a purchaser for value, Penny (see, for example, *Bhullar v McCardle* (2001); ss 20(1) and 59(6) of the LRA 1925).

In such circumstances, the only slender hope – and it is very slender – is for Connie to establish that her unregistered interest has been defeated by fraud. However, even if Penny knows that Oswald is selling the property partly to defeat his daughter's claim, the better view is that this is not fraud – see, for example, *Midland Bank Trust Co v Green* (1981) in a similar context in unregistered land. In this respect, *Peffer v Rigg*, which seems to require the purchaser to act 'in good faith' if they are to be free of unregistered minor interests (where 'good faith' is defined almost synonymously with notice), is probably no longer good law. Only if Penny had promised Connie and/or Oswald that she would honour the option despite the lack of registration (and had, thereby, obtained the property more cheaply) could the purchaser said to have committed fraud – see *Lyus v Prowsa Developments*. If that were the case – and there is no evidence to support it – Penny would be a constructive trustee of the option for Connie and necessarily bound by it.

In conclusion, then, Penny is bound by the easement as it qualifies under *Celsteel* and *Thatcher* as an equitable easement binding as an overriding interest. She is not, however, bound by the option to allow Connie to purchase the ground floor flat and may ask Terrance to leave as he has no estate in the land capable of being binding on her.

Notes

Both Questions 2 and 3 revolve around the precise wording of the LRA 1925 and, for that reason, are sometimes viewed with reluctance. However, they are relatively straightforward so long as the 1925 Act is read closely. Particular attention should be paid to the provisions on rectification and indemnity. It is also apparent that these questions require the student to have some knowledge of other areas of law: such as how leases are created and when certain rights will be equitable or legal. The doctrine of *Walsh v Lonsdale* is crucial here, as is s 2 of the Law of Property (Miscellaneous Provisions Act) 1989.

Question 4

The Law Commission have proposed fundamental changes to the system of registered land and have now taken shape in the form of the Land Registration Act 2002.

Assess in general terms the reforms proposed by the Law Commission and the enactment of them in the Land Registration Act 2002.

Answer plan

This is a very broad question. The discussion needs to include an analysis of the following areas:
- problems with overriding interests: nature, extent, and undiscoverability;
- problems with minor interests: method of protection;
- adverse possession of registered land;
- formalities for the creation of interests in land;
- electronic conveyancing.

Answer

The land registration system inaugurated by the Land Registration Act (LRA) 1925 has been in operation in England and Wales for over 75 years, although it was not until 1 December

1990 that all land became subject to compulsory first registration of title. Throughout this period, the role of 'land' within the economy and the practical realties of property ownership have changed, as have the methods by which legal transactions can be undertaken. The Land Registration Act 1925 was itself an experiment in title registration and no one would argue that it was flawless. Time has revealed, however, that it was not fatally flawed.

The underlying rationale of the LRA 1925 was relatively straightforward: title to land should be recorded and guaranteed by the State through title registration and interests in land should either be obvious on physical inspection or noted in a clear and unambiguous fashion on the register of title. The advantages were also obvious: purchasers could buy in the certainty that they were purchasing land suitable for their requirements because the existence of 'hidden' burdens was minimised, and owners of interests in land, such as easements and covenants, had a relatively easy and inexpensive method of ensuring that their rights survived a conveyance of the land to a third party. These remain fundamental objectives of the land registration system. However, we now live in a different age, where both technological advances and the need to iron out deficiencies in the original 1925 system require that title registration be overhauled. The Law Commission has been with this task for some time, but the publication of Law Commission Report No 271 (*Land Registration for the Twenty-First Century: A Conveyancing Revolution*) including a Draft Bill brought the process to fruition. The Land Registration Bill 2001 has now become the Land Registration Act 2002 and parts of this far reaching statute will come into force in 2003, with full implementation over the next 5–10 years.

The new legislation tackles much that is inaccurate, unwieldy, incomprehensible, inconvenient and downright wrong in the 1925 system. Many of its provisions deal with technical matters that, while important, establish no new principle. These are the 'tidying up' aspects of the legislation. However, there is much that is groundbreaking or truly significant, not least the claim that the new Act will replace 'registration of title' with 'title by registration'. No longer will it be true that a person acquires title that is then registered: the act of registration and only that act will comprise the grant of title.

The first major issue is that of overriding interests: those rights that bind a purchaser of the land without entry on the register and irrespective of whether the purchaser has any knowledge or notice of them. Indeed, currently, they will bind even if the purchaser could never have discovered such rights (that is, they are undiscoverable, as opposed to undiscovered): as in *Chhokar v Chhokar* and *Malory v Cheshire Homes* (2002). Of course, the great majority of current overriding interests (see s 70(1) of the LRA 1925) are discoverable from a reasonable inspection of the property and it is a common error to believe that the 1925 system intended to do away with inspection of land by potential purchasers. Nevertheless, it is true that the mere existence of a category of 'overriding interests' compromises the integrity of the register and raises the possibility that a person will be bound by an adverse right irrespective of the circumstances in which he has purchased the land. Consequently, the new legislation proposes to reduce the effect of overriding interests, both by eliminating certain categories and by inaugurating a change in the way that we think about these important rights. Thus, the rights now falling within s 70(1) of the LRA 1925 will be reclassified. There will be some rights – the larger category – that will override a first registration of title: that is, will override the estate of the person who first registers when the land ceases to be unregistered land (see Sched 1 to the LRA 2002). These rights will include the major categories of legal leases of seven years or less, interests of persons in actual occupation of the relevant part of the land (reversing *Ferrishurst v Wallcite* and excluding the person in receipt of rents and profits who currently qualifies) and legal easements and profits. Other lesser rights, such as feudal franchises, manorial rights and the like will override a first registration for 10 years, after which they must be entered on the register if they are to endure. Secondly, there is a narrower category of rights that will override a disposition of registered land: that is, a sale of the land after it has been registered (see Sched 3 to the LRA 2002). These include the above categories narrowed down to reflect the fact that some rights which override a first registration may – or should – have been entered on the register after such registration if they are to be binding. Thus, any lease which requires its own registration is excluded (at first, this will be those over seven years: reduced from the present 21 years); a right of a person in actual occupation is excluded if the occupation is not patent (that is, if it is not discoverable); expressly granted easements will be excluded (because they will not exist at all unless entered on the register); and also excluded will be other easements not readily discoverable by a purchaser. Significantly, in neither category are the rights of squatters *per se* protected (there is no equivalent s 70(1)(f) of the LRA 1925), although most squatters will be protected under the 'actual occupation' category. Obviously, there is an emphasis on discoverable overriding interests (with undiscoverable ones generally not binding) and there is a connection with the way in which rights in land are to be created. The use of the concept of 'patent' occupation and the reference to easements which are not discoverable will, of course, generate much case law and it remains to be seen whether this charge will be worth the 'gain' of protecting purchasers from these currently binding rights.

A second area of reform is the way in which 'minor interests' are to be protected. At present, the provisions concerning the various forms of protection for a minor interest (notice, caution, restriction, inhibition) are complicated and unsystematic and, as we know, from *Clarke v Chief Land Registrar*, the caution offers only procedural protection despite being the only method of 'protecting' a minor interest that does not rely on the consent of the registered proprietor or some other person or court. The LRA 2002 will have only two means of registering 'minor interests'. A new form of restriction will perform the functions of the current restriction and inhibition and a new form of the notice will combine the functions of the current notice and the caution. The new notice will be either 'consensual' (for rights acknowledged by the registered proprietor) or unilateral (for rights not acknowledged by the registered proprietor). Unilateral notices can be cancelled, but will confer priority and protection if they are not, so offering a protection that the present caution does not. Similarly, despite criticism of the current rule concerning the priority between minor interests (that is that, *inter se*, the first in time prevails, irrespective of whether either are registered: *Barclays Bank v Taylor* (1973)), the Act provides that the priority of competing minor interests should remain essentially unchanged because electronic conveyancing will ensure that creation and registration occur at the same time. Likewise, although there seems to be no definition of a 'purchaser' for the purposes of land registration, there is equally no reference to 'good faith', so it seems that (fortunately) *Peffer v Rigg* will not be reappearing.

Thirdly, the 2002 Act envisages a new method of creating and transferring rights in land. At first, it will be possible to create an enforceable contract and a 'deed' in electronic form so as to satisfy the formality requirements that currently exist for the creation of rights and interests in land. However, it is clear that the ultimate aim is to ensure that many (indeed most) property rights concerning registered land will not exist unless they are entered on the register of title. Given that such entry also ultimately will be electronic, it seems that much of the old law about how rights in land can be created will be swept away. The act of creation will be the act of registration and this will be electronic. Eventually, this will apply to all registrable estates (freeholds and the proposed category of leases over seven years (over 21 years at present)) and to many other rights such as mortgages and expressly created easements. Clearly, this will revolutionise the way we think about rights in land and it is probably just as well that the Act also confirms that rights arising under proprietary estoppel are to be regarded as rights in land along with mere equities (see s 116 of the LRA 2002 and *Lloyd v Dugdale* (2001)). Even more importantly, the fact that creation and registration will be achieved by the same act means that the 'registration gap' will disappear. This will mean that transfers of land can be effected electronically in safety. Here, indeed, is the prime purpose of this part of the Act: to establish a system of electronic conveyancing. There is still much to be done before electronic conveyancing – 'paperless land transfers' – becomes a reality – but a reality it will become. The system will be managed by authorised property professionals who, in effect, will make entries directly on the register, thus creating, registering and transferring land and interests in land 'online'. Network access agreements will be needed, security issues addressed, training provided and fears overcome. However, the system may well be in operation less than 10 years after the Act comes into force. Judgment on its success will have to wait.

Finally, the Act encompasses a wholesale reform of the law of adverse possession as it relates to registered land. In effect, there will be no limitation period – that is, no time after which the registered owner loses their title. Instead, an adverse possessor will be able to apply for registration as owner after 10 years; the Registrar will then notify the 'true owner' (current registered proprietor) who, if he objects, will be given a further two years to evict the possessor unless certain exceptional situations exist. Failure to evict within these two years will result in the adverse possessor being registered as owner. There is no obligation on the adverse possessor to apply for registration after 10 years, so if he waits for 30 years, the registered owner still has a further two years in which to take action. Obviously this will mean – and is intended to mean – the end of adverse possession in the great majority of cases in registered land. The paper owner will be notified and will usually object and evict within two years. Moreover, given that the 'old' law of adverse possession will remain for unregistered land, this new system provides a powerful incentive for owners to voluntarily register their land.

These are far reaching reforms, and this answer really provides only some highlights. Thus, it will also become possible for the Crown to register its land for the first time, legal leases will be registrable above seven years (not the current 21), thus bringing many more titles on to the register. Even then, this period may well be reduced further to more than three years. The registered charge will become the only way of mortgaging registered land (no more long leases), charge certificates will be abolished and land certificates will be of considerably less importance and a new office of Adjudicator will be established to resolve land registration disputes. Let us hope that the Adjudicator is not overwhelmed.

Notes

This question should not be attempted without a grasp of the basics of the proposed reforms and the provisions of the LRA 2002. They are complicated and much remains uncertain. A knowledge of the 'old' system is essential as only then can the impact of reform be assessed. A book could be written – and undoubtedly will be.

CHAPTER 2

UNREGISTERED LAND

Introduction

On 1 December 1990, all land in England and Wales became subject to compulsory first registration of title. In effect, this means that on the first conveyance of title of an estate in unregistered land (or many other dealings with it: s 1 of the Land Registration Act 1997), it will become subject to registration requirements and, thereafter, cease to be governed by unregistered land rules. It is most unlikely, therefore, that a question in an examination will turn on the conveyance of an unregistered title unless it is made clear that the relevant transactions are all completed before 1990. That does not mean, however, that the rules concerning unregistered land are no longer important. There are many situations where questions concerning the enforceability of interests in unregistered land are relevant, especially as a vehicle for assessing understanding of other, substantive areas of law.

Checklist

As noted in Chapter 1, when land is described as unregistered, this means that title is to be found in title deeds rather than on any register. The law of unregistered land conveyancing is, then, related to the rules of property law as they stood prior to the 1925 reforms. However, it would be a mistake to think that the law of unregistered land was unaffected by the 1925 reforms. The Law of Property Act, for example, applies in full to unregistered land as it does to registered land. What is different is that the enforceability of rights and interests in unregistered land – being those rights and interests capable of existing under the provisions of the Law of Property Act – is governed by its own set of rules and procedures:

- Legal estates, both freehold and leasehold, are to be found in title deeds, not in a register. (The exception to this is the periodic tenancy for three years or less which is legal without a deed or any written document. Again, however, it is not registered anywhere.)

- As was the case before 1925 in unregistered conveyancing, it is still true that 'legal rights bind the whole world'. In other words, once it is established that a right is 'legal' in character, that estate or interest is binding on whomsoever comes into possession of the land. So, for example, a legal periodic tenancy or a legal easement will be binding on any purchaser of the land over which those rights exist. There is, by definition, no question of registration and no question of notice. The sole exception to this is the *'puisne* mortgage', a legal mortgage where the documents of title have not been deposited with the lender as security. Such a mortgage, despite being a legal interest, is registrable as a 'land charge' under the Land Charges Act 1972 as noted immediately below.

- With certain well defined *exceptions* (see below), the 'doctrine of notice' has no part to play in unregistered land. It is a common mistake to believe that it does. The reason is simple: by statute, unregistered land has its own system of registration for equitable interests. This was the Land Charges Act 1925, and is now the Land Charges Act 1972. One of the most frequent errors is to forget that in unregistered land there is also a requirement of registration for certain – indeed most – equitable interests. These 'registrable' equitable interests are binding if registered correctly under the Land Charges Act but void if not, irrespective of the question of notice.

- There is a small class of equitable rights which, either deliberately or by subsequent judicial development, are excluded from the operation of the Land Charges Act 1972. In other words, they are 'non registrable'. For these rights, their enforceability against a purchaser still does depend on the doctrine of the *'bona fide* purchaser of a legal estate for value without notice' (equity's darling). This is the only circumstance when notice should form part of the answer to an examination question in land law today.

Question 5

How does the Land Charges Act 1972 safeguard equitable interests in land? Was it successful?

Answer plan

The following should be discussed:

- the need for reform in 1925;
- the system in outline;
- inherent defects.

Answer

Prior to 1925, the conveyancing system in England and Wales was under considerable strain. On the one hand, purchasers of land were faced with many difficulties when trying to establish whether any other person had rights or interests in that land and, on the other, an owner of an equitable interest might find that an interest was destroyed by a simple sale to a purchaser who was unaware of its existence. To meet both of those problems, it was decided to move towards full title registration wherein all titles and many interests in land would be recorded and guaranteed by the State. It was recognised, however, that this mammoth task had to proceed in stages and that a set of transitional provisions was needed. The result was the Land Charges Act (LCA) 1925 (now the LCA 1972), intended to operate for only some 30 years. Unfortunately, it was not until 1 December 1990 that all land in England and Wales became subject to compulsory first registration. The introduction of compulsory first registration of title and the widening of those events which must 'trigger' first registration (s 1 of the LRA 1997) will ensure that the great majority of titles become registered early this century (over 85% currently are registered). Yet, the fact that title registration has taken so long to be introduced has only multiplied those defects that were inherent when the land charges scheme was introduced as a 'temporary measure'.

27

The LCA 1972 is something of a hybrid. On the one hand, it adopts some of the rules of the old common law: thus, it is still true with unregistered conveyancing that (all bar one) legal estates or interests bind the whole world. However, unlike most legal rights, many equitable rights would not be apparent to a purchaser on physical inspection of the property and their simple informality made them vulnerable in the event of a transfer of the land. To deal with these problems, the Land Charges Act substantially replaced the common law doctrine of the *bona fide* purchaser of a legal estate for value without notice. In its place, the LCA 1972 established a system of registration of its own.

The scheme of the Act is relatively straightforward. Equitable interests are divided into various categories known as land charges. These classes – Classes A–F – are statutorily defined and were intended to cover most of the equitable interests that could exist or could be created in land after 1 January 1926. Bearing in mind that these equitable interests would affect the title of land belonging to another person (that title not being registered), s 3 of the LCA provides that a land charge should be registered in its appropriate class against the name of the estate owner whose land is to be bound by the charge. The general purpose of this requirement for registration is clear enough. Under s 4 of the Act, if the owner of an equitable interest has not registered their interest as a land charge, it will be void against a purchaser of the land (*Petrou v Petrou* (1998); *Midland Bank Trust Co v Green* (1981)). To be more precise, an equitable interest that should have been registered as a Class C(iv) or Class D land charge will be void against a purchaser of a legal estate in the land for money or money's worth and an equitable interest that should have been registered in any one of the other Classes will be void against a purchaser of any estate in the land for valuable consideration. Of course, the corollary of this is that, if an equitable interest is correctly registered, it will be binding on any purchaser of the land as stipulated in s 198 of the Law of Property Act (LPA) 1925. It should be noted at this point that even an unregistered equitable interest is binding against someone who is not a purchaser, such as an adverse possessor. In principle, therefore, the position is relatively straightforward. Title to unregistered land is not recorded but lies in the title deeds as was the position before 1925. Similarly, it is still true that legal estates and interests are automatically binding on a purchaser (with one small exception – the *puisne* mortgage). The crucial change has occurred with equitable interests, most of which have to be registered as land charges if they are to bind the purchaser. If they are not so registered, they are void even if the purchaser had actual knowledge of them (*Midland Bank Trust Co v Green*).

Unfortunately, this simplicity masks serious difficulties that have emerged in the application of the LCA in practice. These problems are both inherent in the machinery as it was established, and have emerged because of changes made in the substance of property law since 1925. One of the most serious criticisms of the system of land charges is its reliance on a name based system of registration. Thus, an owner of an equitable interest has to register it against the name of the estate owner and all depends on both the owner of the equitable interest and any prospective purchaser knowing the correct name of the current estate owner. This has caused problems in three respects. First, there are some circumstances when a prospective purchaser has no way of ascertaining the name of the estate owner of the land he is purchasing and so no knowledge of whom to search against. So, for example, under the rule in *Patman v Harland* (1881), an intending purchaser of a lease has no right to examine the title of the freeholder and so no way of obtaining the names of previous owners of the land against whom he should make a land charges search. He is, nevertheless, bound by land charges registered against former estate owners because s 198 of the LPA 1925 overrides the lessee's apparent protection of s 44(5) of the LPA (*White v Bijou Mansions* (1937)). Likewise, now that root of title in 1925 unregistered land is only 15 years (s 23 of the LPA 1969), the purchaser may well have no way of ascertaining the names of persons who held the land previously: these names can be behind the root of title, if contained in a conveyance executed more than 15 years before the date of the impending sale. However, any charges registered against these names are binding on the purchaser (s 198 of the LPA 1925) irrespective of the fact that the purchaser could not have discovered those names. Although a partial remedy is provided by s 25 of the LPA 1969 (compensation), this is a problem that will only get worse the longer it takes to complete full registration of title.

Secondly, there is the problem of incorrect searches. It is axiomatic that a name based system will work only if all parties both register and search under the correct names. This is by no means a foregone conclusion. In *Diligent Finance Co Ltd v Alleyene*, for example, a wife had registered a Class F land charge against her husband, but not against his full name as shown on the title deeds. When the purchaser then searched against the correct name, they received a clear search certificate (which is conclusive: s 10 of the LCA) and the wife's rights lost their priority. An even more complicated set of circumstances arises where there is both a defective search and a defective registration. Thus, in *Oak Cooperative Building Society v Blackburn*, both the registration and the search were made in different, but incorrect, versions of the estate owner's name. In the event, the registration was deemed less defective than the search and took priority, but it was a pragmatic solution made necessary by the deficiencies of the system as a whole.

Thirdly, there is a problem with sub-sales. The LCA requires interests – such as a contract to buy the land – to be registered against the actual estate owner: s 3. If, therefore, a person is buying land at the end of a chain and their own vendor has not yet completed his purchase, the sub-sale should be registered against the head vendor, that is, the estate owner at the time the sub-sale was agreed. Obviously, this can happen only if the end purchaser is aware of the existence of the chain and, if not, they are likely to register their charge against the wrong person, as in *Barrett v Hilton Developments Ltd*. It will then be void if the property is sold elsewhere (albeit in breach of contract).

Apart from problems arising out of the use of a name based registration system, there are other difficulties too. Thus, when a purchaser has exchanged contracts with the vendor, only then will he be in a position to search the Land Charges Register for that is when previous owners are revealed in the title documents. Of course, by that time he is bound to complete the contract and also bound by any registered land charges. Again, it is only because of later statutory amendment, in the form of s 24 of the LPA 1969, that a remedy has been found which enables a purchaser to pull out of the contract if he had no actual knowledge of the charge which he subsequently finds. Again, in unregistered land, there is no equivalent of s 70(1)(g) of the LRA. So, even those owners of equitable interests who are in actual occupation of property at the time of a sale to a purchaser are not protected. As *Hollington Brothers v Rhodes* shows, these interests must be positively protected. Whether or not this was deliberate – and there is some doubt – clearly, it is a significant weakness in the system. Finally, there is one problem that is not so much inherent in the system as originally devised but which has emerged due to legal, social and economic changes in the use of land. As noted above, it is essential to the success of this legislation that virtually all equitable interests fall within its ambit. Unfortunately, that is not the case. There is a category of equitable interests which case law and, indeed, the LCA itself, establishes is not registrable. These unregistrable interests are, of course, still capable of binding a purchaser but their effect depends entirely on the capricious doctrine of notice. In this respect, one of the most important aims of the LCA, namely the virtual abolition of the doctrine of notice, has not been achieved. The equitable rights included in this residual category are wide ranging. On the one hand, there are estoppel easements (*Ives v High* (1967)) and, on the other, such matters as the right of re-entry in an equitable lease (*Shiloh Spinners v Harding* (1973)) and the right of a tenant to recover fixtures at the end of an equitable lease (*Poster v Slough Estates* (1968)). However, the most important is the right of equitable ownership behind a trust of land. Such rights are specifically excluded from the category of land charges by s 2(4) of the LCA 1972, mainly because they are overreachable on a sale by two trustees and so take effect in purchase money. As we now know, however, not all cases of a trust of land will have two trustees (*Pettitt v Pettitt* (1970); *Bull v Bull* (1955)) and, in such cases, the doctrine of notice plays a vital part in assessing whether the purchaser of the co-owned is bound (*Kingsnorth Finance v Tizard* (1986)).

The simple fact that there is an entire class of equitable rights that cannot be 'land charges' and whose viability still depends on the doctrine of notice is a serious criticism of the LCA. This criticism would have been tolerable had the LCA really been the temporary measure that it was intended to be. That, however, is not the case and, combined with the defects that were inherent in the system, the LCA has given rise to a difficult and complicated statutory mechanism. Of course, if one has registered an equitable interest properly and in the correct name, the system of registration is much more reliable than the system of notice and, in this respect, the LCA must be seen as a partial success. That, however, is not saying a great deal and it will be something of a relief to conveyancers, purchasers and owners of equitable interests when the system of unregistered conveyancing is fully replaced by that of the Land Registration Act 2002. Happily, that day is nearly with us.

Notes

This is a standard 'bookwork' question on the LCA 1972.

Question 6

In 1970, when he retired, Frank sold his large farm to William and produced a conveyance from his father dated 1935 as proof of title. William, through his solicitors, made an official search of the Land Charges Register against the name of Frank and his father. The certificate revealed a restrictive covenant, registered against Frank's father in 1934, preventing the building of more than one domestic residence on the farm. In 1970, Frank wished to live in peace and quiet (in the house he had built on the edge of the farm on land he now retained), and so a restrictive covenant was inserted in the sale to William preventing any trade or business on the farm except agricultural works. This was correctly registered against William. In 1982, William granted his daughter (Vanessa), for £100, 'the right to buy my farm when I retire from farming at half its current market value'. By 1984, William had fallen in love with a younger woman and wished to start a new life in Australia. Realising that his farm had quadrupled in value since 1982, he decided to sell the land to Derek, his friend who was also a property developer. Derek thought he might turn the farm into an industrial estate. Derek paid three-quarters of the market value in order to agree a quick sale. Derek searched against the name of 'Bill' (always having known his friend by this name) and Frank. He received a clear certificate.

Vanessa has just heard of the sale and wishes to buy the farm at the cheaper price. Derek has just received a letter telling him that he cannot build the industrial estate. Derek wonders whether this is true and asks whether, in any event, he can build a housing estate instead.

Advise the parties.

Answer plan

The following should be discussed:
- root of title;
- hidden charges;
- compensation;
- classes of land charge;
- effect of registration;
- possible fraud.

Answer

As indicated in the facts of this problem, all the relevant transactions and events are completed before registration of title became compulsory in England and Wales on 1 December 1990 and there is nothing to suggest that the land is of registered title. Thus, this problem falls to be decided under the rules of unregistered conveyancing. These rules, it might be noted, are a mixture of common law and statute, the most important being the Land Charges Act (LCA) 1972 (a replacement for the LCA 1925).

(a) Vanessa's claim to purchase the property

Whether Vanessa can claim a right against Derek to purchase the property depends on whether her father, William, granted her a proprietary right over the land and, secondly, whether this right is enforceable against Derek. First, there may well be some dispute about the nature of the right granted to Vanessa, for it may be that it cannot be regarded as proprietary in nature. On the one hand, the right may be a right of pre-emption – that is, a right of first refusal in the event that the grantor (William) wishes to sell the property. If this is the case, despite the wording of s 2 of the LCA 1972, *Pritchard v Briggs* (1980) suggests that a right of pre-emption cannot be regarded as proprietary until it is exercised (thus, registration would be effective from this later date only). However, the better view is that this is an option to purchase. An option to purchase is clearly an interest in land from the moment of its creation, whether conditional or not (*London and South Western Railway v Gomm* (1882); *Ferrishurst Ltd v Wallcite Ltd* (1998)). Moreover, it is clear than an option to purchase is an 'estate contract' within s 2 of the LCA 1972 (*Armstrong v Jones*) and, therefore, it must be registered against the name of the estate owner who created it (that is, William) if it is to bind a subsequent purchaser of a legal estate for money or money's worth: ss 3 and 4(6) of the LCA 1972. In our case, there is no evidence to suggest that Vanessa has registered her option as a land charge and presumptively, it is void against Derek – clearly, he is a purchaser of a legal estate for money's worth.

There is, however, one small hope for Vanessa. She may be able to claim that she was fraudulently deprived of her right because of dishonest collusion between William – the creator of the right – and Derek, the purchaser who obviously benefits from the fact that it is not binding on him. As the problem tells us, William wished to sell to Derek in order to obtain a higher price and he must have known that he would thereby defeat his daughter's claim. However, there is no suggestion that the sale was solely to defeat the daughter's claim or that Derek ever knew that she had an option to purchase. Indeed, even if this was the case, the House of Lords decision in *Midland Bank Trust Co v Green* makes it clear that that would not be enough to uphold the viability of an unregistered land charge against a purchaser. To recognise the validity of the sale to Derek, even though it destroys Vanessa's right, is to uphold the policy of the LCA, not to subvert it.

(b) The restrictive covenants

(i) The covenant against industry

If Derek wishes to build an industrial estate, he must establish that the covenant against non-agricultural trade is not binding on him. This will be difficult. Derek has obtained a clear search certificate and we know that under s 10(4) of the LCA 1972, an official search is conclusive. However, it is conclusive only 'according to its tenor' and, therefore, is conclusive only in respect of the names actually searched. Here, Derek searched against 'Bill'. 'Bill' is not the estate owner and so the clear certificate is of no avail. In fact, Derek will be bound by the correctly entered covenant under s 198(1) of the LPA 1925.

(ii) The restriction on building dwelling houses

In the original conveyance from Frank's father to Frank in 1935, there was a restrictive covenant against building more than one dwelling house. This had been registered against Frank's father and clearly was binding on Frank. The question arises whether it is also binding on Derek, the successor in title to the burdened land.

Assuming that there was originally some land that could benefit from this covenant and that the benefit of it has passed in orthodox fashion to the person now seeking to enforce the covenant, the question here involves consideration of the particular problems caused by the Land Charges Register being a names register. When Derek buys the land, he must investigate root of title. Under s 23 of the LPA 1969, root of title is 15 years and, so, Derek can rely for good title on the conveyance by Frank to William (his vendor) in 1970. This was the first conveyance which was at least 15 years old. Seeing this document, Derek will realise that he must search against William and Frank – both are revealed in the root of title. Of course, he would not have discovered the restrictive covenant because it was registered against Frank's father, of whom Derek knew nothing and, indeed, about whom he could not have known. The covenant is hidden behind the root of title and was in effect 'undiscoverable'. However, because of s 198(1) of the Law of Property Act 1925,

Derek is deemed to have notice of all covenants correctly registered 'for all purposes' and it is binding on him.

Derek is thus bound by a registered, but essentially undiscoverable, land charge. Fortunately, he may be entitled to compensation under s 25(1) of the LPA 1969 if he can fulfil the three conditions stipulated therein. First, it is clear that the transaction which caused him loss has occurred after the commencement of the Act (that is, after 1 January 1970). Secondly, we can infer that Derek has no actual (that is, real) knowledge of the charge, as he would not otherwise have purchased the property and, thirdly, the name of the estate owner against whom the charge was registered (Frank's father) was not comprised in any title document that Derek would have seen when purchasing the property. He would be aware of Frank and William only. Although, then, he cannot build, he can claim compensation.

Notes

See, also, the possibility that the restrictive covenants can be discharged by application to the Land Tribunal under s 84 of the LPA.

Question 7

Molly is the freeholder of a large house, title to which is unregistered. In 1988, Molly contracted to sell the land to Saul and even though he did not register his rights, Saul agreed in writing to sell the land to Oscar. Oscar has registered his rights against Saul but none of these sales have taken place. Molly also agreed to allow her son, Tony, to occupy the basement while he was working as her cook. Tony, being a clever law student, has registered his right against his mother's name. Molly's neighbour, Harold has just bought three horses and asks whether he can make a path for walking access across Molly' back garden to reach his field. Molly agrees but only after they have agreed by deed that Harold should pay £100 a year for the next 10 years for this right. The next day, Harold asks whether he can build a wider drive over part of Molly's garden in order to take his horsetrailer to the field. Molly agrees. Molly also grants a restrictive covenant in favour of Harold saying she will not build in her garden. Harold's solicitor registers this covenant against 'Moll'. In 1989, Molly sells the house to Peter who, using the same solicitors as Harold, search against 'Milly'.

Peter wants to build in his garden and to stop Harold's access. He asks Tony to leave and is faced with a claim by Oscar to purchase the land.

Discuss.

Answer plan

The following should be discussed:

- legal interests;
- classes of land charge and effect of registration;
- name registration.

Answer

This problem concerns the sale of unregistered land and the consequences for a purchaser of the existence of rights over that land belonging to third parties. In the normal course of events, the position is simple: Peter the purchaser will be bound by any legal rights over the land as 'legal rights bind the whole world' and will be bound by equitable rights if they have been correctly registered under the Land Charges Act (LCA) 1972. He must also be aware that certain equitable rights may bind him apart from registration if they fall into the category of unregistrable equitable rights whose binding effect depends on the doctrine of notice.

(a) The contracts of sale entered into with Saul, and the sub-sale to Oscar

Clearly, both these contracts of sale (Molly/Saul and Saul/Oscar) amount to 'estate contracts' within s 2 of the LCA. They are Class C(iv) Land Charges, being 'a contract by an estate owner [Molly] or by a person entitled at the date of the contract to have a legal estate conveyed to him to convey or create a legal estate'. As such, they must be correctly registered against the name of the estate owner if they are to bind a subsequent purchaser of a legal estate for money or money's worth – s 4(6) of the LCA 1972. On these facts, there is no doubt that Saul's contract with Molly is not binding on Peter. Peter is a purchaser of a legal estate for money and the charge is not registered. It is void: s 4(6). However, what of Oscar's estate contract, for he has registered his rights? Unfortunately for Oscar, he is a victim of one of the flaws in the system of unregistered conveyancing. Despite being registered, Oscar's estate contract is also not binding on Peter because, under s 3 of the LCA 1972, a land charge must be registered against 'the name of the estate owner whose estate is to be affected'. When Oscar entered into his contract for sale, he registered it against Saul, but Saul was not then (nor has he ever been) the 'estate owner' whose estate is to be affected. That was, and still is, Molly. So, as in *Barrett v Hilton Developments* (1975), a sub-purchaser under an initial contract for sale which is not completed at the time of the sub-sale, loses their rights against a subsequent purchaser of the land (that is, someone to whom, the land was sold in breach of the initial contract for sale) when they have registered against their vendor instead of the estate owner. Of course, Oscar may have a remedy for breach of contract against Saul, but even then, his remedy lies in damages only because Saul does not have title to the land and so the contract cannot be specifically enforced.

(b) Tony

As we are told, Tony has registered his right to occupy his mother's flat and we know that correct registration of an equitable interest will bind a subsequent purchaser: s 198 of the Law of Property Act 1925. However, it is axiomatic that only those rights capable of binding third parties (that is, proprietary rights) can, if registered, bind third parties. Registration can never make binding something which is inherently incapable of being binding (unless specifically provided for by statute). On this ground, Peter may be able to force Tony to leave, as it appears that Tony has only a licence to occupy the basement.

We are told that the occupation of the flat is granted while Tony acts as his mother's cook. The strong presumption on these facts is that this is a service occupancy, where the occupation is for the better performance of the duties of the employee, as in *Norris v Checksfield* (1991), or maybe occupation borne of family generosity or friendship (see *Gray v Taylor* (1998)). If this is true, the arrangement amounts to a licence and a licence is not an interest in land: *Ashburn Anstalt v Arnold* (1988); *Lloyd v Dugdale* (2001). It cannot, therefore, be binding on anybody, whether 'registered' or not. Of course, if it transpires that Tony has a lease, the registration is effective to bind Peter to the terms of that lease.

(c) Harold and the path

From the facts of the problem, we know that Molly allows Harold access by foot over her garden. This might be a right of way – an easement – that is well capable of binding subsequent purchasers of the land. We are told, further, that the right is created by deed. In such circumstances, it is reasonably clear that Molly has granted Harold a legal easement to use the garden path: it is a right capable of being an easement (*Re Ellenborough Park* (1956)) and is created by deed. In such circumstances, there is no doubt that Harold may continue to use the path because, as is the rule in unregistered land, legal rights bind the whole world. Peter is bound by the terms of the deed to allow Harold access on foot for as long as the agreement stipulates.

(d) Harold and the driveway

To some extent, this issue may be resolved as a matter of construction. If the right to use the path (above) encompassed the right to drive to the field, then the matter is as (c) above. However, this is unlikely, not only because the issue of the driveway arises after the easement over the path is created, but also because of the general rule in the law of easements that a specifically granted right of way does not include a more general right: *London and Suburban Land and Building Co v Carey* (1991). On this ground, Harold has no claim on Peter. He had no easement against Molly, so nothing can be binding on Peter.

However, it may be that Molly has otherwise created an easement in respect of the driveway in Harold's favour. Under the rules of proprietary estoppel, an assurance, relied upon to detriment can give rise to a proprietary right (see *Gillett v Holt* (2000)). In fact, in *Ives v High*, an equitable easement was created by just such a process. Here, it is arguable that Molly has encouraged Harold to believe that he may use the driveway and also that Harold had relied on that assurance to his detriment, viz, the construction costs. This may well be an equitable easement and, if it is, the question arises whether it is binding on Peter. In that respect, the general rule is that equitable interests must be registered as land charges to be binding in unregistered land: ss 3 and 4 of the Land Charges Act 1972. This is not registered. However, certain equitable rights – outside the statutory definition of land charges – are binding in unregistered land under the old doctrine of notice. According to Lord Denning in *Ives*, the equitable estoppel easement is just such a right. Although it is true that Class D(iii) land charges include 'equitable easements', Lord Denning suggests that this category refers to easements which would have been legal before 1925 but, because of the changes then made in the way rights could be created, can now be equitable only. Estoppel easements, by contrast, can never be legal, and so are outside Class D(iii). The consequence is that their validity is determined by notice and whether notice exists is a question of fact. If, for example (assuming an estoppel exists), the drive is under construction when Peter inspected the land, or the existence of the easement is obvious, or if Peter did not inspect at all but would have had notice had he done so, Peter will be bound, because he will have 'notice' (*Hunt v Luck* (1902)).

(e) Harold and the restrictive covenant

This particular aspect of the problem shows how difficult the system of land charge registration can be in practice given that it depends on name registration. Clearly, Harold has registered his charge against the wrong name and it would not, therefore, be binding against a purchaser who made a correct search (*Diligent Finance Ltd v Alleyene* (1972)). Likewise, Peter has searched against the wrong name and it is clear that he would have been bound had the charge been registered correctly: s 198 of the Law of Property Act 1925. In this case, therefore, we have two errors – a defective registration and a defective search. This was exactly the situation in *Oak Cooperative Building Society v Blackburn* and it is clear that the solution must be a pragmatic one. According to that case, it seems that precedence will be given to either the registration or search according to which is in the most sensible version of the estate owner's correct name. In our case, this might well be the registration (Moll instead of Molly). If that is the position, then Harold's covenant is binding on Peter. If, however, we were to take the view that 'Milly' was a more sensible version of the true name, the search certificate would take priority and, having been clear, it would absolve Peter under s 10(4) of the LCA.

Notes

Problems in land charges can be difficult as they are meant to highlight the inherent defects of the system which, in many cases, arise only in special or convoluted factual situations. Particular attention should be paid to the provisions for compensation for 'hidden' charges as these are not so simple as would first appear: for example, the name against whom the charge is registered must not appear on any relevant title deed (s 25 of the LPA 1969). Likewise, the different rules of 'voidness' for an unregistered charge can be troublesome. Students must be aware of the difference between a purchaser of any estate for valuable consideration and a purchaser of a legal estate for money or money's worth. If the land charge is Class C(iv) or D, for example, a purchaser of an equitable lease will be bound even if the charge is not registered, as they are buying 'only' an equitable interest. A person who is not a 'purchaser' at all is bound by all proprietary rights, whether registered or not: for example, an adverse possessor or a recipient of a gift.

Question 8

Compare and contrast the provisions of the Land Registration Act 1925 (as amended) and the Land Charges Act 1972 in respect of the protection they give to equitable interests.

Answer plan

The following should be discussed:

- brief outline of each system;
- the differences in registration procedures;
- the certificate and priority periods;
- protection of occupation;
- loopholes in unregistered land: notice.

Answer

The machinery instituted by the Land Charges Act (LCA) 1972 and the Land Registration Act (LRA) 1925 were intended to achieve the same objective, albeit that the latter was far more wide ranging than the former. In essence, both of these systems were intended to bring stability to the system of conveyancing in England and Wales by protecting purchasers of land and owners of rights over that land.

The LRA 1925 achieves this by ensuring that title to land and many interests over land are recorded or otherwise statutorily protected. In respect of equitable interests, the protection is two fold. On the one hand, equitable interests can be protected by registration as minor interests (by notice, restriction, inhibition, or caution) and, on the other, they may qualify as overriding interests under one of the categories defined in s 70(1) of the LRA. Indeed, it is the ability of an equitable interest to qualify as an overriding interest that gives registered land its advantages. Thus, under s 70(1)(g), an owner of such a right is protected so long as they are in occupation whether or not they knew they had a right (as may be the case with many *Pettitt v Pettitt* claims) and whether or not they knew that it should be registered (for example, *William and Glyn's Bank v Boland*). This is particularly attractive if the equitable rights are acquired informally, as with equitable estoppel easements under s 70(1)(a) (*Celsteel v Alton*; *Thatcher v Douglas*).

Of course, problems with registered land do exist. The fact that an owner of an equitable right need not actually register their right as minor interest poses something of a problem to a prospective purchaser. It undercuts somewhat the policy that all rights should either be registered or obvious (and, therefore, overriding). Thus, the curative effect of s 70(1) not only causes overlap with the minor interest provisions but may even amount to a disincentive to register. In the case of *Pettitt* type family interests, there is no doubt that registration is a hostile act and, in any event, registration of a right may alert a purchaser and so encourage them to seek overreaching by the appointment of a second trustee of the land or attempt to persuade the equitable owner to consent personally: *Abbey National Mortgages plc v Mostaga Saleh-Rad* (1998). Of course, the ability to overreach on the appointment of a second trustee (or to seek consent) is not peculiar to registered land, but this does highlight why a prudent equitable owner might wish to subvert the purposes of the LRA and rely on s 70(1) instead of registering their right as a minor interest. In fact, there are provisions in the LRA 2002 to deal with this occurrence.

The protection of equitable interests in registered land also has problems in other respects. Thus, the provisions dealing with the choice of method of protection are complicated and unsatisfactory. For example, because a notice can be lodged only by production of the land certificate, the consent of the registered proprietor is required. Conversely, a caution does not require the consent of the registered proprietor, but then only gives procedural protection to the owner and does not actually protect the right if the caution is not upgraded to a notice (*Clark v Chief Land Registrar* (1993)). Likewise, the LRA 1925 makes it clear that an equitable interest that does not qualify as an overriding interest or is not protected as a minor interest is void against a purchaser for value of the legal estate: ss 20 and 23 of the LRA. This position of principle has, however, been compromised by the decision in *Peffer v Rigg,* where Graham J suggested that an unregistered minor interest would be binding against a purchaser of the land who took the land in bad faith. While it is true that a purchaser will be bound by any equitable interests whether registered or not if there has been fraud ('fraud unravels all'), it is doubtful whether simply knowing of the equitable interest, which Graham J equates with bad faith, should be sufficient to bind the purchaser. This is clearly not the position in unregistered land (see *Midland Bank Trust Co v Green*) and it plays no part under the scheme of the LRA 2002. This will ensure that the old doctrine of notice is not re-introduced into registered land by a side door, a view endorsed in *Bhullar v McCardle* (2001).

Perhaps, however, these are but small problems compared to those found when considering the protection of equitable interests in unregistered land. It is often easy to forget that unregistered land also has a system of registration of equitable interests that is intended to give those interests the same degree of protection as is available in registered land. Unfortunately, this is clearly not the case and the LCA 1972 falls considerably short of this goal. In unregistered land, equitable interests can be divided into three broad categories. First, there are those equitable interests that are registrable as land charges. Land charges fall into six distinct categories: Classes A–F, the most important of which are Class C and Class D. It is, for example, in Class C(iv) that all equitable leases fall and, in Class D, that all restrictive covenants and most equitable easements are to be found. Following a similar principle as that applicable to minor interests, these registrable land charges must be protected by entry on the Land Charges Register in order to bind a purchaser: s 4 of the LCA 1972. In the case of Classes A, B, C (except C(iv)) and F, an unregistered charge will be void against the purchaser for valuable consideration of any interest in the land while Classes C(iv) and D will be void against the purchaser of a legal estate for money or money's worth. In short, as with registered land, registration means validity and non-registration means voidness, save only that the policy of voidness in the event of non-registration has been more rigorously enforced in unregistered land (*Midland Bank v Green*).

However, the system of land charges does suffer from one considerable defect: its lack of protection for persons with equitable interests who occupy premises. In unregistered land, the fact of actual occupation of property does not, of itself, protect any equitable interest of the occupier. There is no equivalent of s 70(1)(g) of the LRA (that is, overriding interests) as amply illustrated by *Hollington Brothers v Rhodes*, where an equitable lease was void against a purchaser for lack of registration as a Class C(iv) charge despite the occupation of the tenants. If this had been registered land, the purchaser would have been bound. It is unfortunate that equitable interests in unregistered land are not protected in this way and, indeed, on one view, there was supposed to be such protection in the Land Charges Act but the section conferring such protection was inadvertently omitted from the 1925 consolidating statute (see Harpum [1990] CLJ 277). Whether that be the case, the protection does not exist and the omission is unfortunate.

The second category of equitable interests in unregistered land are those 'family' interests which are overreachable as existing behind a trust of land. As with registered land, if there are two trustees of land or a trust corporation there is nothing the equitable owners can do to prevent sale or to remain in occupation of the property against a purchaser (*City of London BS v Flegg* (1988); *Birmingham Midshires BS v Sabherwal* (1999)), unless their consent is required under the trust or by order of the court (see Trusts of Land and Appointment of Trustees Act 1996) and such consent has not been obtained and the equitable owners apply to the court to enforce the consent requirement. However, if there is only one trustee, in registered land, the equitable interest may be overriding (*Boland*) or even a protected minor interest, whereas, in unregistered land, these equitable interests are not registrable (protectable) as land charges (s 2 of the LCA 1972) but can bind a purchaser only under the old doctrine of notice (*Kingsnorth v Tizard*). Although it will be rare that a purchaser does not have notice (for example, occupation will equal constructive notice of the equitable interest), it is undesirable that the inherently uncertain concept of notice should play a part in such a vital area as co-ownership of domestic property.

Indeed, it is not only with these equitable interests that notice is still relevant, for there is a third category of equitable interest within the scheme of unregistered land. These are equitable interests that either by design or by accident are outside the operation of LCA and are not within any of the Classes. These are unregistrable equitable interests whose validity against a purchaser rests on the doctrine of notice. They have no equivalent in registered land as the categories of overriding or 'minor' interests are all embracing and this will be confirmed under the LRA 2002. Of course, some such rights such as leasehold covenants cause few problems (although see *Dartstone v Cleveland*

(1969)) and this is why they were deliberately omitted. Indeed, equitable co-ownership would not have been a problem had the two-trustee trust of land been the norm. However, such matters as estoppel easements (*Ives v High*), equitable rights of re-entry (*Shiloh Spinners v Harding*) and a tenant's right to remove fixtures at the end of an equitable lease (*Poster v Slough Estates*) which have emerged as unregistrable interests since 1925 can cause difficulties, as these cases show. The existence of these rights means that a purchaser cannot rely with total security on a search of the Land Charges Register. There is always the possibility that an unregistrable but potentially binding equitable interest will exist that will affect the purchaser's title through the medium of notice. Such matters would not have been so important in practice had the LCA been replaced swiftly by full title registration, but only now is that coming to fruition.

Finally, there are some other differences in the application of the LRA 1925 and the LCA that can cause practical difficulties. An obvious one is the fact that the LCA depends on a system of name registration. The problems that this gives rise to are well known, as in *Barrett v Hilton* (sub-sales); *Oak v Blackburn* (defective registration and defective searches); and *White v Bijou Mansions* (hidden charges). These are difficulties that do not arise in the Land Registration Acts because the system is based on titles rather than names. Likewise, the fact that charging orders over equitable co-ownership interests can be registered, and therefore protected, in registered land (*Chancery plc v Ketteringham*) but cannot in unregistered land (*Perry v Phoenix Assurance*) only causes confusion. Last of all, it should be noted that the priority periods conferred on a person are different under the Land Charges and the Land Registration Acts (15 days and 30 days respectively) and that, in unregistered land, it is the official search that is conclusive – s 10(4) of the LCA (even if a charge is actually registered) – whereas, in registered land, it is the register that is conclusive – *Parkash v Irani Finance* (even if the official search is clear).

The LCA and the LRA 1925 have both done much to introduce certainty into the whole area of the purchaser and the equitable interest. There is no doubt, however, that, as far as protecting equitable interests is concerned, the LRA offers considerably more comfort than the LCA. Above all, the safety net provided by the concept of actual occupation under s 70(1)(g) of the LRA 1925 (and confirmed in the LRA 2002) provides a considerable advantage over the unregistered land system. Indeed, even for the purchaser, the registered land system has its attractions. Although the existence of overriding interests may seriously compromise a title, most of these interests are reasonably ascertainable on inspection of the property and, in any event, this will be reduced significantly by the LRA 2002. Those that currently are not, particularly the right of equitable co-ownership, is a problem that arises because of increased reliance on the *Pettitt v Pettitt* principles and not because of the rules of the LRA 1925. Furthermore, at least the purchaser in registered land has the benefit of indemnity provisions in cases where defective title registration causes loss. There is no such safety net in unregistered land. Moreover, the purchaser in unregistered land must always fear the existence of an unregistrable equitable interest that will be binding on him through the mechanism of constructive notice. These problems and the name based registration system make the introduction of country wide compulsory registration of title on 1 December 1990 very welcome. The widening of compulsory triggers under s 1 of the LRA 1997 necessarily provided further impetus and the entry into force of the LRA 2002 is likely to encourage the voluntary registration of title.

Notes

This question can be answered in many ways, although the central point is the lack of protection for occupiers and the lack of a 'safety net' in unregistered land. We could go on to consider whether the LRA 1925 itself is now so flawed because of changes in the social pattern of land use that it is as bad as the LCA! This would be an extreme view, but some credence is given by Law Comm No 271.

CHAPTER 3

CO-OWNERSHIP

Introduction

The law relating to concurrent interests in property (co-ownership) has changed considerably in recent years. This is a result of both changes in the legislative framework surrounding co-ownership (that is, the Trusts of Land and Appointment of Trustees Act (TOLATA) 1996) and because the increased incidence of co-ownership has revealed many practical problems for which the 1925 legislation did not clearly provide. Many difficulties have been caused by social and economic changes in the pattern of property ownership, particularly of residential or domestic houses. The emergence of the *Pettitt v Pettitt* and *Lloyds Bank v Rosset* line of authority, whereby a partner or spouse can acquire an interest in a house that formally belongs to someone else, has done much to channel the law of co-ownership in new directions. Co-ownership is no longer confined to commercial or business situations but is virtually an expected attribute of domestic life. The Law of Property Act 1925, which established the original scheme of co-ownership, was ill-equipped to deal with this shift of emphasis and the changes made by the TOLATA (which came into force on 1 January 1997) have done much to remedy deficiencies in the law, although many would argue that much remedial work had been done already by sensible judicial application of existing statute. As we shall see, where land (for example, a house) is deliberately co-owned, in the sense of having been conveyed originally to two or more people (for example, husband and wife, or an unmarried couple), few serious problems exist. However, where co-ownership arises informally – usually in respect of land that was conveyed originally to only one person (for example, the husband alone) – considerable practical problems can arise and not even the new legislation has dealt with all of these.

Checklist

In this chapter, the various issues relating to co-ownership will be considered in turn and the student needs to have an understanding of the following issues. First, there is the question of the statutory machinery and the reasons for the 1925 reforms. This must be addressed in the light of the legislative changes made by the TOLATA and the reasons for them. Without this background understanding, much of the law of co-ownership will make no sense. Secondly, there is the question of the actual share that each co-owner really has in co-owned land: problems of severance and the like. Thirdly, there are important issues as to how implied co-ownership can arise or, in other words, when does single ownership turn into co-ownership without any formal documentation. This is the law of resulting and constructive trusts based on *Pettitt v Pettitt* and *Lloyds Bank v Rosset*. Fourthly, there are issues about the consequences for purchasers when buying land subject to co-ownership, especially if that co-ownership has been informally created. In this context, 'purchasers' means mortgagees (banks, building societies, etc) who lend money and so 'purchase' an interest in the co-owned land as security. In an examination, it is quite common for at least two of these issues to be addressed in different questions and it is quite possible for one question to raise all four matters.

Question 9

To what extent did the Trusts of Land and Appointment of Trustees Act 1996 alter significantly the statutory scheme regulating co-owned land?

Answer plan

The answer should include a discussion on the following areas:
- brief description of the meaning of 'co-owned land';
- the statutory scheme prior to the TOLATA;
- judicial application of the pre-TOLATA scheme;
- the effect of the TOLATA.

Answer

Concurrent ownership of land describes the situation where two or more persons are entitled to the simultaneous enjoyment of property, whether that land be used for commercial or residential purposes. Prior to the 1925 legislative reforms, there were several forms of co-ownership: in other words, the legal relationship between the individual co-owners could take various forms. However, this caused numerous problems and one of the most important reforms of the Law of Property Act was to limit the types of co-ownership that could be created thereafter. From 1926, land may be co-owned only under a joint-tenancy or, alternatively, under a tenancy in common. In a joint-tenancy, as far as the rest of the world is concerned, the individual persons are as one owner (although, of course, as between themselves they do have separate rights). So, there is but one title to the land and the individuals own that title jointly. By way of contrast, under a tenancy in common, although each tenant in common is in physical possession of the whole of the property in common with the others (that is, there is no partition), nevertheless they are regarded as having a distinct share in the land (for example, one-third). Consequently, a tenancy in common is sometimes known as 'an undivided share in land'.

This simple picture is complicated by further reforms introduced by the LPA 1925 that made crucial changes in the legal scheme for holding co-owned land. Under the 1925 Act, a legal tenancy in common cannot exist – s 1(6) – so eliminating the prospect of multiple legal titles for co-owned land. So, after 1925, all legal titles to co-owned land must take the form of a joint-tenancy even if the document of conveyance purports to create a tenancy in common. This means that, whenever land is conveyed to two or more persons for concurrent ownership, it is statutorily deemed to be conveyed to them as joint-tenants of the legal title (ss 34 and 36 of the LPA). Originally, this was a special form of joint-tenancy because, under the LPA, the statutory joint-tenants were trustees for sale of the legal title. So, these joint-tenant legal owners held the land on such trusts for the equitable owners (who may be themselves!) and, in equity, the co-ownership could take the form of either a joint-tenancy or tenancy in common according to the circumstances existing when the land was conveyed.

To give two examples: if 26 Grange Road is conveyed to A and B as joint tenants, each paying half the purchase price, this will take effect as a conveyance to A and B as joint-tenant trustees of the legal title, holding on trust for themselves as joint-tenants in equity (because they paid the price equally). Likewise, if a house is conveyed to Y and Z 'as tenants in common, 50% each', this will take effect as a conveyance to Y and Z at law as joint-tenant trustees upon the statutory trusts because a tenancy in common cannot exist at law but holding on trust for themselves in equity as tenants in common, half each (because this is expressed in the conveyance). The use of the trust is, therefore, a device to ensure that all legal title to co-owned land is held as a joint-tenancy whilst also ensuring that in equity (where, after all, the real interest lies), the co-owners can be either joint-tenants or tenants in common as before. Frequently, as in the two examples above, the 'trustees' will be the same people as the 'beneficiaries', and there is no real change in their rights to use and enjoy the land.

Obviously, the use of the trust device must have had a purpose and it is clear that the overriding policy aim was to make co-owned land more saleable while at the same time giving some degree of protection to the rights of all the co-owners, especially those not on the legal title. To this end, as noted, the original statutory trust was a trust for sale, meaning that the trustees were under a duty to sell the property unless they all agreed to postpone sale. Of course, in the normal course of events, at least with residential property, the two trustees (for example, husband and wife) would obviously agree to postpone sale because they had purchased the property to live in it. Yet, if such agreement to postpone sale could not be maintained and the legal owners disagreed, an application could be made to the court under what was then s 30 of the LPA for an order for sale. Such an order would be granted – because of the duty to sell – unless there were pressing contrary reasons relating to the purpose for which the land was originally acquired (*Jones v Challenger*; *Banker's Trust v Namdar*). Moreover, when a sale did take place, the statutory mechanism revealed its considerable advantages First, because the legal title must be held by way of joint-tenancy, the purchaser need investigate only one title, irrespective of the number or type of co-owners that exist in equity. Secondly, s 34(2) of the LPA limited the number of potential legal co-owners (that is, trustees) to four – being the first four persons named in a conveyance.

Thus, the purchaser only ever had a maximum of four people to deal with and, in most domestic situations, it will only be two. Thirdly, because there must be a joint-tenancy of the legal title, the right of survivorship applies. So, if one legal owner dies, no formal documents are need to transfer title to the remaining legal owners. Fourthly, if there are two or more legal owners (trustees), any purchaser automatically will receive the land free of the rights of all the equitable owners, be they equitable joint-tenants or equitable tenants in common because, by statute, a payment to two or more trustees overreaches the equitable interests existing behind the trust (s 2 of the LPA; *City of London BS v Flegg* (1987); *State Bank of India v Sood* (1997)). Of course, the equitable owners' rights are not destroyed: rather, they take effect in the purchase money paid by the purchaser which is then held on trust by the trustees in the same way that they held the legal title to the property.

It should be apparent from this that the changes made by the 1925 Act greatly assisted the easy transfer of co-owned land, both by simplifying the conveyancing machinery and by protecting the purchaser through the device of overreaching. However, this original scheme was not without its problems. First and most strikingly, the equitable owners may have their rights transformed from rights over land to rights in money by action of the legal owners conducting an overreaching transaction. Secondly, as noted, the duty to sell, under the then trust for sale, meant that disputes between trustees (that is, legal owners) very often resulted in a court-ordered sale, even if one party wished to remain in the property. Thirdly, in theory, the equitable owners' rights were regarded as interests in money, not land (because of the doctrine of conversion), and this could affect the rights of the equitable owners to require the legal owners to allow them into possession. This was mitigated somewhat by *Bull v Bull* (1955), but there were further problems in ordering a co-owner in possession to pay rent to the other if the latter were excluded, although, again, *Re Petrou* alleviated this (the court 'found' a general equitable power to order such a payment).

To meet these difficulties, and generally to re-cast the scheme of co-ownership for the modern era, the Trusts of Land and Appointment of Trustees Act (TOLATA) 1996 was enacted based on Law Commission Report No 181. This came into force on

1 January 1997 and applies to virtually all co-ownership trusts. Its effect is, broadly, to ensure that the legal scheme of co-ownership accords with how co-owned land is owned in practice. However, many of the changes simply put into statutory form the pre-existing judicial gloss that had been placed on the original 1925 scheme.

First, and most importantly, existing trusts for sale of land become simple *trusts of land* and all future co-ownership trusts must operate under the trust of land scheme found in the TOLATA. The land remains held by trustees (still a maximum of four) on trust for the equitable owners but the nature of the trust has changed. There is no longer a duty to sell the land so, in cases of dispute, it may well prove to be the case that courts do not feel such a compulsion to order a sale (see the hint in *Banker's Trust v Namdar* (1997) and *Mortgage Corp v Shaire* (2001)), but note the contrary view in *Bank of Ireland v Bell* (2001)). This is undoubtedly a sensible reform and accords with the expectations of most co-owners who would have been astonished (pre-TOLATA) to find that they had a duty to sell immediately they had purchased the land. Secondly, the doctrine of conversion is abolished, effective for all new and nearly all existing trusts of land (s 3 of the TOLATA). So, no longer are the interests of the equitable owners regarded as interests in money rather than land. Although, *de facto*, this had been the position under the old trust for sale and so may not have great practical import (see, for example, *Williams and Glyn's Bank v Boland* (1981)), it is a welcome recognition of reality. Thirdly, as under the original scheme, the trustees have all the powers of an absolute owner, but their ability to delegate such powers to an equitable owner is made explicit and the only non-delegable power is the trustees role in overreaching (ss 6–9 of the TOLATA). This may be useful in cases where the equitable owner is not also a trustee but where the trustees are content to leave the everyday management of the land to the person in possession of it – the equitable owner. Fourthly, the trustees of land must consult with the equitable owners, and give effect to their wishes in so far as is consistent with the purposes of the trust of land (s 11 of the TOLATA) but, as under the old system, failure to consult (or to agree after consultation) does not appear to invalidate any dealings with the land by the trustees (see *Birmingham Midshires BS v Sabherwal* (1999)). More significantly, under the TOLATA, the ability to make any of the trustees' powers subject to the consent of the beneficiaries is explicit. Granted, this occurs only if such a 'consent requirement' is found in the instrument creating the trust (s 10 of the TOLATA) or if imposed by the court under an application under s 14 of the TOLATA, but this may be a mechanism by which the overreaching effect of the trust of land can be controlled: for example, by placing a restriction on the registered title saying that the co-owned land cannot be dealt with by the trustees unless the consent of the equitable co-owners is obtained. Fifthly, the TOLATA now formally recognises that the equitable owners have a right to occupy the property (s 12), which can be modified subject to safeguards, including being made subject to an obligation to pay compensation to a non-possessing co-owner (s 13). Again, this is formal confirmation of judicial developments prior to the TOLATA. Finally, again in similar fashion to the position under the original scheme, any person with an interest in the land can make an application to the court under s 14 of the TOLATA for a variety or orders (replacing s 30 of the LPA for the old scheme) – for example, sale, no sale, override consent requirement, impose consent requirements. As before, there are special criteria specified for cases of bankruptcy (s 15 of the TOLATA; s 335A of the Insolvency Act 1986; and see *Alliance & Leicester BS v Slayford* (2001)) and these largely mirror the position under the old scheme.

Clearly then, the fundamentals of the statutory co-ownership scheme under the TOLATA are the same or similar as under the original LPA scheme. There may be only joint-tenancies of the legal estate, the legal owners are trustees and overreaching applies. In matters of detail, however, changes have been made. Some of these introduce new law (for example, no longer a duty to sell, no doctrine of conversion), while others give statutory recognition to principles previously validated by judicial decision alone (for example, a right to possession). All in all, the TOLATA is a success.

Notes

This is a relatively straightforward question, provided that you understand both the 1925 trust for sale and the new TOLATA trust of land. There is now a little more case law on the latter.

Question 10

In 1987, Tony and Tracy decided to live together as an experiment before getting married. They purchased a semi-detached house, of registered land, in the centre of town with the aid of a 90% mortgage from the Safe Building Society. The rest of the purchase price was provided by Tony out of his savings. The house was conveyed to Tony alone as Tracy does not have a full time job. Tony had an excellent job in the construction industry and Tracy had no need to work. She stays at home from where she does occasional work as a dressmaker, the money from which she uses to pay for holidays. In 1989, with the construction industry in decline, Tracy's income was useful to help pay the mortgage and Tony often said that he did not know how they would meet their commitments if Tracy gave up dressmaking. Later that year, however, Tony inherited enough money from his uncle to pay off the mortgage and the couple decided to get married as Tracy is now pregnant. They have a tropical wedding costing several thousand pounds but, on their return, they find that Tony's employer has gone into liquidation and he is unemployed. Despite the birth of their child, Tracy takes on more dressmaking to meet the mounting bills. Unfortunately, Tony's attempt to start his own business has failed and he owes the bank several thousand pounds. He is now bankrupt and his trustee in bankruptcy is pressing for the house to be sold.

Advise Tracy.

Answer plan

The following should be discussed:
- a resumé of the 1925 machinery of co-ownership;
- the trust of land – ss 34 and 36 of the Law of Property Act 1925, as amended, and ss 4 and 5 of the TOLATA 1996;

- acquisition of beneficial ownership – *Pettitt v Pettitt et al*;
- sale of co-owned property – s 14 of the TOLATA;
- Insolvency Act 1986, as amended by the TOLATA.

Answer

Much depends in this case on whether Tracy owns a share of the house or, in other words, whether she has any equitable interest in it. If Tracy can establish that she has an 'ownership interest' in the property, she may (although it is not by any means certain) be able to resist the application of her husband's trustee in bankruptcy for sale of the property. If Tracy has no interest in the property, her only hope would be to show that she had taken advantage of s 30 of the Family Law Act 1996. This gives non-owning spouses a right of occupation against their partner which, if registered, can bind subsequent purchasers of the property. Although Tracy clearly has such a right, there is no evidence that she has entered it (by way of notice) on the registered title. In any event, if such a right is registered, a trustee in bankruptcy can apply for an order for sale to defeat such right under s 336(2) of the Insolvency Act 1986 and the position would be very similar to that discussed below in respect of sale if she does have an equitable interest.

Does Tracy have an interest in the property? When the property is purchased, it is conveyed into the sole name of Tony. The purchase is by mortgage and by cash deposit. Tony pays the entire cash deposit and, because he is to be the sole legal owner of the property, the mortgage is made with him. Title is registered in his name alone and there is no express declaration of trust in writing in favour of Tracy. Clearly, therefore, at the time of purchase, Tony is owner of the property both at law and in equity. There is no co-ownership – express or implied – and there is no trust of land. In such circumstances, if Tracy is to establish any interest at all, she must fall back on a line of authority stemming from the House of Lord's landmark decision in *Pettitt v Pettitt* (1970).

The *Pettitt* case, and a whole range of decisions following it (for example, *Lloyds Bank v Rosset* (1990)), have established that it is possible for a non-legal owner of property (that is, Tracy) to claim an equitable ownership interest in someone else's property. The principles are not limited to situations where a couple are married and, indeed, there need be no personal relationship between the parties. These rules are the application of traditional property law concepts to new situations. The basic principle flowing from *Pettitt* and a similar House of Lords' decision in *Gissing v Gissing* is that a person may claim an equitable interest in property belonging to another if they can establish a common intention that this was to be the case. This may either be by way of resulting trust – based on contributions to the purchase price, as in *Dyer v Dyer* – or by constructive trust based upon inequitable conduct and detrimental reliance, as in *Grant v Edwards*.

In the 1970s, under the influence of Lord Denning's Court of Appeal, this doctrine quickly expanded. It became apparent that the *Pettitt* decision could be used to justify any re-ordering of property rights that seemed appropriate to the judge. Cases such as *Falconer v Falconer* (1970), *Hestletine v Hestletine* (1971) and *Eves v Eves* (1975) appeared to give the court power to grant an equitable interest whenever the court thought it just and equitable to do so. Now, however, this jurisdiction has been more clearly defined and the House of Lords' decision in *Lloyds Bank v Rosset* has returned the law to the spirit of *Pettitt* and established reasonably clear guidelines for the future. According to *Rosset*, if Tracy is to establish any interest in the property, she must bring herself within one of the following categories. First, she must show that the legal owner has made an express promise to her that she should have an interest and that she has relied on that promise to her detriment, as in *Eves*, *Grant v Edwards* (1986) and *Babic v Thompson* (1998). Such an interest arises under a constructive trust but it seems that, on the facts, Tracy cannot establish such a claim. It is doubtful whether Tony's words of gratitude about the value of her dressmaking count for this purpose. There is no oral promise that she should have an interest and *Rosset* and *Burns v Burns* make it clear that such a promise cannot be inferred from the fact that a person shares some of the obligations of communal living, such as cleaning the house. As Lord Bridge makes clear, sharing the obligations of a relationship is not the same as sharing the obligations of property ownership. Secondly, however, if Tracy has contributed directly to the purchase price of the house, an interest can arise in her favour. The size of her interest will be in proportion to her payments (that is, has she paid one-fifth, one-half, etc) or, following *Midland Bank v Cooke* (1995), equivalent to the share she agreed with Tony that she should get as a result of making the payments. Does she have an interest by this 'payment' route?

Lord Bridge in *Rosset* accepts that such an interest can arise through mortgage repayments (being a referable contribution to the purchase price) and we are told that Tracy does make these payments. Tracy's payments towards holidays would not count for this purpose, although that is immaterial in view of her other financial contributions. As noted, the court now appears to be able to quantify this 'payment interest' by either the traditional route of awarding a proportional share in the property (see, for example, the discussion in *Drake v Whipp* (1995)) or, on the basis that the parties had a shared intention as to the size of the claimant's interest, the payments being the trigger for it (*Cooke*). In order to quantify Tracy's share (which may well be important if the property is sold), we would need to know whether she and Tony had ever discussed the question of share of ownership. If they have not, it seems (contrary to the widest view of *Cooke* but in line with *Clough v Killey*) that the court should fall back on the proportional approach.

If Tracy can establish her interest in the above fashion, it is clear that the property is now co-owned. According to *Bull v Bull* (1955) and s 1 of the TOLATA 1996, this means that an implied statutory trust of land comes into existence: Tony, the legal owner, holds the property on trust for himself and Tracy as tenants in common in the shares determined and subject to the statutory machinery of the TOLATA 1996. This gives Tracy some measure of protection. There is, of course, only one trustee of land and, therefore, no possibility of overreaching (*Williams and Glyn's Bank v Boland* (1981)). Any purchaser may well be bound by Tracy's interest under the normal rules of registered conveyancing. In this case, there is no registration of a minor interest but, if Tracy is in actual occupation of the property at the time of any sale to the purchaser (*Abbey National BS v Cann*), she will have an overriding interest under s 70(1)(g) of the LRA in similar fashion to *Williams and Glyn's Bank v Boland*.

However, that is not the end of Tracy's difficulties. When Tony becomes bankrupt, the trustee in bankruptcy becomes vested with all his property, including the legal title to the house. As we have just established, the trustee cannot sell the property immediately as Tracy's interest would be binding on a purchaser. In such circumstances, the trustee will apply to the court for an order for sale under under s 14 of the TOLATA 1996. Under this section, 'any person who ... has an interest in property subject to a trust of land' (which includes a trustee in bankruptcy) may apply for an order for sale. If such an application is made, the court will have to balance the claims of the creditors against the claims of Tracy (assuming she resists the sale) and s 335A of the Insolvency Act 1986 (inserted in the 1986 Act by Sched 3 to the TOLATA) provides a list of the criteria which the court should consider (as required by s 15(4) of the TOLATA). These include her interests and any children but, in any event, the court will permit a postponement of sale for only one year unless there are 'exceptional circumstances' (s 335A(3) of the Insolvency Act 1986). In our case, much might turn on the size of Tracy's interest. If it is small (perhaps based directly on the proportion of the purchase price she paid through mortgage instalments), the court might refuse to postpone sale at all. If postponement is ordered – perhaps to give Tracy a chance to find another home irrespective of the size of her share – one year is the maximum she can hope for. There are no exceptional circumstances here (see, for example, a refusal to postpone in *Re Harrington* (2001)). In short, then, Tracy will have an interest, but a court is likely to order sale in due course. Of course, Tracy's interest will not be subject to that of Tony's creditors and will be satisfied out of the proceeds of sale before those proceeds are distributed. As above, the precise amount will depend on how the court quantifies her share.

Question 11

Gloria, a rich widow, is the registered proprietor of a large house in London. Recently, at a friend's party she met Simon, an 18 year old student, and, after a passionate affair of a few weeks, she invited him to live with her. Simon accepted. Being a proud man, Simon insisted that he share the expenses of running the house and, over the next few months, he paid the occasional bill and even paid for the cost of having the house redecorated both inside and out. Simon was a little concerned that, because of the difference in age, Gloria would soon tire of his charms and he repeatedly asked her about the future. Last year, after one particularly splendid dinner together, Gloria told Simon that 'what's mine is yours'. Next day, realising that his future was secure, Simon spent his life savings on a sports car. Unfortunately, unknown to Simon, Gloria was paying school fees for her five children and, two months ago, she had to take out a mortgage with the Eton Building Society to cover next year's fees. The building society visited the property when Simon was on a field trip abroad and Gloria executed the mortgage that day. The building society registered their charge at the Land Registry the day after he returned.

Gloria has now met someone more her own age and has emigrated to Australia. The building society is seeking possession of the property in order to realise its security.

Advise Simon.

How would your answer differ if title to the property had been unregistered?

Answer plan

The following should be discussed:
- acquisition of beneficial interests;
- implied trust of land: *Bull v Bull*; s 1 of the TOLATA 1996;
- overreaching machinery: s 2 of the Law of Property Act 1925;
- registered land: one trustee; overriding interests; meaning of actual occupation; time of occupation;
- unregistered land: one trustee; doctrine of notice.

Answer

This question concerns the acquisition of beneficial interests in property belonging to another and the effects of such ownership, if any, on a third party purchaser – here, a mortgagee. In concrete terms, this problems revolves around a contest between the building society, who have an interest in the property and a power of sale under s 101 of the Law of Property Act by virtue of their duly registered mortgage, and Simon who must claim, if he is to have any prospect of remaining in the property, an equitable right of ownership to it. The crucial questions are, therefore, whether Simon has such an interest and, if so, whether the building society are bound by that interest. If the building society are bound, there is no prospect of a sale of the property with vacant possession unless an application is made to the court under s 14 of the TOLATA 1996 (see *Bank of Baroda v Dhillon* (1997); *Bank of Ireland v Bell* (2001)) and, in any event, Simon would be entitled to the monetary equivalent of his interest before the building society could be paid.

If Simon is to have an interest in the property, it is clear that this must be established under the principles elaborated in *Pettitt v Pettitt* and codified by the House of Lords in *Lloyds Bank v Rosset*. In our case, there is no express conveyance to Simon as owner and no express written declaration of trust by Gloria in his favour. His only hope is the law of constructive or resulting trusts. In this respect, *Rosset* makes it clear that a person claiming an equitable interest in property, legal title to which is vested in another, must be able to show either some contribution to the purchase price of the property – so as to raise a resulting trust in their favour (confusingly called a constructive trust in *Rosset*: see *Drake v Whipp* (1995)) – or must prove some oral assurance that they were to have an interest in the property which they then relied on to their detriment. On the facts as stated, it seems clear that when Simon met Gloria, Gloria was sole legal owner of the property and that it was not subject to any charge by way of 'purchase mortgage'. In other words, the property was hers, paid for and complete. It follows that Simon cannot pursue the resulting trust path to an equitable interest – there is no purchase price to which he can make a contribution, not even monthly mortgage payments. Moreover, even if there were an outstanding 'purchase mortgage', Simon's contributions to the cost of running the house cannot be considered, for they are part of the costs of sharing property, not of acquiring it – *per* Lord Bridge in *Rosset* (1990) and Court of Appeal in *Burns v Burns* (1984). The payment of the decoration expenses might have been relevant if the couple had been married: there is every chance that Simon could have relied on s 37 of the Matrimonial Proceedings and Property Act 1970 to establish a beneficial interest by way of improvement expenditure. However, this is not the case, and it is doubtful whether contributing to the costs of improving a house that is already purchased can, without any agreement, give rise to an equitable interest (*Bank of India v Mody* (1998)).

It would seem, then, that Simon should rely on the doctrine of constructive trusts: he must plead a promise plus detrimental reliance. Once again, are the costs of decorating the house relevant here? If Simon can show that he spent his money on improvements because there was a promise or agreement that he should part-own the property, then a case is clearly made out. Once again, however, there is no evidence to support this and such statements that Gloria does make are made *after* Simon spends money. Such expenditure could not have been made as a result of those particular statements. There is no reliance.

Eventually, Gloria does make a promise of sorts to Simon and it is a matter of construction whether this is sufficient for the *Rosset* principles. First, a problem exists with intention: does Gloria, after a romantic dinner, intend by her words 'what's mine is yours' that Simon should have an interest in the property? Although it is not entirely clear, *dicta* in *Gissing v Gissing* suggest that the oral promise (the 'common intention') must be real rather than imagined and it is questionable whether Gloria's statement meets this criterion. On the other hand, no case has denied that, if a reasonable person would have believed that the property owner was making a statement about ownership of the property, the particular promisee is entitled to rely on it even if this was not the actual intention of the property owner (see, for example, *Eves v Eves*). In our case, we do not know what Gloria actually meant, but a reasonable person in Simon's position might well conclude that this was an assurance about the ownership of the shared home. On this ground, Simon has a case that the relevant promise was made and it seems clear from the facts that he relied on that promise when he spent his life savings on the sports car. There is here, however, a further problem. Certain cases, such as *Gissing* and *Christian v Christian* suggest that the detriment suffered as a result of the promise must be related to the property in question; for example, spending money on improvements. However, another view is that, so long as the detriment was referable to the promise, that is, was caused by it, it does not matter that the actual detriment suffered was not property related. If the reason why an interest arises under a constructive trust is that a promise has been made and relied on (not that the property has been paid for), it should make no difference what form that detriment takes: whether it is property related or not, the promisee has still spent money that they would not otherwise have done. On this view, Simon has an equitable interest in the property if he can show that his lavish expenditure was a direct result of Gloria's promise. The size of his interest seems to lie in the discretion of the court, but it may well be substantial, given the content of the promise made to him and the level of his detriment.

Assuming, then, that Simon does have an interest, what is his position vis à vis the purchaser-mortgagee? Clearly, when Eton advanced the money, they did not pay it to two trustees of land: Gloria is the single trustee and, therefore, there can be no overreaching. The statutory conditions of s 2 of the Law of Property Act are not met. This makes the Building Society potentially subject to Simon's interest on either of two grounds: either he had registered his interest as a minor interest, or he can claim an overriding interest. As for a minor interest, there is nothing to suggest that Simon has protected his equitable ownership in this way as there is no evidence of registration. This leaves us with the overriding interest that can arise under s 70(1)(g) of the LRA 1925, as applied in *Williams and Glyn's Bank v Boland*. First, Simon must have an interest in land and this we have just established. Secondly, he must be in actual occupation and, following *Chhokar v Chhokar*, this is perfectly possible even though Simon was away from the house temporarily. On the facts, given that the house is his regular home he would seem to be in actual occupation – see, also, the Court of Appeal analysis in *Rosset*. Thirdly, Simon must be in actual occupation at the relevant time and, following *Abbey National BS v Cann*, it is clear that, for claims under s 70(1)(g), the crucial time is the moment of creation of the mortgage or time of purchase (confirmed in *Barclays Bank v Zaroovabli* (1997)). Thus, in our case, it is irrelevant that Simon returns before the charge is registered, we must determine whether he was in actual occupation at the time the charge was created. On the above facts, this seems to be established.

To conclude, then, Simon has an interest under a constructive trust (possibly of one-half as this is what he seems to have been promised) and he was in actual occupation of the property at the time the mortgage was made. Thus, under s 70(1)(g), he has an overriding interest against the building society and takes priority over them. They cannot obtain vacant possession under their normal powers as mortgagees and must apply to the court under s 14 of the TOLATA for an order for sale. Even if this is granted, they are unlikely to recover their money in full as Simon's interest takes priority and he must first be paid out of any proceeds of sale. The building society might pursue Gloria personally for the mortgage debt and make her bankrupt (*Alliance & Leicester v Slayford*). This could trigger a sale by the trustee in bankruptcy, but at least Simon would be paid his share before any settlement for the creditors.

Finally, if the land had been unregistered, Simon would still have acquired an equitable interest as the principles are identical, but whether that interest would have bound the building society would have depended on whether they had had notice of it at the time the mortgage was created. In unregistered land, these type of equitable interests cannot be registered as land charges (s 2 of the LCA 1972) and, thus, their enforceability depends on the doctrine of notice. Following *Kingsnorth v Tizard* (1986), it is highly likely that Simon's occupation of the property (that is, his presence in a general sense even though he was temporarily absent) would have given the Building Society notice of his interest and, therefore, they would be bound accordingly.

Question 12

Hilda and Harold, brother and sister, have recently discovered that their 17 year old nephew, William, has been orphaned in a road accident and that they are his legal guardians. In anticipation of William coming to live with them, they decide to buy a bigger house with their savings and with some of the money left to William by his parents over which they have lawful control until William is 18. The new house, title to which is unregistered at all material times, is expressly conveyed into their joint names as legal and equitable joint-tenants. There is no mention of the fact that William's money was also used. William arrives and Hilda and Harold employ a live-in personal tutor, Mary. Mary lives in a self-contained part of the house for which she pays Hilda and Harold £30 a week. Unknown to Mary and William, Hilda and Harold sell the property to Percy. Percy is told, and believes, that William and Mary are the vendors' children.

Advise William (who is now 18) and Mary as to their right to stay in the property. Is the law in this area satisfactory?

Answer plan

The following should be discussed:

- co-ownership and expressly declared trusts;
- acquisition of beneficial interests;
- overreaching and two trustees: *City of London BS v Flegg*;
- purchasers and existing tenants: s 4 of the Land Charges Act 1972;
- Law Commission Report 188; TOLATA 1996.

Answer

In this problem, we are once again faced with the difficulties that can arise from the operation of the trust of land and the overreaching provisions of the Law of Property Act (LPA) 1925 as the mechanism for regulating concurrent co-ownership. Under the LPA 1925 and the TOLATA 1996, when land is conveyed to two or more persons, they take that property as legal joint-tenants upon the statutory trusts of land: ss 34 and 36 of the LPA and s 1 of the TOLATA 1996. In our case, therefore, when the new house is conveyed to Hilda and Harold, it becomes subject to the rules governing these statutory trusts. Hilda and Harold become the joint-tenant trustees of the land, with all of the powers of an absolute owner, subject to the provisions of the TOLATA (s 6 of the TOLATA 1996). Moreover, as the conveyance is expressly conveyed to them as joint-tenants in equity, they hold the legal title on trust for themselves as equitable joint-tenants (*Goodman v Gallant*).

However, what of William, for it appears that some of his money has been used to purchase the property? It is axiomatic that, when a person contributes to the purchase price of property but does not acquire legal title to that property, a resulting trust will arise in their favour (*Dyer v Dyer* and see *Lloyds Bank v Rosset*), unless the contribution was by way of loan or gift (*Bradbury v Hoolin* (1998)). There is no evidence of that here and it may be that William's money was used without his knowledge or consent. In such circumstances, it is clear that a resulting trust is raised in his favour. The express declaration of the equitable ownership that is found in the conveyance (that is, to Harold and Hilda) does not prevent William claiming an interest by way of resulting trust, for in *Goodman,* it was made clear that an express declaration of beneficial interests only precludes a claim of resulting or constructive trust for the parties to that declaration. William was not a party to it and is not bound by it. In the end, therefore, Hilda and Harold are trustees of the legal estate on the statutory trusts of land holding on trust in equity for themselves as joint-tenants in the portion purchased by their own money and for William as a tenant in common of the share purchased with his money.

The property is now sold to Percy. This would seem to place William and Mary (the other occupier) in considerable difficulty, as it is obvious that Percy will not wish to share the property with them. The question becomes, then, whether William's interest, and any interest that Mary may have, can bind Percy.

First, what is the position of William? As seen above, William has an equitable interest in the property when Percy purchases the unregistered title. Normally, in unregistered land, equitable interests have to be registered as Land Charges to be binding against purchasers. However, under s 2 of the LCA 1972, these equitable ownership rights cannot be registered. They are, in fact, unregistrable and their binding effect continues in principle to be governed by the doctrine of notice. In our case, however, there is another important factor. Percy has purchased the property from two trustees of land – in other words, he has complied with the statutory requirements of s 2 of the Law of Property Act 1925 for overreaching. As in *City of London BS v Flegg* (1987), a sale by two trustees for sale overreaches all 'family style' equitable interests (that is, William's equitable ownership) so that the purchaser cannot be bound. It does not matter that William knew nothing of the sale or that Percy knew nothing (or everything!) of William: the statutory magic operates in favour of the purchaser and protects him. The only possible exception is if William's consent to the sale has been made a condition of a sale under the original trust (that is, the conveyance to Hilda and Harold) or if such a requirement has been imposed by the court consequent upon William's application to it under s 14 of the TOLATA. Again, there is no evidence of this and, in any event, Percy would not be affected by the violation of any consent requirement unless he had 'actual notice' of the violation (s 16 of the TOLATA). Of course, William's equitable interest is reflected in the purchase money and he is entitled to a share of the proceeds of sale in proportion to his share of the property – if he can locate the trustees. It is likely, however, that he has no claim against Percy and must surrender possession.

Mary's position is less clear. On one view, the arrangement she made with Hilda and Harold amounted to nothing more than that of lodger and landlord. If this is the case, she would have a mere licence, which is not an interest in land and which cannot, therefore, bind any purchaser irrespective of all questions of notice or registration – *Ashburn Anstalt v Arnold* (1988); *Lloyd v Dugdale* (2001). She would have to leave. Indeed, this may well be the case, especially if Hilda or Harold provided 'board and services' within the definition of a lodger in *Street v Mountford*. Likewise, if Mary was given accommodation 'for the better performance of her duties' as a tutor, she would have only a licence, as in *Norris v Checksfield* (1991). Then, she would be a service occupant under a licence and could not stay on against Percy. In fact, Mary's only hope is to claim that she has a tenancy – for this is capable of binding Percy in the right circumstances and, of course, such 'commercial' rights are not overreachable. In this case, there is evidence of 'rent' and it is payable weekly. This could mean that Mary has a legal periodic tenancy and, as such, it would be binding on Percy under the normal rules of unregistered land: viz, legal rights bind the whole world (*Hunt v Luck* (1902)). Of course, even if there is a legal periodic tenancy binding on Percy, Percy could terminate the tenancy according to its terms which, in the case of periodic tenancies, is usually on giving one period's notice (subject to a statutory minimum four weeks under the Protection from Eviction Act 1977). Finally, Mary might consider claiming an equitable tenancy under *Walsh v Lonsdale*, but only if there is a written record of the original tenancy agreement (s 2 of the Law of Property (Miscellaneous Provisions) Act 1989). In any event, however, to bind Percy in unregistered conveyancing such an equitable tenancy would need to have been registered as a Class C(iv) land charge (*Hollington Brothers v Rhodes*). There is no evidence of this. In the end, it looks as if Mary also has to leave and the best she can hope for is for one further period under the legal periodic tenancy until it is terminated.

This question clearly identifies one of the most striking problems of the use of the trust of land as a co-ownership device. William, the equitable owner, was deprived of his own property while he was in occupation of it because of the magic of overreaching. It is not enough to say that his interest is now in money form because a share of the proceeds of a house sale by no means guarantees that other accommodation can be purchased, even if the trustees do distribute the money properly. To meet these problems and to safeguard the position of the equitable owner in William's position, the Law Commission (in Report No 188) once flirted with three alternative solutions:

(a) that if the equitable owner registers their interest, they could not be overreached. Unfortunately, this solution would only help those equitable owners who both knew of the requirement of registration and, more fundamentally, knew that they actually had an interest. William did not;

(b) that in order for overreaching to take place, one of the trustees should be a solicitor or licensed conveyancer. This presupposes that such professional persons would not consent to a sale that destroyed an equitable owner's property rights without proper consideration of all material circumstances. This might or might not be true but it would be expensive, as well as introducing strangers into family affairs. In practice, the protection would have been negligible and formal;

(c) that no beneficiary, of full age and in occupation, could be overreached without their consent. This undoubtedly would have worked. It would have prevented sales of co-owned property such as the Fleggs suffered in the *City of London* case and William in this problem. Under the TOLATA 1996, this idea has been given partial effect, even though the Act was not specifically designed to implement Law Commission Report No 188. It is now possible for a 'consent requirement' to be imposed either in the conveyance establishing the trust or by order of the court under s 14 of the TOLATA. This would require the trustees of land to obtain the consent of any equitable owners before dealing with the legal title. In unregistered land, however, a purchaser's title would not be invalidated merely because the land was transferred by the legal owners in breach of the requirement. This would be the result only if the purchaser had 'actual knowledge' of the violation (s 16 of the TOLATA). In registered land, the consent requirement would be entered on the title as a restriction, so effectively blocking any dealing until the requisite consents had been obtained. This looks impressive, in the sense that equitable owners can be protected even when there are two trustees of the land. Yet, such protection as exists depends crucially on the existence of a consent requirement and such a requirement is not imposed by the Act as a matter of course. It is unlikely that a consent requirement will be built into the trust of land of domestic property at its inception, and only marginally less likely that an equitable owner will seek the imposition of such a requirement by application to the court.

Finally, we can also note that Mary's position, if she had a tenancy, is not satisfactory. In registered land, her tenancy whether legal or equitable would have been an overriding interest (under s 70(1)(k) and (g) respectively) and would have automatically bound Percy. In unregistered land, however, there is no protection for occupiers of property under an equitable tenancy unless they positively register (see *Hollington Brothers v Rhodes*). This is an unfortunate disparity between the two systems of conveyancing.

Question 13

Martin and Judith live together in a small country cottage, title to which is registered in the name of Judith only. They are not married but plan to have children shortly. Judith has an excellent job and persuades Martin that he should give up work and stay at home and look after the now expected child. Martin is unsure, especially because he dislikes relying on Judith so much, yet she assures him that 'when the child is born, this will be your home for the rest of your life'. Martin finally agrees, gives up work even though he was about to be promoted. After giving up work, but before the child is born, Martin completely redecorates one room as a nursery meeting the cost out of his savings. It comes as a great shock to discover that Judith, in fact, is expecting twins and the couple go to see the building society about a mortgage to extend their house. This is easily arranged and the building society duly register its charge. Two years later, Judith meets another man and, unknown to Martin, she takes out a bigger mortgage with a different building society, paying off the first and using the balance to go on a round the world cruise.

She never returns. The second building society seek possession of the cottage. Martin seeks your advice.

Answer plan

The following should be discussed:
- acquisition of beneficial interests;
- nature of interest: life interest or equitable ownership;
- sale by one trustee: overriding interest or implied consent;
- priority of replacement mortgages;
- ways to protect beneficial interests.

Answer

Once again, this problem poses difficult questions about the acquisition of equitable interests in property belonging to another and its effect on third parties. In this particular case, Martin must hope to establish that he has an interest in the property and that it is binding on the first mortgagee or, at least, on the second. If he can do so, he may well be able to stay in the property and, in any event, will be entitled to a share of the proceeds of sale in priority to the lender.

(a) Martin's interest

There is clearly no conveyance of the property to Martin and so Martin has no legal title to it. In fact, before the first mortgage is taken out, it appears that Judith is the sole owner, both at law and in equity. Likewise, there is no evidence that Judith has made a written declaration of trust in Martin's favour and so no possibility of an equitable interest arising in this way. Once again, we are thrown back on the law of resulting and constructive trusts. This may enable Martin to claim an interest in the property, even though legal title belongs to Judith, provided he can bring himself within the principles of *Pettitt v Pettitt* (1970) and *Lloyds Bank v Rosset* (1990). In this instance, it appears that Judith did not require a mortgage to purchase the property or, if she did, that mortgage has been repaid before Martin has any dealings with the property. Therefore, there is no scope for Martin to claim an equitable interest under the resulting trust approach – he cannot claim to have made a contribution to the purchase price under the first method identified in by Lord Bridge in *Rosset*. However, what of constructive trusts? At any time after the acquisition of the house, has Judith made a promise or assurance that Martin has relied upon to his detriment? As ever, this must be a matter of construction of the words and acts of the parties, with the proviso (as stated in *Gissing v Gissing* (1971)) that the agreement ('common intention') must be real and not supplied by the courts (see *First National Bank v Wadhwani* (1998)).

Clearly, Judith has made some kind of oral promise to Martin. She states openly, without duress, that 'this will be your home for the rest of your life'. As in *Ungarian v Lesnoff* and *Eves v Eves*, this must amount to a promise of some kind of interest in the property. Of course, under *Rosset*, Martin must rely on this assurance to his detriment before equity will come to his assistance: 'equity will not assist a volunteer.' In this respect, two matters are relevant. First, is there detrimental reliance when Martin stays at home and redecorates the intended nursery.

Clearly, there is detriment because he spends his own money but there are doubts over whether this detriment was in reliance on the promise made by Judith. It is more likely that the redecoration of the room was motivated by natural parental affection, although the presence of an emotional motive does not mean there can never be reliance (*Chun v Ho, Re Melodius Corp* (2001)). Perhaps Martin may be able to rely on *Greasley v Cook*, where Lord Denning (albeit in the context of proprietary estoppel) stated that, if a promisee changed their position to their detriment after a promise was made, it could be inferred that this was because of the promise. However, even if this wide ranging statement is correct, this does no more than shift the burden of proof to the person denying the existence of the interest – that is, the defendant would have to show that the promise was not the cause of the detriment. In our case, there is a real possibility that this could occur and that Martin will be held not to have relied on the promise when spending his money on redecoration.

However, Martin also suffers detriment by giving up his job and staying at home in readiness for the baby's arrival. We are told that he was unsure about this and was directly reassured that his position was secure. There is, here, no doubt that the detriment was in reliance on the promise. Yet, that is not the end of the matter. Some authorities suggest (for example, *Gissing*) that the detriment suffered must be related to the property itself before any interest crystallises in the promisee. If this is the position, now we have the situation where Martin has acted in reliance, to his detriment, but where the detriment does not qualify. It is suggested, however, that this limit on the type of qualifying detriment is not appropriate for constructive trust cases where the essence of the matter is loss suffered as a result of a promise denied. If the essence is a promise denied, causing loss, then Martin clearly qualifies and should be able to establish an equitable interest under a constructive trust within the second limb of *Rosset*.

(b) The nature of Martin's interest

In this case, Martin was promised that the property would be his home 'for the rest of your life'. According to *Ungarian* (1989), this means that Martin has a life interest in the property, rather than an absolute share of the ownership. In short, that he becomes the tenant for life, albeit under a trust of land under the TOLATA (assuming that the events occur on or after 1 January 1997, s 2 of the TOLATA 1996, replacing the provisions of the Settled Land Act 1925). In *Ungarian*, this result was a direct consequence of the particular promise made and it is difficult to see how the same conclusion can be avoided here, especially as the authorities suggest that a person's interest under a constructive trust which arises out of a promise bears a direct relation to that promise: viz, if Martin is promised a home for life, he gets a life interest. This conclusion (that Martin has a life interest) has the unfortunate consequence that his position appears precarious. This is registered land and under s 86(2) of the LRA 1925, the interest of a tenant for life can never be an overriding interest (and this will remain the case under the LRA 2002). Thus, if the property is sold to a purchaser or mortgagee, the equitable tenant for life cannot gain automatic protection. In fact, as in our case, the equitable tenant for life can protect himself only by registering his interest as a minor interest and this Martin has not done. In other words, pending an application by Martin under s 14 of the TOLATA for protection, Martin is very vulnerable to a third party purchaser.

(c) The first mortgage

Clearly, the first mortgage is made to only one trustee – Judith. Whatever interest Martin has, it is not as joint-tenant of the legal title. This means, then, that overreaching cannot take place and the Building Society may be bound by subsisting equitable interests. However, the Society will only be bound by subsisting interests if they have been protected in the appropriate way. If they have not, the Society takes free of those interests even though no overreaching occurs – this is the effect of s 20 of the LRA 1925. As we have seen above, if Martin has a life interest, he is statute barred from claiming an overriding interest and must register as a minor interest. In fact, Martin has not registered and the Society will take free. Indeed, only if Martin can show that he has a full ownership interest (that is, a share of the equity absolutely, not just for life) is it even possible for him to claim priority against the mortgagee. If that were the case, Martin would be a person with an interest in actual occupation at the time the mortgage was made, and might have an overriding interest within s 70(1)(g) of the LRA: *Williams and Glyn's Bank v Boland* (1981) and *Abbey National BS v Cann* (1991). Even then, however, Martin might not be able to claim priority. Following *Paddington BS v Mendelson* (1985), the Society might well be able to prove that Martin had impliedly consented to the mortgage, thereby losing any priority which he may have had as a result of an overriding interest. On the facts, it is clear that Martin knew of the first mortgage, went to the Society to discuss it and, indeed, was aware that the mortgage was needed for family purposes. With such evidence, it is most likely that implied consent will be held to exist. In other words, Martin's interest will be subject to the Society either because it was a life interest not properly protected and/or because he impliedly consented to a postponement of his rights.

(d) The second mortgage

It is, however, the providers of the second mortgage that are seeking possession. The first mortgage has been discharged. Martin knows nothing of the second mortgage and cannot be said to have consented to it in any sense. However, it is very important that the second mortgage is used to pay off the first. Following *Equity and Home Loans v Prestidge* (1992), applied in *Abbey National Mortgages plc v Mostaga Saleh-Rad* (1998), it seems that when a second mortgage is used to pay off a first mortgagee, the second mortgagee steps into the shoes of the first mortgagee, at least up to the value of the first mortgage. In other words, the second lender acquires the first lender's priority to the extent of the first mortgage (assuming the second mortgage to be on no less favourable terms). Objectively, this is a reasonable conclusion given that any equitable owner (Martin) is in no worse position simply because the identity of the lender has changed: he is still subject to a mortgage. So, then, if Martin did impliedly consent to the first mortgage, he will be taken to have impliedly consented to its replacement, up to the same amount.

In fact, in our case, if Martin has a life interest which he has not protected, he will be subject to the whole of the second mortgage, for the same reason that his life interest was subject to the first – viz, the second Society is a purchaser of a legal estate and takes free of all interests except overriding interests (which this cannot be) and registered minor interests (which this is not).

Unfortunately, then, it seems that Martin's position is precarious. He has an interest in the property, but that is subject to the rights of the first mortgagee either because he consented to it or, being a life interest, because he has not protected it correctly. If it is a question of consent, the priority is passed to the second mortgagee, but only to the extent that the second mortgage is for the same amount as the first. If he has a life interest, Martin is subject to the second lender up to the whole amount. Consequently, the property is likely to be sold, with the proceeds being used in the following way:

(a) if Martin has an ownership interest: pay off the value of the first mortgage, but to the second mortgagee; use any balance to pay the cash equivalent to Martin of his interest; pay off the balance of the second mortgage; surplus to Judith;

(b) if Martin has an equitable life interest, he ranks after both mortgagees but before Judith. It will be interesting to see how far down this chain of claimants the proceeds of sale actually reach.

Notes

The previous four questions all deal with various aspects of the same problem: the creation of co-ownership rights informally and the consequences this has for third party purchasers. There is no substitute for a thorough knowledge of *Rosset*, *Flegg*, *Cann* and *Prestidge*. There are useful case notes on all these cases in the Student Law Review, the Cambridge Law Journal and the Conveyancer. One of the difficult problems is going to be to distinguish between rights arising by constructive trust, and those arising by estoppel (see, for example, *Yaxley v Gotts* (2000)). The House of Lords in *Cann* has already made one allusion to this and it may be the issue of the future.

Question 14

Arnold, Bill, Claudio and Dominic and Eric are all trainee solicitors in London and they decide to buy a house together. All contribute equally to the purchase price and the house is conveyed to 'Arnold and Bill as joint-tenants in law and in equity'. Several months later, Bill is made redundant and forges Arnold's signature to a mortgage made with the Easy Loan Bank. At the same time, Arnold agrees in writing to sell his interest in the property to Eric and the agreement is executed. Meanwhile, Claudio has plans to marry and asks Dominic whether he will buy his share in the house. Dominic is very keen but disputes the price. Before they can come to a agreement, Claudio is killed in a road accident leaving all his property to his fiancee, Wendy. Very soon after, Eric becomes entangled in a city deal that goes badly wrong and, owing many millions, is made bankrupt. Before Eric is formally adjudged bankrupt, Dominic commits suicide leaving all his property to the Battersea Dogs' Home.

Eric's trustee in bankruptcy, Wendy, the Dogs' Home, Bill and Dominic's next of kin all claim an interest in the property. What is your advice?

Would it make any difference if, before his death, Dominic had written to Eric informing him that he wished to leave the house as soon as possible?

Answer plan

The following should be covered:
- construction of the conveyance:
  - nature of parties interest;
- purpose of the law of severance;
- *Williams v Hensman*:
  - an act operating on one's own share;
  - mutual agreement;
  - possible course of dealing;
- right of survivorship;
- effect of bankruptcy of co-owner;
- s 36(2) of the Law of Property Act 1925: *Kinch v Bullard*.

Answer

This question concerns the law of severance. Severance is the process by which an equitable joint-tenancy can be converted into an equitable tenancy in common. There may be many reasons why a joint-tenant should wish to sever his interest in this way, but, very often, the motivation is to avoid the operation of the right of survivorship. In a joint-tenancy, when one joint-tenant dies, their interest automatically accrues to the other joint tenants, irrespective of any disposition made in a will. If, therefore, a co-owner is a joint-tenant but wishes to deal with their interest separately, severance of that tenancy is crucial. Before we consider the problem in detail, however, one point must be borne in mind. Under the Law of Property Act (LPA) 1925, the only form of co-ownership that can exist at law is the joint-tenancy. This legal joint-tenancy is unseverable – s 36(2) of the LPA – because, if it were otherwise, a legal tenancy in common would result and, under the LPA, that is not possible – s 1(6). In other words, when we talk of severing the joint-tenancy, we are talking about severing the joint-tenancy in equity. As is made clear in the LPA, the equitable co-ownership that exists behind the joint-tenancy at law can take either form and so the equitable joint-tenancy can be transformed into a tenancy in common under the law of severance.

The law relating to severance is to be found both in statute and at common law. Under s 36(2) of the LPA 1925, any equitable joint-tenant may give notice in writing to the other joint-tenants of their intention to sever (unless it seems they have promised not to: *White v White* (2000)) and this actually results in a severance in equity – see, for example, *Burgess v Rawnsley* (1975) and *Kinch v Bullard* (1998). Similarly, at common law, *Williams v Hensman* (1861) establishes that severance may occur by three methods: first, where one joint-tenant does 'an act operating on their own share' (such as a sale of his interest); secondly, where joint-tenants agree to sever by 'mutual agreement' (this acts to sever the shares of all those agreeing, even if the agreement is never carried out or is actually unenforceable – *Burgess*); thirdly, severance can occur by 'mutual conduct' (where the party's conduct is of a kind sufficient to evince an intention no longer to be part of a joint-tenancy).

In our problem, some or all of these principles may be relevant but, first, it is necessary to identify the nature of the co-ownership between the parties. Clearly, Arnold and Bill are the legal owners and are, by statute (s 35 of the LPA), the joint-tenant trustees of the legal estate holding for the equitable owners on a trust of land under the TOLATA 1996. Who are the equitable owners and are they joint-tenants or tenants in common? Although the conveyance expressly declares that Arnold and Bill are joint-tenants, this conveyance can be conclusive only between the parties to it – *Goodman v Gallant*. Therefore, the doctrine of resulting and constructive trusts is not excluded for Claudio, Dominic and Eric. Following *Dyer v Dyer*, *Pettitt v Pettitt* and *Lloyds Bank v Rosset*, there is no doubt that Claudio, Dominic and Eric will be able to claim a share of the equitable ownership by virtue of their contribution to the purchase price of the property. In fact, because all five people contributed to the purchase price equally, they are in equity joint-tenants. So, the picture of the ownership of the house is as follows: Arnold and Bill hold the property as trustees of land for Arnold, Bill, Claudio, Dominic, and Eric as joint-tenants in equity.

As the problem makes clear, there are now several claimants to the property and if, as seems likely, it is sold, there will be confusion as to how the proceeds of sale should be distributed. Of course, if there have been no acts of severance, the surviving joint-tenants will be entitled to the property or its proceeds by virtue of the right of survivorship. In addition, it is quite possible that only one or some of the original joint-tenants have severed their interest so that survivorship might operate between only some of the surviving parties.

(a) Bill's attempted mortgage to the Easy Loan Bank

Bill is a trustee of the legal title, but jointly with Arnold. Thus, no action on his part alone can deal with the legal title and, without Arnold's agreement, there can be no mortgage to the bank. In other words, both legal owners must genuinely agree to any conveyance of the legal title – this is at the very heart of the legal joint-tenant trusteeship. So, forging the signature of the other legal owner is not sufficient to create a mortgage of the legal title – *First National Securities v Heggarty* (1985). However, following *Ahmed v Kendrick* (1987), *Banker's Trust v Namdar* (1997) and s 63 of the LPA 1925, the attempted mortgage by Bill will be sufficient to mortgage to the bank such interest as Bill does control – in other words, his equitable interest. Without doubt, this mortgage of his equitable interest is 'an act operating on his own share' within *Hensman* and means that Bill severs his share of the equitable interest. He is now a tenant in common of one-fifth, albeit mortgaged to the Bank. The other owners are still within a joint-tenancy of the remaining four-fifths. Legal title remains in Arnold and Bill as before.

(b) The transfer by Arnold

When Arnold agrees in writing to sell his interest in the property to Eric, this is an enforceable agreement to sell his equitable interest (see s 2 of the Law of Property (Miscellaneous Provisions) Act 1989). This is not an agreement to sell the legal title as Bill would have had to concur. As above, this is an act operating on his own share within Hensman and will sever Arnold's interest from the joint-tenancy. Thus, when the agreement is executed, Arnold's equitable share passes to Eric. The overall position is now that Arnold and Bill hold on trust for Eric as tenant in common of one-fifth, Bill as tenant in common of one-fifth (but mortgaged) and Claudio, Dominic and Eric as joint-tenants of the remainder.

(c) Mutual agreement on mutual conduct

It is unclear whether Claudio's discussions with Dominic lead to any severance of the joint-tenancy between them. It seems that there is no 'mutual agreement' within *Hensman* as, although Dominic is keen to buy, no price has been agreed. This probably prevents severance by mutual agreement. It should be noted, however, that, if an agreement can be inferred from the circumstances, the fact that this agreement would be unenforceable (because it is not in writing) does not prevent severance occurring (*Burgess*). Under an unenforceable 'mutual agreement', the transfer would not take place but severance would occur for both parties. However, assuming that mutual agreement is inapplicable here, can the discussions between Claudio and Dominic amount to severance by 'mutual conduct', being a course of dealing between the parties that show an intention to hold as tenants in common. This is unclear, because, as a matter of principle, it is difficult to see why a failed attempt to agree (as here) should be treated as effective to sever even though there is no agreement to sever. If that were possible, the difference between mutual agreement and mutual conduct would become virtually non-existent. However, if one reads Lord Denning's judgment in *Burgess*, it is clear that he does suggest that negotiations between joint-tenants can give rise to severance.

Essentially, the answer will depend on the facts of each case and whether the court is prepared, as a matter of policy, to extend the circumstances in which severance is possible. The degree of hardship caused by the operation of the right of survivorship might well be relevant in that calculation. In our case, the tentative conclusion is that severance has not occurred because of the potential overlap with mutual agreement. Thus, the position remains as at (b) above.

(d) The right of survivorship

When Claudio dies, he dies as a joint-tenant of three-fifths of the property with Dominic and Eric. He has not severed his interest and, thus, it accrues to Dominic and Eric under the right of survivorship. The fact that he left his property by will to Wendy is irrelevant as survivorship takes precedence over testamentary dispositions (*Gould v Kemp* (1834)). Thus, Arnold and Bill hold on trust for Eric as tenant in common of one-fifth, Bill as tenant in common of one-fifth (but mortgaged) and Dominic and Eric as joint-tenants of the remainder.

(e) Eric's bankruptcy and the suicide

Under the Insolvency Act (as applied in very similar circumstances to these in *Re Dennis* (1992)), it is clear that a bankrupt's property does not become vested in the trustee in bankruptcy until he or she is formally adjudicated bankrupt. At that moment, of course, there is alienation (that is, transfer) of the bankrupt's property such as to cause a severance of any joint-tenancy of which he may be part – it is really an act operating on his own share, albeit an involuntary one. In our case, however, when Dominic dies and leaves his property to the Dogs' Home, Eric has not been adjudicated bankrupt and so there has been no severance between the remaining two joint-tenants. Unfortunately, therefore, Dominic's interest passes to Eric under the right of survivorship. In other words, when Eric is adjudicated bankrupt, he is, in fact, the sole surviving joint-tenant and all the property subject to that joint-tenancy accrued to him and will fall to the trustee in bankruptcy to pay the creditors.

The final position is, therefore, that Arnold and Bill are legal owners of the property holding as joint-tenant trustees in equity in the following way:

- for Eric as tenant in common of one-fifth. This will pass to the trustee in bankruptcy;
- for Bill as tenant in common of one-fifth, but as mortgaged to the bank;
- for Eric as owner of the remainder, having succeeded to the shares of Claudio and Dominic under the right of survivorship. This also passes to the trustee in bankruptcy for distribution among his creditors.

(f) *Would it have made any difference if Dominic had written to Eric before his death informing him that he wished to leave the property?*

The only possible difference this could make is if this written communication can be regarded as written notice of severance under s 36(2) of the LPA 1925. Under that section, written notice to the other joint-tenants (here, Eric), may sever a joint-tenancy providing that it is a communication of an intention to sever and there has been no promise not to sever: *White v White* (2000). This will be a matter of construction but, following the liberal construction used in *Re Draper's Conveyance* (where a court summons seeking sale of the property was held to sever under the section), this letter probably suffices: after all, an intention to leave the property almost certainly implies dealing separately with one's own share. Indeed, according to *Kinch v Bullard* (1998), a notice to sever is effective even if never actually read by the other joint tenant(s), provided it is effectively delivered to them. However, there is one small problem in that the words of s 36(2) say that this form of severance is available where 'a legal estate is vested in joint-tenants beneficially', that is, where the legal and equitable owners are the same people. That is not the case here – because only Arnold and Bill are legal owners. However, this restrictive construction is generally regarded as being incorrect and the better view is that severance by written notice is available for all joint-tenants in equity, whether or not they are legal owners as well. Thus, if Dominic had severed by this method before his death, he could successfully leave his one-fifth share to the Dogs' Home in his will.

Notes

This is a disguised essay on the law of severance. The answer to this, and similar problems, is not difficult and requires a knowledge of the law of severance found in most textbooks.

CHAPTER 4

SUCCESSIVE INTERESTS
IN LAND

Introduction

Although it is becoming less frequent, it was once quite common
for property to be left to one person for their life, then to another,
then to another and so on. These are successive interests in land
and they arise when one person is entitled to the possession of
land in succession to another, a typical example being where land
is left to A for life, with remainder to B for life, remainder to C in
fee simple. In such a case, A has a life interest in possession (and
is known somewhat confusingly as the 'life tenant'), B has a life
interest in remainder (and will be the life tenant when A dies) and
C has a fee simple in remainder (and will become the absolute
owner on the death of A and B).

The reasons for creating successive interests can, of course, be
many and varied, although one very common reason was so that
land could be 'kept in the family' by limiting its ownership to
successive heirs (subject to the perpetuity rules). Nowadays, this
is less of a motivating factor, although successive interests may
still be created in family or commercial relationships where the
settlor desires to make provision for several persons out of his
land. Today, the law concerning successive interests is to be
found in two distinct sets of statutory provisions. First, for
'settlements' in existence prior to 1 January 1997, the operating
statute is the Settled Land Act 1925. This is a complicated piece of
legislation and the machinery it establishes is rightly regarded as
unwieldy. Land subject to this statute (that is, land subject to
successive interests created before 1 January 1997, even if
'resettled' after this date) is known as 'settled land'. Secondly, life
interests created on or after 1 January 1997 are subject to the
provisions of the Trusts of Land and Appointment of Trustees Act
(TOLATA) 1996. Such interests are held under a 'trust of land'
and are excluded from the operation of the Settled Land Act. To
put it another way, on 1 January 1997, it became impossible to
create any new 'settlements' under the Settled Land Act and any

attempt to create a successive interest in land after this date will, by statute, create a trust of land under the TOLATA (s 2 of the TOLATA 1996). This move to abolish the strict settlement for all future successive interests reflects both the changing social uses to which land subject to successive interests is put and the fact that the Settled Land Act 1925 had become out-dated, cumbersome and expensive to operate.

There is no doubt that the law of successive interests is complicated, especially when there is an 'old style' settlement and the Settled Land Act is in play. Unfortunately, we cannot yet abandon the strict settlement to the legal graveyard as many existing settlements have time to run and, indeed, because any resettlement of existing settled land (that is, the creation of new successive interests for new family members over land that is already settled) will be governed by the Settled Land Act, even if such resettlement takes place on or after 1 January 1997 (s 2 of the TOLATA 1996). An old style settlement will cease to exist only when there is no land or heirlooms subject to the settlement (s 2(5) of the TOLATA 1996). The new style trust for successive interests – the trust of land under the TOLATA – is simpler and, therefore, less expensive to establish. The mandatory use of the trust of land for all new successive interests will, hopefully, simplify this area of the law. One side effect is that the law of concurrent co-ownership (Chapter 3) and successive co-ownership are now governed by the same statutory provisions of the TOLATA.

Checklist

The need remains to have a working knowledge of the Settled Land Act, of the scope of the powers of the 'tenant for life' under it, of the controls placed on the tenant for life and of the differences between the settlement and the trust of land as a means of regulating successive ownership. An awareness of the history of settled land is also helpful. In addition, for new successive interest trusts, it is imperative to have a clear understanding of the provisions of the TOLATA and much of what has been said in the previous chapter (concurrent co-ownership) is relevant here also. Particular attention should be given to the ability of the trustees under a trust of land to delegate powers to any beneficiary – such as the holder of a life interest. This will preserve the advantage enjoyed under strict settlements that the person most interested in the land has power to deal with it in specified circumstances.

Question 15

Compare the Settled Land Act 1925 with the Trusts of Land and Appointment of Trustees Act 1996 as a means of governing successive interests in land.

Answer plan

The following areas should be covered:
- the nature of successive interests;
- the effect of the TOLATA on successive interests in general;
- the salient features of the Settled Land Act;
- a comparison with the TOLATA.

Answer

Land can be said to be held in successive ownership when two or more persons are entitled to enjoyment of that land (or the income from it) in succession to each other. This is distinct from concurrent co-ownership, being cases where two or more persons are entitled to the simultaneous enjoyment of land. An example of successive co-ownership is where land is left to A for life, then to B for life, then to C absolutely. Each is entitled to possession in succession to the other although each does have an immediate proprietary interest in the land. Originally, the purpose of such arrangements was to ensure that land remained in the family (as where A is the grandfather, B the father and C the son), although it is perfectly possible for successive co-ownership to be used in a commercial context. Before 1926, the two methods of creating successive ownership – the settlement and the trust for sale – were subject to the same statutory controls (Settled Land Acts 1882 and 1884) although, for various reasons, this was not satisfactory. After 1925, two mutually exclusive statutory regimes are in operation. First, for land subject to a 'settlement' (sometimes called a 'strict settlement') that was created before 1 January 1997, the Settled Land Act 1925 is the governing statute. This is 'settled land'. A settlement arises, in general terms, where land is limited in trust for any persons by way of succession, or land is limited in trust for an infant for an estate in fee simple or term of years absolute in possession or, where land is charged by way of a family arrangement with the payment of any sums for the benefit of any persons (ss 1 and 2 of the Settled Land Act (SLA) 1925 and see, for example, *Re Austen* (1929)). Secondly, however, all attempts to create successive interests in land on or after 1 January 1997 (save for a 'resettlement' of existing settled land) must take effect as a trust of land under the Trusts of Land and Appointment of Trustees Act 1996 (s 2 of the TOLATA, which came into force on 1 January 1997; note, also, existing trusts for sale will operate under the TOLATA). In short, it will not be possible to create new 'settled land' on or after 1 January 1997 and any such attempt (even if expressly made) will cause the creation of a 'trust of land' under the TOLATA. Clearly, this is a major reshaping of the law of successive interests, designed to lead to the eventual disappearance of settled land and the Settled Land Act. For the present, however, the two statutes operate in parallel, each defined by reference to the time of creation of the successive interest.

The principal attributes of settled land (under the SLA) can be analysed quite briefly. Settled land is land held on trust. Consequently, there will be 'trustees of the settlement' and beneficiaries under the settlement. These beneficiaries will be the person having a life interest (the life tenant, A above) and those persons entitled in remainder, that is, after the life tenant has died (B and C). The settlement will have been created by the 'settlor', by deeds, and these deeds will usually identify the trustees and deal with the detail of the settlement. Under the Settled Land Act, various persons are given statutory powers to deal with settled land and it is important to remember that the major purpose behind the grant of these powers is to ensure that the land itself can be freely dealt with: in other words, that the land is alienable and does not get tied up in the settlement. As with concurrent co-ownership, if the land is sold, the rights and interests of the beneficiaries will be transferred to the purchase money via the mechanism of overreaching.

The first point of particular interest in respect of settled land is that, under the Settled Land Act, the tenant for life has significant powers to deal with the land. The tenant for life (for example, the person having the current life interest: see, also, s 19 of the SLA 1925) is holder of the legal estate in the land and he holds that legal estate on trust for the beneficiaries under the settlement: ss 4 and 107 of the SLA. Further, as just noted, in the great majority of cases, this tenant for life is also the person entitled to the equitable life interest in the property and so he will have two roles: holder of the legal estate in the land and owner of an equitable, but limited ownership. It is no accident that the person in possession of the land should also have the legal title. Before 1925, that legal title could be vested in several trustees or split up among several beneficiaries and this made dealing with settled land a painful and expensive experience. Now, under a SLA settlement, the legal title is vested solely in the tenant for life, for he will be the person in immediate possession of the land and the person who may best judge how to deal with it.

Secondly, and following on from the above point, the tenant for life also exercises most of the important statutory powers to deal with the settled land. These are found in Pt II of the Settled Land Act 1925 and effectively place the tenant for life in control of the land. He has the power to manage it for the best interests of all the beneficiaries. Consequently, the role of the 'trustees of the settlement' is limited. In general, they exercise supervisory functions in respect of the settlement: *Wheelwright v Walker* (1883). It is their responsibility to ensure that the rights and interests of *all* the beneficiaries under the settlement are protected, especially if the tenant for life misuses his statutory powers. The identity of the trustees is determined according to s 30 of the SLA, although they will usually be named as such in the trust deeds.

Thirdly, under the Settled Land Act, if the person with the statutory powers chooses to sell the settled land (that is, usually the tenant for life), the interests of the beneficiaries are overreached *if* the purchase money is paid to the trustees of the settlement (who must be two in number or a trust corporation) or into court. If overreaching occurs, the purchaser need not concern himself with the equitable interests because these take effect in the purchase money: this is the 'curtain principle'. The purchaser obtains a clean and unencumbered title to the land. If overreaching does not occur, the tenant for life cannot make a good title to the purchaser and the purchaser may be bound by the equitable interests as specified under the provisions of the Settled Land Act.

Finally, in this survey of the Settled Land Act, brief mention should be made of the process by which such settlements were once created (that is, before 1 January 1997). Under the SLA, all strict settlements had to be created by two deeds – a 'trust instrument' and a 'principal vesting deed': ss 4 and 5 of the SLA. The trust instrument declared the details of the settlement, appointed the trustees of it and set out any powers conferred by the settlement that were in addition to those provided automatically by the Act. The principal vesting deed was less comprehensive and described the settled land itself, named the trustees, stated the nature of any additional powers and, most importantly of all, declared that the settled land was vested in the person to whom the land was conveyed (the tenant for life) on the trusts of the settlement. The principal vesting deed was, in one sense, the *indicia* of ownership of the settled land. It is with this that any purchaser of existing settled land will be concerned as the equitable interests detailed in the trust instrument will be swept off the land by overreaching.

By way of contrast, 'new style' successive interest trusts of land operating under the TOLATA follow a different statutory regime. This new regime represents a revamping of the old 'trust for sale' (which, prior to 1 January 1997, was the alternative to 'settled land') and is designed principally to avoid the complicated machinery of the Settled Land Act. As noted above, all attempts to create successive interests on or after 1 January 1997 must take effect as a trust of land under the TOLATA, unless the parties are effecting a resettlement of existing settled land (s 2 of the TOLATA 1996).

A 'trust of land' is of course a trust, having trustees and beneficiaries. The trustees will be named in the instrument establishing the successive interests and the beneficiaries will be those entitled to a life interest and interests in remainder. Most importantly, however, under the trust of land, legal title to the land and primary control over it lies with the trustees. The trustees have legal title and have all the powers in respect of the land of an absolute owner (s 6 of the TOLATA). The exception is where the trustees' powers are limited by the TOLATA itself or, for a trust that is expressly created (most successive trusts of land will be), by any provision in the instrument creating the trust (s 8 of the TOLATA 1996). Primarily, therefore, it is the trustees of land who control it or its capital value and they who decide whether the land should be sold or retained. This is very different from the location of power and control under a settlement where all lies with the tenant for life, one of the beneficiaries.

Secondly, while the tenant for life under a settlement is subject to some controls on the exercise of his powers (*Wheelwright v Walker* (1883)), under a trust of land, the trustees are largely unfettered. They are subject to the provisions of the TOLATA (for example, the duty to consult beneficiaries: s 11 of the TOLATA) and a person with an interest in a trust of land (for example, the life beneficiary) may make an application to the court under s 14. Yet, these are not powerful fetters. Indeed, the trustees of land under the TOLATA can exercise those powers in respect of the land that the tenant for life under the Settled Land Act may not exercise unless the consent of the trustees of the settlement is obtained. It is true that, under s 10 of the TOLATA, the powers of the trustees of land can be made subject to the consent of another person (for example, the life interest holder), provided that this is stipulated in the instrument establishing the trust or as a result of an application to the court under s 14 of the TOLATA. It is possible – perhaps probable – that settlors who deliberately create a successive interest trust of land will use s 10 to limit the role of the trustees, say in favour of the life tenant, but this will need careful drafting. In registered land, such a consent requirement will be entered on the register of title by means of a restriction (so alerting a purchaser), although, in unregistered land, a purchaser may deal with the trustees of land safely, even in violation of a consent requirement, unless he (the purchaser) had actual notice of it (s 16 of the TOLATA 1996). Finally, like all trustees, the trustees of land under the TOLATA and the trustees of the settlement under the SLA 1925 are subject to the normal rules controlling persons in a fiduciary position: for example, they are personally liable in an action for breach of trust.

Thirdly, because of the complicated workings of the Settled Land Act, on the death of the tenant for life, the legal estate can be transferred to a new tenant for life only by 'vesting deeds', a relatively expensive process. However, in a trust of land under the TOLATA, the trustees must have the legal title and must be joint-tenants of it (ss 34 and 36 of the LPA), irrespective of the complicated nature of the beneficiaries' interests or the circumstances surrounding the establishment of the trust. Thus, on the death of a trustee of land, legal title accrues automatically to the remaining trustees under the right of survivorship without the need for any documentation.

Fourthly, while, under the SLA, the tenant for life has the statutory powers to deal with the land, we have seen that under the TOLATA, the trustees have the powers of an absolute owner. However, in order to ensure that the person most interested in the land has an active part in its management, the trustees of land under the TOLATA may delegate to a beneficiary (for example, the life interest holder) 'any of their functions' which relate to the land (s 9 of the TOLATA 1996). This gives trustees of land the option of keeping the powers for themselves if, say, the beneficiary is not trustworthy, but to delegate them if this is in the best interest of the trust. Such flexibility is not possible under the old settled land regime.

Finally, if it should happen that a strict settlement under the SLA 1925 has arisen informally (as in *Ungarian v Lesnoff* (1989), where the plaintiff acquired a life interest by means of a constructive trust under the *Rosset* principles), the informal equitable rights created in the plaintiff's favour are precarious. On a sale by a single legal owner (that is, no overreaching), her equitable life interest cannot amount to an overriding interest under the Land Registration Act 1925 (s 86(2)) and can only bind a potential purchaser if registered as a minor interest. Such registration is, of course, unlikely when the interest arises informally. By contrast, in an informally created trust of land, it is trite law that a beneficiary's interest can be overriding (that is, by virtue of actual occupation: s 70(1)(g) of the LRA 1925; *Williams and Glyn's Bank v Boland* (1981)) and so he will almost certainly be protected should the single trustee (no overreaching) sell to a purchaser.

To sum up then, after 31 December 1996, it is no longer possible to create successive interests in land under the Settled Land Act, save for resettlements of existing settled land. All new successive interests will be trusts of land. The former are governed by the complicated provisions of the SLA 1925, the latter by the TOLATA 1996. Under a settlement, the legal title and powers to deal with the land are vested in the tenant for life, who also holds an equitable interest. Under a trust of land, title and power is in the hands of the trustees, although they may delegate to a beneficiary. Again, in settled land, the tenant for life is subject to control by the trustees of the settlement: in a trust of land, the trustees are not subject to such control unless express provision is made in the trust instrument or after an application to the court. The duty of the trustees of land to consult the beneficiaries does not encompass an obligation to do as they wish. Finally, transfer of title on the death of a tenant for life under the SLA is expensive and complicated, but no such problems arise should a trustee of land die. Similarly, there are differences in the way the two regimes protect a purchaser of the land and how the equitable interests are protected should that sale not be an overreaching transaction.

Notes

This is a long question: a whole book could be written in answer to it! It is important to establish the basic structure of each means of creating successive interests before comparing them. The trust of land under the TOLATA 1996 is a variant on the old trust for sale that was once the only alternative to the Settled Land Act 1925.

Question 16

Analyse the powers given to a tenant for life under a strict settlement governed by the Settled Land Act 1925. Can a wayward tenant be controlled in the exercise of those powers?

Answer plan

The following areas should be covered:

- the nature of a settlement;
- the position of the tenant for life in relation to the trustees and other beneficiaries;
- the powers of the tenant for life;
- the controls of the trustees.

Answer

It is in the nature of a settlement under the Settled Land Act (SLA) 1925 that there may be many occasions for conflict among the persons intended to be benefited by the settlor. A settlement necessarily gives one person a life interest in the property (the tenant for life) and another (or others) interests in the land after that life estate has ended. In this sense, therefore, two often contradictory interests need to be reconciled: the interest of the life tenant in actual possession of the property who wishes to enjoy the land (or the income it generates) during their life, and the interest of the persons entitled in remainder in keeping as much value locked into the settlement until their own interest 'falls in' on the life tenant's death. Prior to 1926, it was the persons entitled in remainder who held the upper hand as it was relatively easy to restrict the life tenant's ability to deal with the land and his ability to diminish its value. Unfortunately, this meant that much settled land stagnated because the tenant for life had no means of raising the money necessary to use the land profitably. Indeed, given that the tenant for life's rights over the land were so limited, there was little incentive for them to manage the land effectively. Under the SLA, the position has changed, as it is a fundamental feature of the Act that the tenant for life shall have both the legal estate in the land and extensive powers to deal with it, even to the point of selling it and converting all the beneficiaries' interests into money.

In the normal course of events, when the settlement is created, the settlor will appoint trustees of the settlement and, in some exceptional circumstances, they will have legal title and the powers conferred by the Act. In the normal case, however, these powers and the title will rest with the tenant for life. Of course, being trustees, the persons so appointed will have fiduciary responsibilities to all the beneficiaries, especially those entitled in remainder and, as *Wheelwright v Walker* makes clear, the trustees have a general supervisory function in relation to the settlement. This can result in an application to the court to control the tenant for life. However, the SLA makes it clear in no uncertain terms that the policy of behind the Act (encouraging the proper use of settled land) will be best served by giving considerable control to the tenant for life via the legal title and statutory powers.

In brief terms, the Act gives the tenant for life a wide range of powers and then subjects them to varying degrees of control by the trustees. Thus, a life tenant has a power of sale over the land (which will overreach the beneficial interests), although he is obliged to obtain the best price that can reasonably be made (*Wheelwright v Walker (No 2)* (1883)). There is also the power to exchange the land, to grant and accept leases, to mortgage the land in order to raise funds for its benefit and to grant options over the land. All of these powers may be exercised without the consent of the trustees, providing that the tenant gives written notice to the trustees and their solicitor, although it is clear from *Wheelwright* that, if there are no trustees, these powers cannot be exercised. However, even if the trustees have been given notice in the appropriate manner, they are under no obligation to interfere (*England v Public Trustee* (1968)) and they may accept less than the required one month's notice or waive it in writing altogether. Indeed, except for the power of mortgaging, the tenant for life may give general notice that he intends to exercise his powers at some point and this will suffice. In any event, under s 110 of the SLA, a purchaser from the tenant for life is protected against non-compliance by the life tenant. These are, then, fairly limited and relaxed controls and it is unlikely that they give great comfort to the other beneficiaries under the settlement. In respect of other powers – such as the power to dispose of the main house, to cut and sell timber, to sell chattels and to compromise claims – there is more control as these depend variously on obtaining the consent of the trustees or of the court. As such, this is not surprising, as these powers relate to those matters of a more personal nature (that is, as opposed to the land itself) in which the other beneficiaries may well have a legitimate interest. Even so, the fact that the tenant for life can sell the land with only minimal intervention by the trustees speaks volumes for the policy operating behind this statute.

Indeed, the matter is even clearer when we realise that it is virtually impossible to restrict the tenant for life in the exercise of his powers, other than under the mild provisions of the statute. Thus, under s 106 of the SLA, any provision in the settlement which attempts or purports to forbid the exercise of a statutory power by the tenant for life or which attempts, tends or is intended to induce the tenant for life not to exercise a power is void. Thus, in *Re Patten* (1929), certain gift overs of property which would *de facto* induce the tenant for life not to sell (and, thereby, not lose the property subject to the gifts over) were void. Likewise, in *Re Orelebar* (1936), a provision which forfeited the life tenant's interest if they quit the land was held void if their leaving was due to an exercise of a statutory power, although it would be upheld if the tenant for life left for any other reason. Some limitation on this very wide protection for the life tenant was provided by *Re Aberconway* (1953) which decided that, if what might be lost to the life tenant by virtue of an exercise of a power was not a benefit nor ancillary to his enjoyment of the land, s 106 would not operate to invalidate that stipulation. In a similar vein, the tenant for life cannot give up his powers, even if parting with all his interest (*Re Mundy* (1899)), although a surrender to the person next entitled (s 105 of the SLA), order of the court (s 24 of the SLA) and cases of lunacy can lead to those powers being exercised by other persons.

Perhaps, indeed, the only real control over the tenant for life arises under the general equitable jurisdiction to restrain breach of trust and supervise the actions of fiduciaries. By virtue of s 107 of the SLA, the tenant for life is deemed to be trustee for the beneficiaries of both the legal estate and the statutory powers. This means, in effect, that he must have regard to the interests of others when exercising his powers. On sale, therefore, the life tenant must sell as fairly as any trustee would sell, for the best price and recognising the interest of the remainderman: *Wheelwright v Walker*. Likewise, the tenant cannot accept payment in order to exercise his powers (*Chandler v Bradley* (1897); *Bray v Ford*) (1896)) as he is under a trustee's duty not to profit from his trust. There can be no fraud on the power (*Middlemas v Stevens* (1901)), but the transaction will not be invalidated simply because the tenant had an uncharitable motive, such as lack of interest in the land or dislike for the remainderman (*Cardigan v Curzon-Howe* (1885)). Of course, the extent of this general equitable jurisdiction is as flexible as it needs to be and is supported by the ability under s 24 of the SLA for an application to be made where a tenant for life has definitely refused (although not merely neglected) to exercise his powers under the Act (*Re 90 Thornhill Road* (1970)).

Finally, we must note that s 18 of the SLA gives a measure of protection to the other beneficiaries by providing that any transaction not authorised by the Act shall be invalidated (*Weston v Henshaw* (1950)), although it is not clear how this gels with the strong protection given to a purchaser who deals in good faith with the tenant for life under s 110 (*Re Morgan* (1972)).

All in all then, the tenant for life has a very wide measure of control over settled land and the trustees of the settlement can do little to restrain him save in clear cases of abuse. This is entirely consistent with the purposes behind the Settled Land Act: that use of land takes precedence over the motives of the settlor in trying to tie up land for his family.

Notes

A bookwork question needing much citation from the Settled Land Act. If more detail is required, the complicated arguments about how *Weston v Henshaw* and *Re Morgan* can be reconciled may be pursued.

CHAPTER 5

LEASES

Introduction

Leasehold interests are one of the two estates (along with freeholds) that are capable of existing at law or in equity (s 1 of the Law of Property Act 1925). In fact, the leasehold estate, whether it be equitable or legal, is one of the most versatile concepts found in the whole of the law of real property. Even the terminology of leases reflects the many purposes to which they may be put. The 'term of years', 'tenancies', 'sub-leases', and 'leasehold estate' are all synonymous and in terms of the legal rules governing their creation and operation the principles are the same, although one particular description may be more appropriate than another depending on the situation. So, for example, the term 'lease' is most often used for commercial or long term lettings whereas the term 'tenancy' is used for 'domestic' or shorter term lettings.

One of the most important feature of leaseholds is that they allow two or more estate owners to enjoy the benefits of the same piece of land at the same time: for example, the freeholder will receive the rent and profits and the leaseholder will enjoy physical possession and occupation of the property. Indeed, if a 'sub-tenancy' is involved, one lease will be carved out of another as where a freeholder, L, grants land to A for 30 years, who sub-lets to B for 25 years, who sub-lets to C for 10 years and so on. It is this ability of the leasehold estate to facilitate multiple enjoyment of land that gives it its special character. In addition, it is inherent in a lease that the rights and obligations undertaken by the original landlord and tenant concerning the land can be transmitted to persons who later step into the shoes of the original parties, as where a landlord assigns (transfers) the reversion or the tenant assigns the lease. The ability to make rights and obligations 'run' with the land is a special feature of the landlord and tenant relationship and legislation (Landlord and Tenant (Covenants) Act 1995) has enhanced this feature of the leasehold estate, at least for leases granted on or after 1 January 1996, the date the 1995 Act came into force.

Checklist

Questions on leasehold interests are a favourite for examiners, not least because they offer such diversity. In order to tackle questions concerning leases, the student must have an understanding of several important issues:

- the methods of creation of leasehold interests and the differences between equitable and legal leases;
- the difference in theory and practice between a 'lease' and a 'licence';
- the place of leasehold interests, both equitable and legal, within the machinery of registered and unregistered land;
- the rules relating to covenants in leases: types of covenants and the enforceability of leasehold covenants between the original parties and their successors in title; in particular, the differences between pre-1996 leases and those leases now governed by the Landlord and Tenant (Covenants) Act 1995 (LTCA), being leases granted on or after 1 January 1996;
- the remedies for breach of leasehold covenants, with particular reference to the remedy of forfeiture;
- the determination of leases.

Question 17

What is a lease?

Answer plan

The following areas should be covered:

- definition of a lease: *Street v Mountford*; *Bruton v London and Quadrant Housing Trust*;
- time certain: *Lace v Chandler*; *Prudential Assurance v London Residuary Body*;
- exclusive possession;
- rent;
- ss 52 and 54 of the Law of Property Act 1925;

- periodic tenancies;
- s 2 of the Law of Property (Miscellaneous Provisions) Act 1989;
- *Walsh v Lonsdale*.

Answer

By virtue of s 1 of the Law of Property Act 1925, a term of years absolute in possession is one of the two estates in land that may exist either at law or in equity. The term of years (or lease) is, consequently, one of the major forms of land ownership in England and Wales. It is, in addition, a concept of considerable versatility that can provide both occupation in a domestic or commercial enterprise, as well as income for the freeholder and even the leaseholder if the premises are sub-let. It is a peculiar feature of the leasehold estate that it can give several different estate owners the use or enjoyment of the land or its profits at the same time.

According to *Street v Mountford*, a lease can be defined as exclusive possession of property, for a term, at a rent. These three conditions are commonly regarded as the *indicia* of a leasehold, irrespective of the purpose for which the estate is created. It is clear, however, from *Ashburn Anstalt v Arnold* (relying on s 205 of the LPA 1925), that rent is not essential to the existence of a lease, although it will be a rare situation indeed where the parties to a transaction have intended to be legally bound by the relationship of landlord and tenant but have not specified the payment of rent. With this in mind, rent will be discussed below as if it were synonymous with the existence of a tenancy.

In addition to the principles established by *Street* which are, in fact, conditions required by the common law, the nature of leases is also governed by various statutory provisions. These provisions are largely to be found in the Law of Property Act 1925 and determine whether any particular lease is legal or equitable. Briefly, the position is that any lease for a period of more than three years must be by deed if it is to take effect as a legal estate (s 52 of the LPA). Leases for three years or less that give the tenant an immediate right to occupy without the payment of an initial premium (that is, a capital sum) may also be legal (s 54 of the

LPA) and into this category come many short term periodic tenancies, mainly governing domestic occupancy. Equitable leases, on the other hand usually result from a binding contract (or written agreement that can be treated as such a contract) between landlord and tenant that has not been put into effect by deed. If this contract is in writing (s 2 of the Law of Property (Miscellaneous Provisions) Act 1989) and is specifically enforceable, equity will regard the relationship between the parties as one governed by an equitable lease (*Walsh v Lonsdale*). The exception to this are equitable leases arising out of proprietary estoppel. These can be completely oral and arise out of the inequitable conduct of the landlord (see *Taylor Fashions v Liverpool Victoria Trustees; Orgee v Orgee*).

Turning, then, to the position at common law. The *Street* requirements define the inherent nature of a lease and set the parameters outside of which a lease simply cannot exist, irrespective of the intention of the parties or whether the above statutory formalities are complied with. The first is the requirement of 'time certain' or, in other words, the requirement that the lease must exist for a clearly defined period of time. This means not only that the lease must start at a clearly defined moment, but also that the term granted must be certain. The lease must be of certain maximum duration at the commencement of the lease. Any lease, or rather any intended lease, that fails to satisfy this condition is necessarily void because it does not amount to a 'term'. In *Lace v Chandler*, for example, a lease for the duration of the second world war was held void as being of uncertain maximum duration. In recent years, the principle of time certain has been under attack and courts once appeared willing to accept arrangements which on a proper construction could not be said to have a certain term. In *Ashburn Anstalt v Arnold*, an arrangement whereby a tenant occupied property indefinitely until the landlord gave three months' notice was held to be a lease on the ground that the term could be rendered certain by action of one of the parties. This does seem to contradict the rule that a lease must be certain at the date of its commencement and so it came as no surprise when, in 1992, the House of Lords in *Prudential Assurance v London Residuary Body* reaffirmed the rule that a leasehold term must be certain from the outset. It is not enough that the term can, in fact, be rendered certain by action of either the landlord or the tenant after the lease has commenced. This is a significant and welcome return to the orthodox position. Finally, one further point needs to be borne in mind when talking about time certain. It often happens that a tenant may occupy premises and pay a regular sum to the landlord in respect of that occupation. There may well be no written record of this arrangement. In these circumstances, a tenancy of a certain duration will be presumed from the facts. Thus, if money is paid weekly in respect of a week's occupation, a periodic tenancy of one week will be presumed and, likewise, if payment is made monthly or quarterly. Obviously, if a further week's, month's or quarterly payment is made, the lease will continue and can in this sense continue indefinitely so long as the payment is made. However, although such a situation appears to be a lease for an uncertain period, in fact, it is a succession of periodic tenancies; that is, one week after one week or one month after one month and so on. These relatively short term periodic tenancies are common in residential lettings and should not be thought to contradict the principle of time certain.

The other common law conditions for the existence of a lease are not so controversial although they may be just as difficult to identify in practice. The concept of exclusive possession is notoriously elusive as can be seen in the confused and confusing debate over the distinction between a lease and a licence. In essence, the existence of exclusive possession is a matter for the construction of the agreement between the parties in the light of their conduct in relation to the property (*Antoniades v Villiers*). Thus, if the occupier has been granted the exclusive right to use the property, even to the exclusion of the landlord, then there is a strong presumption that the agreement amounts to a lease. The only exceptions to this are those cases identified by Lord Templeman in *Street* where, because of some special circumstance, exclusive possession may exist but a tenancy does not. An example is the service occupancy of *Norris v Checksfield*, where the right to occupy was given to an employee for the better performance of his duties, and cases where the occupation is given as an act of generosity, friendship or charity, as in *Gray v Taylor* (1998), where occupation of an almshouse did not indicate the existence of a lease.

Finally, we come to rent, the receipt of which is usually the main reason why the landlord has granted the tenancy in the first place. As noted above, under s 205 of the LPA, it is clear that rent is not an essential requirement of a lease, although certain types of tenancies such as those within the Rent Acts must be supported by rent to qualify for statutory protection. Indeed, that is why, in *Street*, Lord Templeman refers to rent, that being a case concerning the application of the Rent Acts. In fact, the existence of rent as an adjunct to a lease is so likely that, in the absence of an express promise by the tenant, a covenant to pay rent can easily be implied from the words of a deed. Likewise, the absence of a rent obligation may mean that the parties have not intended to create any type of obligation at all (see *Javad v Aqil* (1991)). It is, however, a common misconception that rent has to be in monetary form. It can be in goods, services, or payable in kind. The only clear requirement is that the amount of rent must be capable of being rendered certain. Thus, in *Bostock v Bryant*, the obligation to pay fluctuating utility bills could not be regarded as rent, being an uncertain sum.

The defining features of the leasehold estate have been described above and reference to its versatility has been made. This versatility is reflected in the terminology of leasehold estates where 'term of years', 'lease', 'tenancy', 'periodic tenancy' and 'sub-lease' all describe situations within which the relationship of landlord and tenant can exist. That relationship has many advantages, both for the landlord and the tenant (for example, simultaneous enjoyment of property, leasehold covenants, occupation or income generation) and that is why it has survived the many statutory reforms of the law of real property in the 20th century. Finally, mention must be made of the House of Lords decision in *Bruton v London and Quadrant Housing Trust*. In that case, it was suggested that 'a lease' could exist in favour of an occupier even though the 'landlord' did not actually have an estate in the land himself out of which to grant a lease (the landlord had a licence). This controversial view requires acceptance of the idea that not all 'leases' are really estates in the land after all, but may be personal to the original parties (a so called 'non-proprietary lease'). Suffice it to say that this view has not been universally welcomed and remains suspect.

Question 18

Are there any significant differences between the creation and the operation of legal, as opposed to equitable leases?

Answer plan

The following areas should be covered:

- ss 52 and 54 of the Law of Property Act 1925;
- periodic tenancies;
- s 2 of the Law of Property (Miscellaneous Provisions) Act 1989;
- *Walsh v Lonsdale*;
- registered and unregistered land;
- leasehold covenants (pre-1996 leases only);
- s 62 of the LPA 1925.

Answer

Under s 52 of the Law of Property Act 1925, all legal leases except those which are exempt under s 52(2) must be created by deed. This is the basic principle in respect of the creation of legal leases. The exception granted by statute is for those leases which take effect in possession for not more than three years without a fine. This is merely a complicated way of saying that leases for three years or less which entitle the tenant to go into immediate possession and which require only the payment of rent and not an initial lump sum are legal leases without the need for a deed. Thus, the periodic tenancy, where an occupier goes into occupation and pays a defined sum for a period usually of one week, one month or one quarter, will amount to a legal tenancy because the rent will be paid in respect of periods of less than three years. It matters not that, in fact, the periodic tenant may occupy for many years because, in theory, this is just a succession of periodic tenancies. Of course, this means that the tenancy can be determined by the giving of one period's notice (subject to a statutory minimum of four weeks notice: s 2 of the Protection from Eviction Act 1977), but, while it continues, it is legal in character. In fact, the provisions of ss 52 and 54 are relatively simple but they only tell us how legal leases can be created. What of leases that take effect in equity only?

The practical reality is that many leases are created in the absence of a deed (despite the fact that the Law of Property (Miscellaneous Provisions) Act 1989 simplified the requirements for their execution), but the majority of these are for three years or less and qualify as legal interests, as discussed above. So, it is unusual for a lease of over three years' duration to be created without the use of a deed – primarily because the parties routinely use lawyers who proceed to execute the lease by deed. However, circumstances do arise where the parties do not proceed by deed, perhaps because property professionals are not involved and the need for a deed is not known or even because the parties are content to rely on a written (but non-deed) record of their agreement. In such cases – that is, a lease of over three years not executed by deed – if there is a written contract (or a written record of an agreement that can be treated as if it were a contract), the parties may be taken to have created an equitable lease. In simple terms, an equitable lease arises from an enforceable contract between landlord and tenant to grant a legal lease, but where no grant of a legal lease has in fact occurred. There are a number of distinct steps in this process. First, the contract between prospective landlord and tenant must be enforceable: viz, the contract must in writing containing all the terms and signed by both parties: s 2 of the Law of Property (Miscellaneous Provisions) Act 1989, replacing s 40 of the LPA 1925 (which allowed oral contracts if supported by acts of part performance). In this connection, 'written contract' means either a written document clearly expressed to be a contract or a written record of agreement that the law is prepared to treat as contract. A good example of the latter is where A and B set down in writing the terms on which A will let her house to B. A and B may not intend to take any further steps to create the lease, perhaps believing they have done all that is necessary, but their written agreement will be treated as a 'written contract to grant a lease'. We should also note that in future, it will be possible to execute a 'written' contract electronically

Secondly, this properly created contract must be specifically enforceable, for it is the specific enforceability of the contract that allows it to be regarded as an equitable lease. If the contract is specifically enforceable, this means that it would be executed by order of a court and, because equity regards as done what ought to be done, the unexecuted but enforceable contract will be regarded as an equitable lease (*Walsh v Lonsdale*). Of course, if the contract is in fact carried out, a legal lease by deed will be the result, but, usually, a dispute arises between the parties precisely because there is no deed. A contract will be specifically enforceable if valuable consideration has been paid by the tenant, if damages for breach of contract would be an inadequate remedy and if the person seeking to enforce the contract has not themselves behaved inequitably. Usually these three conditions are easily satisfied (the first two almost by definition) and, in most cases, an equitable tenancy can be established. Furthermore, *Walsh* makes it clear that, if in the circumstances there is a choice between a legal periodic tenancy (because the tenant is in occupation and paying rent) and an equitable tenancy on the same terms as the proposed but defunct lease by deed, the equitable tenancy will take priority as this gives efficacy to the parties' agreement. So, for example, any intended covenants in the failed legal lease will take effect in the equitable lease.

It is plain to see, then, that the requirements for an equitable lease have changed somewhat since 1989, primarily because of the requirement of writing. There is, however, one small exception to this. It may still be possible to create a lease longer than three years entirely out of oral agreements providing that those oral agreements amount to a proprietary estoppel within the rules of *Taylor Fashions v Liverpool Victoria Trustees*. So, if a landlord assures an occupier that they have a tenancy and the occupier relies on that to their detriment, an estoppel tenancy may well result (cf *Orgee v Orgee*). This will be equitable and, even if over three years without writing, would be enforceable against the landlord.

Despite the apparent ease with which an equitable lease can be created, it is clear that the parties to a legal lease do enjoy significant advantages, not least because a purchaser of the landlord's right (his 'reversion') will almost certainly be aware of the existence of any legal tenancy. So, for example, in registered land, currently a legal lease of over 21 years' duration will be registered with its own title number. (This will change to leases over seven years under the Land Registration Act 2002.) Even if it is not (say because someone has forgotten to register, as in *Barclays Bank v Zaroovabli* (1997)), the legal lease will be an overriding interest under s 70(1)(g) of the LRA 1925 as the tenant is likely to be a person in 'actual occupation'. Likewise, legal leases for 21 years or less are by definition overriding interests: s 70(1)(k) of the LRA 1925. This means that a purchaser of registered land is going to be bound by the legal lease come what may. Similarly, in unregistered land, the deed (or fact of occupation under a legal periodic tenancy) will be obvious and, after all, in unregistered land legal rights bind the whole world. As much cannot be said, however, for equitable leases.

Equitable leases can sometimes be difficult for a purchaser of the reversion to discover (although the requirement of writing in the 1989 Act may relieve this somewhat), but they can be destroyed on a sale of that reversion. Like all equitable interests, equitable leases are *prima facie* vulnerable to purchasers, that is, to purchasers of the freehold land over which the lease exists. In unregistered land, for example, the equitable tenant is required to register his interest as a Class C(iv) land charge under the Land Charges Act. Should he fail to do so, the equitable tenancy is not binding on any purchaser of the reversion of a legal estate for money or money's worth (s 4 of the Land Charges Act). This was just the position in *Hollington Brothers v Rhodes* and no amount of occupation, obvious or otherwise, can help. Moreover, if the equitable lease has resulted from proprietary estoppel, it is probably unregistrable as a land charge (cf *Ives v High*). In that case, the old doctrine of notice comes into play and this is unsatisfactory for both the purchaser and the equitable tenant.

In registered land, the position is more satisfactory, at least for the tenant. Whereas the equitable tenant may protect their interest by way of notice as a minor interest, they may rely in the alternative on s 70(1)(g) of the LRA to gain an overriding interest as a person in actual occupation of the premises. Of course, this is all very well for the equitable tenant, but it does mean that the purchaser of the reversion may well become bound by an interest that was informally created. Of course, in many situations the fact of occupation (and, hence, the equitable lease) may well be obvious and the purchaser will be warned of the overriding interest, but this is not always going to be true (for example,

Ferrishurst Ltd v Wallcite Ltd; Malory v Cheshire Homes (2002)), especially with estoppel leases that can still be entirely oral.

Further difficulties with equitable leases also arise in the context of leasehold covenants, although these have been eliminated for leases granted on or after 1 January 1996 by the Landlord and Tenant (Covenants) Act 1995 (LTCA). So, for pre-1996 equitable leases, the general position is that although covenants in the lease will be enforceable between the original landlord and the original equitable tenant (because of privity of contract), they may well be unenforceable between successors in title to those persons. Being a pre-1996 equitable lease (and despite contrary *dicta* in *Boyer v Warbey*), the traditional view is that there is no 'privity of estate' between a successor to the landlord and an assignee of the tenant. In fact, it is the landlord that suffers most in this situation because the burden of covenants entered into by the original tenant (that is the obligation to perform them) may well not be passed to an assignee of an equitable lease, unless they can be enforced as restrictive covenants under *Tulk v Moxhay*. Indeed, it is worse than this because the new equitable reversioner (the new landlord) is under the burdens of the equitable lease as these are statutorily transmitted on a sale of the reversion by s 142 of the LPA. Thus, the new landlord can be sued on the original covenants of an equitable lease but unless *Tulk* applies he cannot sue the new tenant. Fortunately, for equitable leases granted on or after 1 January 1996, the LTCA 1995 ensures that both the benefits and burdens of leasehold covenants pass to both an assignees of the landlord and an assignee of the tenant.

Finally, there are some provisions of the Law of Property Act relating to conveyances of land that apply only to conveyances of a legal estate. The most important of these in practice is s 62 of the LPA which can be used to imply easements into a tenancy in favour of the tenant; for example, an easement of way. Unfortunately, s 62 is restricted to transfer of a legal estate and cannot be relied upon by an equitable tenant.

Ultimately, then, it is better for all parties if a legal lease is established. Not only is the very existence of the equitable lease dependent on the availability of specific performance, its informal nature poses problems for purchaser and tenant alike.

Notes

These first two questions require a thorough understanding of the nature of leases and the method of their creation. Apart from being relatively straightforward, such knowledge is required when dealing with problems from other areas, such as the mechanism of registered and unregistered land. Recent developments which may cause problems are the effect of s 2 of the Law of Property (Miscellaneous Provisions) Act on the creation of equitable leases and the distinction between pre-1996 leases and later leases concerning the running of leasehold covenants. The answer will need further refinement when the provisions of the Land Registration Act 2002 come into force. These will allow the use of 'electronic' deeds and written contracts and, eventually, will provide that no lease at all will exist in registered land unless an appropriate entry is made on the register.

Question 19

In 1985, Lord Templeman in *Street v Mountford* stated that the defining features of a lease were exclusive possession, for a term, at a rent. Is this still the case?

Answer plan

The following areas should be covered:
- the existence of rights v intention of the parties;
- lodgers and tenants;
- exceptions to exclusive possession;
- *Antoniades v Villiers*; *Westminster CC v Clarke*; *Bruton v London and Quadrant Housing Trust*; *Royal Bank of Scotland v Mehta*.

Answer

A lease is properly regarded as a proprietary right, an interest in land capable of binding third parties (despite the unorthodox decision in *Bruton v London and Quadrant Housing Trust*).

Moreover, despite some suggestions to the contrary (for example, *Errington v Errington and Woods*), a licence is a personal right, usually arising out of contract, which as a matter of principle is not capable of binding third parties under property law principles (*Ashburn Anstalt v Arnold*, confirmed in *Lloyd v Dugdale* (2001)). It is from this basic distinction that so many practical consequences flow. Indeed, the great majority of cases on the lease/licence distinction have been the result of occupiers trying to claim the protection of the 1977 Rent Act or later Housing Acts, because the protection they offer is available to a tenant, not always to a licensee. Of course, the ability of landlords to grant non-protected tenancies under the Housing Act 1996 may affect the volume of litigation before the courts on this subject, but the distinction between a lease and a licence forms the boundary between property and contract and will always be contentious.

Lord Templeman's judgment in *Street v Mountford* (overruling the intention based approach of *Somma v Hazlehurst*) caused something of a stir. Not only did he propound an abstract test for distinguishing between a lease and a licence ('exclusive possession for a term at a rent'), he told us how to apply it. First, there are certain exceptional situations where the occupier may (or may not) have exclusive possession of the property but, for special reasons, no tenancy will result. One example is where a mortgagee goes into possession under the terms of her mortgage and another where the occupation is based on charity or friendship, as in *Gray v Taylor*, or where there is no intention to create legal relations between the owner and the occupier (cf *Javad v Aqil*). These exempted categories were explained at length in *Facchini v Bryson* and that they are alive and well is demonstrated by *Norris v Checksfield*. In that case, the occupier of a cottage was held to be a 'service occupant' and hence a licensee, although the Court of Appeal did warn that this was an exceptional situation justified only because the occupation of the cottage was for the better performance of the employee's duties.

Secondly, apart from the exceptional situations, according to Lord Templeman, an occupier must either be a lodger (a licensee) or a tenant. This practical distinction between a lodger and a tenant is crucial. A lodger is someone who receives attendance and services from the landlord, such as room cleaning or meals.

Such a person will be a licensee, although, as *Markou v Da Silvaesa* illustrates, a mere promise to provide such services is not sufficient. They must actually be provided. However, if it is true that an occupier is *either* a lodger or a tenant, this means that no other kind of 'occupation licence' can exist. If someone is not a lodger, they are a tenant. There is no intermediate category of licensee who, while not a lodger, is still not a tenant. Obviously, this has far reaching consequences for it restricts the options open to a landlord when seeking to make use of her property. It is the triumph of property law over freedom of contract and it is precisely this that subsequent cases have found difficult to accept. Indeed, many of the apparently inconsistent decisions of the Court of Appeal have resulted from attempts to identify some middle way, some form of occupation that can still give rise to a licence, but where the occupier is not a lodger. *Hadjiloucas v Creen* and *Brooker Estates v Ayers*, both decisions of the Court of Appeal quite soon after *Street*, are of this type.

Nevertheless, under the influence of Lord Templeman in the House of Lords (for example, *Antoniades v Villiers*, *Westminster CC v Clarke*) and Lord Donaldson in the Court of Appeal (for example, *Aslan v Murphy*), a degree of certainty has emerged. First, cases of multiple occupancy may give rise to licences in favour of the occupiers because of the absence of the four unities necessary to support a joint-tenancy of the whole premises. This is the result of *AG Securities v Vaughan*. So, if four people occupy a four bedroom house, but each sign different agreements, on different days and for a different rent, there can be no exclusive possession/joint tenancy because there is no unity of interest, title, or time. The house, as a whole, cannot be held on a tenancy. Each occupier may have a tenancy of their own rooms, with a licence over the common parts, but there is no single tenancy of the property as a whole.

Secondly, there are certain types of public sector landlords who may be able to grant licences in circumstances where a private landlord could not. Examples are *Westminster CC v Basson*, *Ogwr BC v Dykes* and the House of Lords' decision in *Westminster CC v Clarke*. In these cases, the licence is allowed not because of the intention of the landlord – for that would be to return to *Somma v Hazlehurst* – but because of a policy decision, namely that public sector landlords must not be hindered in the exercise of their statutory housing duties. It is clear, of course, that public sector landlords and similar bodies will be held to have granted tenancy if this is justified on the facts (see *Family Housing Association v Jones*) and, it seems, will even be held to have given a lease if they themselves had no estate in the land (*Bruton v London and Quadrant Housing Trust*). This is discussed below.

Thirdly, Lord Oliver in *Antoniades* suggests that there may be circumstances where a landlord can genuinely reserve to himself the right to make use of the premises and, if such use is made, no exclusive possession is given. In effect, this is no more than a restatement of the distinction between exclusive possession and exclusive *occupation*: the former establishing the legal relationship of landlord and tenant, the latter describing a factual situation devoid of proprietary effect. An example might be where an academic lets his house to students but reserves the right to enter the house and use his library. This is, of course, open to abuse and in the light of his speech in *Antoniades*, it is doubtful whether Lord Templeman would agree that it is even a possibility. However, the door has been left open by Lord Oliver for future development in genuine cases, and it is implicit in the decision in *Royal Bank of Scotland v Mehta* where, despite apparent exclusive possession, the occupier of an hotel room was said to have a licence, presumably because it is never intended to create a lease of such a property.

Fourthly, in *Bruton v London and Quadrant Housing Trust* (1999), a quasi-public sector manager of land (the Trust) was held by the House of Lords to have granted the plaintiff a valid lease to occupy, even though the Trust had no estate in the land. This is unusual as normally the absence of an estate in the landlord means, by definition, that the occupier cannot have an estate (a lease) but must have a licence. As noted, the Trust itself held only a licence to manage the land (granted to it by the local authority landowner) and argued that because it held no proprietary right, it could never have granted the plaintiff a tenancy. In its view, the plaintiff must have a licence, carved out of the Trust's own licence. In rejecting this argument, the House of Lords said that a 'lease' was not always an estate in the land, but could be a merely personal arrangement between 'landlord' and 'tenant'. Apparently, this non-proprietary lease was justified by the

111

exclusive possession of the 'tenant', even though the landlord could not grant the *kind* of exclusive possession (that is, of an estate in the land) that was so crucial in *Street v Mountford*. This decision and its reasoning has attracted some sharp criticism and it is not clear why this 'non-proprietary lease' is not properly identified as a licence! It means, however, that leases can exist even if the grantor has no estate in the land.

Finally, all of the above is subject to the doctrine of pretences. Any clause, in any agreement, will not be given legal effect if it is not intended to be relied on by either party to the agreement but is merely inserted in it to avoid the grant of the tenancy that would otherwise arise. Thus, in *Antoniades* itself, an agreement providing for the separate occupancy of an unmarried couple in what was to be their home was held to be a tenancy because the separate agreements were clearly a pretence. It should be noted in this regard, that the doctrine of 'pretences' has replaced that of shams: a 'sham' transaction is where only one party does not intended a clause in a lease to have legal effect and, of course, a landlord always intends in these cases to deny, by means of a clause like that used as in *Antoniades*, the creation of a lease.

To conclude then, the case law after *Street* has finally taken a decidedly practical path where the emphasis is on identifying those factual situations which can give rise to a licence and those which can give rise to a tenancy. This may not be the most intellectually satisfying approach – after all, we have not defined 'exclusive possession' – but it is the most realistic. The most serious reservation is the uncertainty caused by the House of Lords decision in *Bruton v London and Quadrant*.

Question 20

Nellie is the registered proprietor of freehold land comprising a large Victorian property in the centre of town. The house has four storeys, including a basement. Nellie has just inherited a small bungalow in the country and has decided to move out. She wishes to let the property but is determined not to have long term tenants just in case she wants to return to the city. She divides the house into two self-contained, one bedroomed apartments on the first and second floors, and one self-contained two bedroomed flat on the ground floor/basement. She agrees in writing with Ivor and Anne, a young unmarried couple, that they can occupy the two roomed flat and produces two documents which state in each that 'this agreement does not intend to create a term of years' and gets them to sign separately and on different days for a 'fee' of £80 per week each. She lets the first floor flat to Steven, an apprentice builder, who is to carry out repairs to the premises. Steven pays no money, but each week £50 is deducted from his wages. Nellie keeps a key to Steven's flat, primarily to inspect the building works at the weekend when Steven is away. The top floor flat is given to Nellie's son, Tony, a university drop out with nowhere else to go. Tony is not the most reliable individual, so Steven is asked to keep an eye on him and to make sure that he gets regular meals.

Nellie has now decided to move to the country permanently and sells the entire premises to Peter, a property developer. Peter wishes to evict all the occupants and redevelop the site.

Advise him.

Answer plan

The answer needs to include the following:

- leases and licences;
- *Antoniades v Villiers*;
- *Street v Mountford*;
- *Mikeover v Brady*;
- *Aslan v Murphy*;
- s 70(1) of the Land Registration Act 1925.

Answer

This problem concerns the distinction between a lease and a licence. A lease is traditionally a proprietary right, whereas a licence is a mere personal arrangement between two parties (*Ashburn Anstalt v Arnold*). The practical difference this makes in this problem is clear. If the arrangements entered into by Nellie with her respective occupiers amount to leases, then they have the ability to bind Peter the purchaser when he acquires the freehold title. If, however, the arrangements are properly to be regarded as licences, then, in principle, they cannot bind Peter and the occupiers will have to vacate the premises.

In general terms, the distinction between a lease and a licence was summarised by Lord Templeman in *Street v Mountford*. A lease exists where an occupier has been granted exclusive possession of the property, for a term, at a rent. The answer is not to be found in the label attached to the agreement by the parties but in the nature of the agreement created by the parties. Not surprisingly, this formula is subject to some exceptions, notably, those known as the *Facchini v Bryson* categories, which relate to special, limited, factual situations where for some reason, external to the parties, no tenancy will exist even though exclusive possession may have been granted. The main practical distinction resulting from Lord Templeman's formula is that an occupier must be either a tenant or a lodger, the latter being someone in receipt of attendance and services from the landlord and so without exclusive possession (*Markou v Da Silvaesa*). Finally, we must also be aware of the doctrine of pretences (see, for example, *Antoniades v Villiers*), whereby the court will examine an agreement between the parties to discover whether its terms genuinely reflect the actual relationship between the parties. Only if the agreement is 'genuine' in this sense will any clauses in the agreement affecting 'exclusive possession' be given legal effect.

(a) Ivor and Anne

Clearly, the agreement between Nellie on the one hand and Ivor and Anne on the other is designed to allow them to occupy the premises and, from Nellie's point of view, to prevent the grant of a tenancy: this much is expressly stated in the documents which both Ivor and Anne sign. At one time, such an express statement of the parties 'intention' (query whether Ivor and Anne can really be said to share this intention) would have been enough to prevent a lease being granted (*Somma v Hazlehurst*). Now, after *Street*, it is clear that it is the nature of the relationship that is important and not what the parties decide to call that relationship. Thus, if this agreement amounts to a lease under the *Street* formula, it will be a lease irrespective of the label attached to it.

Clearly, Nellie has had some well informed legal advice, for she has made every attempt to prevent the couple enjoying exclusive possession. She has, in fact, attempted to deny them a tenancy by seeking to grant each of them a separate licence whereby neither of them has exclusive possession of the whole but each occupies in common with the other, as in *Mikeover v Brady*. The only way that Ivor and Anne can refute this is to establish that they have been granted exclusive possession jointly: in other words that they are joint-tenants of a leasehold interest. As was made clear in *AG Securities v Vaughan*, for a joint-tenancy of a leasehold estate to exist, the 'four unities' must be present: there must be unity of interest, title, possession and time and this is what Nellie has tried to prevent. In this case, as in *Vaughan* itself, the landlord has persuaded the parties to sign different documents on different days. It looks as if there is no unity of time or of title. In *Vaughan*, these facts, plus the different rents paid by the occupiers, clearly meant that no leasehold joint-tenancy of the whole property could exist. The parties were occupying separately not jointly. Moreover, even if *Vaughan* is not quite in point, because, in that case, the property was always intended to be for independent, ever changing, occupants, Nellie can clearly rely on the decision in *Mikeover v Brady*. In that case, a flat was let to two people by two separate agreements, each responsible for one-half of the total 'fee'. Despite the fact that the occupiers wished to co-habit jointly (that is, as a couple), the agreements were held to confer separate licences only. The facts of our case are very similar indeed.

Perhaps, however, there is one further possibility. In *Antoniades v Villiers*, the appellants were a young couple, living together as if married in a joint home. This fact was known to the landlord. In the House of Lords, this arrangement was held to create a joint-tenancy of the leasehold estate, despite the fact of separate 'licence' agreements similar to those signed by Ivor and Anne. According to Lord Templeman, the landlord's attempt to deny the couple exclusive possession jointly was a pretence designed entirely to avoid the imposition of a lease. As such, it would be ignored and the 'true' nature of the parties' bargain respected. If we follow *Antoniades*, then, and assuming Nellie knew that Ivor and Anne wished to live together, this agreement may still amount to a lease. Despite the fact that separate agreements were signed, and on different days, there will be a joint-tenancy of the leasehold estate because this was the true nature of the bargain.

If the couple do have a lease, then it would appear to be equitable. The agreement is in writing (not by deed and not legal) and probably amounts to a specifically enforceable contract. Assuming this, equity will regard this as an equitable lease under *Walsh v Lonsdale*. When the property is sold to Peter, presumably the couple are in actual occupation and would, therefore, have an overriding interest under s 70(1)(g) of the LRA. If the lease is not equitable, the arrangement may well amount to a legal periodic tenancy because of rent paid and accepted for the weekly term. If that were true, it would be overriding under s 70(1)(k) of the LRA (*Barclays Bank v Zaroovabli* (1997)). Of course, the lease is binding on Peter only according to its terms. He may terminate it on giving the appropriate notice unless it is protected by the Rent Acts or Housing Acts.

(b) Steven

Steven is in occupation of the first floor flat and, again, the nature of his occupancy is crucial in determining whether Peter can acquire immediate possession. Whether or not Steven has a tenancy may well depend on whether Steven's occupancy falls within one of the exceptional categories identified by Lord Templeman in *Street* as being occasions where even though exclusive possession may have been granted, no tenancy results. As a preliminary point, it might be thought that the apparent lack of rent destroys any chance of a tenancy. However, as confirmed in *Ashburn*, relying on s 205 of the LPA, the payment of rent is not essential for the existence of a tenancy. Lord Templeman's comments in *Street* should be read in context: viz, that the case was concerned with the Rent Acts, under which tenancies do need to be supported by rent to qualify for statutory protection. In any event, we can argue forcefully that the weekly deduction from Steven's wages does amount to rent. There is no rule that 'rent' must be described as such, so long as the payment made is in respect of the right to occupy the demised premises.

Steven's problem is, however, that his occupation seems to be a 'service occupancy'. He appears to be in occupation of the premises for 'the better performance of his duties' as Nellie's employee/builder. A *bona fide* service occupancy clearly creates a licence and was one of the original *Facchini* exceptions. That it still can occur has been confirmed in the recent case of *Norris v Checksfield*. Subject to the warning in that case that the court must be astute to detect 'pretences', as where the occupant is given minimal employment duties to make it appear as if there is a service occupancy, our case seems to fall into this category. If anything, Steven is more like a caretaker than a tenant. Assuming, then, that Steven has a licence by way of service occupancy Peter cannot be bound by the agreement. A mere licence is binding only on the parties and Steven will have to quit (*Ashburn Anstalt v Arnold; Lloyd v Dugdale* (2001)).

(c) Tony

As far as Nellie's son, Tony, is concerned, the circumstances also seem to give rise to a licence. There is every indication that Tony's occupation of the top floor flat can be put down to normal family considerations rather than the creation of a tenancy. As in *Heslop v Burns*, this is not a situation where the parties had an intention to enter into legal relations at all. This is within one of the *Facchini* excepted categories: viz, occupation based on friendship, generosity or family arrangement (see, also, *Gray v Taylor* (1998)). Moreover, if this were not enough, Nellie could even argue that Tony was a lodger and by definition not a tenant (*Street*). The facts suggest that Tony is in receipt attendance and services as provided by Steven, who may be regarded as Nellie's agent for these purposes. On this interpretation of the facts, Tony could be within *Markou v Da Silvaesa* and a licensee by virtue of a genuine lodger relationship. Once again, as this is a licence there is no possibility of Peter being bound.

So, to conclude, with the possible exception of the arrangement agreed with Ivor and Anne, Nellie has successfully avoided granting any leases over her property. Peter can obtain vacant possession. Finally, we can note that Nellie would have been well advised to have granted short term assured tenancies under the Housing Act 1996. These fall outside the Rent Acts and possession can be recovered easily. This would have avoided all the difficulties Nellie experienced.

Notes

Questions 3 and 4 are variations on the same theme: the distinction between a lease and a licence. There is a welter of case law here and it is easy to get lost. A firm grasp of *Street, Antoniades, Vaughan* and *Bruton* is a good base point. There are, however, always new cases and examiners do tend to concentrate on novel or unusual points (*Bruton*). The role of the public sector landlord or tenant (see *Tower Hamlets LBC v Miah*) is currently the most litigious aspect of this area. Another litigious area is unusual occupation settings, such as occupier of hotels (*Mehta*).

Question 21

Were the defects in the law relating to the enforceability of leasehold covenants so serious as to justify the scheme introduced by the Landlord and Tenant (Covenants) Act 1995 for leases granted after 31 December 1995?

Answer plan

The answer needs to include a discussion of the following areas:

- outline of rules applicable to pre-1996 leases;
- defects of pre-1996 rules;
- purpose of LTCA 1995;
- provisions of LTCA 1995;
- overall effect of LTCA 1995.

Answer

In 1988, the Law Commission produced a Report and a Draft Bill (No 174) containing various proposals for the reform of the law of leasehold covenants. In their view, the need to iron out the idiosyncrasies, the illogicalities and the plain injustices of the then current law justified a fundamental reordering of its rules. To this end, the Law Commission set out to resolve what they believed to be two of the most fundamental problems: the principle of continuing liability throughout the entire term of the lease for the original landlord and tenant and the notoriously elusive concept of covenants that 'touch and concern' the land. These goals remained at the heart of the legislative proposals that subsequently became the Landlord and Tenant (Covenants) Act 1995. Today, this Act (LTCA 1995) governs the enforceability of leasehold covenants in leases granted after 31 December 1995, whether the lease be legal or equitable. However, for leases granted prior to this, the 'old' rules apply. Consequently, there are currently two sets of distinct legal principles governing the enforceability of leasehold covenants and by comparing them we can discover whether the radical reforms of LTCA 1995 were really necessary.

For leases granted before 1 January 1996 (non-LTCA leases), the enforceability of leasehold covenants revolves around privity of contract, privity of estate and statutory magic. The original parties to a lease will be bound throughout the entirety of the term to perform the covenants they have agreed to, whether those covenants be personal or not. Thus, both the original landlord (*Stuart v Joy*) and the original tenant (*Arlesford Trading Co v Servansingh*) can be sued for failure to perform the leasehold covenants by the person who enjoys the benefit of those covenants irrespective of the time the breach was committed or by whom. This is the principle of continuing liability and it flows from the very nature of a lease as a contract. Of course, it is open to the original parties of a lease to stipulate expressly that their liability shall be limited to the period in which they enjoyed possession but, as the Law Commission pointed out when considering reform, this is quite unlikely especially for a tenant in what is typically a landlord's market. The continuing liability of the landlord and tenant under a pre-1996 lease is a primary one, so that they may be sued on the covenants even though the plaintiff has an obvious remedy against the person actually committing the breach, such as an assignee.

The second major area of difficulty identified by the Law Commission was the requirement for pre-1996 leases that a covenant must 'touch and concern the land' (*Spencer's* case) (and the equivalent under statute that it must have 'reference to the

119

subject matter of the lease': ss 141 and 142 of the LPA), before it can bind successors in title. So, for pre-1996 leases, if privity of estate exists between plaintiff and defendant (that is, they are current landlord and tenant under a legal lease), the assignee of a tenant will acquire the benefit and burden of all those covenants that touch and concern the land (*Spencer's* case). Likewise, the benefit and the burden of all of the original landlord's covenants will be passed to an assignee of the reversion if they have reference to the subject matter of the lease (ss 141 and 142 of the LPA). Obviously, such a central concept for pre-1996 leases needs to be applied consistently and, if possible, have a core meaning. The Law Commission were of the view that this was not the case, despite the guidance provided by the House of Lords in *Swift Investments v Combined English Stores*, where Lord Oliver developed a three stage test, namely: (a) whether the covenant could benefit any estate owner as opposed to the particular original covenantee; (b) whether the covenant affected the nature, quality, mode of user or value of the land; and (c) whether the covenant was expressed to be personal. Of course, this is somewhat circular and it is obvious that whether a covenant 'touches and concerns' will still be a matter for judgment in each individual case. It is this element of inconsistency and uncertainty that prompted the Law Commission to propose a radical reform: the abolition of the distinction between covenants which do and covenants which do not touch and concern the land for LTCA leases.

Thirdly, there are a number of other matters which attracted the attention of the Law Commission and which still operate for pre-1996 leases. So, it is uncertain whether an assignee of the reversion is liable for breaches of covenants committed by the original landlord before assignment. As a matter of principle, it would seem that he should not be, but *dicta* in *Celsteel v Alton* (1985) suggests otherwise. Again, there is a certain inequality in the fact that a landlord loses the right to sue on the covenants when he assigns his reversion (*Re King*), but, according to *City and Metropolitan Properties v Greycroft* (1987), a tenant retains the right to sue the landlord after assigning the lease, at least in respect of breaches of covenant committed while he (the tenant) was in possession. All of this, however, pales into insignificance in the light of the problems that arise when the pre-1996 lease is merely equitable or where a legal lease has been assigned only in equity (that is, not by deed: *Julian v Crago*). In such cases, although the original parties are bound to each other in contract, there can be no privity of estate between successors in title to those parties. This can cause serious difficulties, especially for a landlord. Thus, whereas ss 141 and 142 of the LPA 1925 operate to transfer the benefit of covenants and the burden of covenants respectively to the equitable assignee of the reversion (as they do with pre-1996 legal leases), the assignee of the equitable tenant does not come under the burden of the covenants due to lack of privity of estate. This is even more disadvantageous to the landlord when we appreciate that the benefit of an original equitable tenant's covenants can be transmitted to an assignee by a simple contractual assignment on the basis that benefits of a contract can be assigned. Thus, we reach the position under a pre-1996 equitable lease that an assignee of the tenant can sue an assignee of the landlord but not vice versa. Of course, there is some relief for the landlord by virtue of the fact that restrictive covenants may bind under the rule in *Tulk v Moxhay* (1848) and also that the landlord may have the remedy of forfeiture. However, forfeiture is a drastic remedy as it brings to an end the lease (and the income generated by it) and *Tulk* does not help with important positive covenants such as covenants to repair. One solution would be to regard the parties to a pre-1996 lease as being in privity of estate if they were parties to either a legal or an equitable lease and indeed such a solution was proposed by Lord Denning in *Boyer v Warbey* (1953). Yet, it has not found favour and there remains an unfortunate distinction in pre-1996 leases between the running of covenants in legal leases and the running of covenants in their equitable counterparts.

It was, then, against this background that the Law Commission moved to promote legislation to amend the law relating to the enforceability of leasehold covenants. This became the Landlord and Tenant (Covenants) Act (LTCA) 1995 that, save for the matters noted below, applies only to leases granted on or after 1 January 1996. It does, however, apply to legal and equitable leases in identical fashion. The Act itself was subjected to much amendment in its passage through Parliament; not surprising given it could be seen as an attack on landlords' rights. The result is that the Act is different in some respects from the

Law Commission's original proposals and, crucially, is open to the charge that it has not materially benefited tenants, at least not those under commercial leases.

The principal provisions of the Act – and, therefore, the new scheme for regulating the enforcement of leasehold covenants – are as follows. First, the Act is applicable to legal and equitable tenancies granted on or after 1 January and the troublesome distinctions between such leases are abolished (s 28(1) of the LTCA 1995). Secondly, the tenant (whether original or an assignee) is released automatically from the burden of leasehold covenants when they assign the tenancy (s 5), subject only to the possibility that they might be required to guarantee performance of the leasehold covenants by the next (but only the next) immediate assignee under an authorised guarantee agreement (s 16: an AGA). The exception is for assignments made in breach of covenant or by operation law when the assigning tenant remains liable (s 11(2)). Thirdly, the landlord is not released automatically from the burdens of leasehold covenants, but may serve a notice on the tenant applying for release from covenants which have passed to an assignee (s 6; *BHP Petroleum v Chesterfield Properties* (2001)) which release will be effective if the notice is not answered within a specified time or on the landlord's application to the county court (s 8). A landlord assigning in breach of covenant or by operation of law cannot serve such a notice (s 11(3)). Fourthly, the rule that covenants must 'touch and concern' the land or 'have reference to the subject matter of the lease' before the benefits and burdens can be passed to assignees of the lease or the reversion is abolished (ss 2 and 3). Fifthly, and in consequence, the benefit and burden of all leasehold covenants pass automatically to assignees of the lease and the reversion, so that an assignee may enforce, and will be subject to, any covenant contained in the lease (s 3). There is no need to show 'privity of estate' and ss 141 and 142 are no longer applicable. There is automatic annexation of all leasehold covenants to the premises comprised in all leases and reversions. Only those covenants that are positively expressed to be personal will not pass to assignees, but this may include covenants which in substance would have been proprietary under the old law. Sixthly, an attempt to enforce liability for a 'fixed charge' (for example, rent or a service charge) against a person not in possession (for example, an assigning tenant under an AGA, or the original tenant for pre-1996 leases to which this provision applies retrospectively) must comply with a 'problem notice' procedure. This requires the landlord to serve a notice on the person liable within six months of the charge becoming due. Following payment, this person may go back into the property as tenant under an 'overriding lease' and so attempt to recoup the payment by making use of the land or taking action against the actually defaulting tenant. Failure to serve such a notice within the proper time makes the charge unenforceable. Also, as indicated, this is a provision of the LTCA that applies to both pre-1996 and LTCA leases, being an attempt to control original tenant liability even under the former regime.

Clearly, the LTCA rules establish an entirely new system for the enforcement of leasehold covenants. Worthy of note is the idea that the rights and liabilities of landlord and tenant should be coterminous with possession of the land (hence, no continuing liability for original tenant, but why not also automatically for the landlord?) and that the benefit and burden of all covenants should pass automatically. This also means that the right to sue runs with possession. This removes many of the anomalies under the 'old' rules. Likewise, the removal of the distinction between legal and equitable leases is greatly to be welcomed. Additionally, the landlord's position is preserved by the ability to require the assigning tenant to enter into an AGA guaranteeing the next immediate assignee's liability under the covenants. This is permissible only as a guarantee of the next immediate assignee but, of course, if the obligation to enter an AGA is itself made a covenant of the lease it will flow to all assigning tenants.

To conclude, then, there is no doubt that the LTCA has remedied the most serious deficiencies of the old law and it is a matter of regret that no way could be found to make every provision applicable to all leases whenever granted, although that would have been very difficult. Overall, however, there are still doubts about some aspects of the new system. So, the removal of the distinction between 'proprietary' covenants (those that touch and concern) and personal covenants is thought by some to be unnecessary (but see *BHP Petroleum*). After *Swift*, is it really true that the distinction is hard to draw and if (as the Law Commission argue) few personal covenants creep into leases, why bother at all! Also, why not release the original landlord automatically from liability throughout the term of the lease? Will tenants really oppose such requests and will landlords be denied by the court when the tenant is automatically released? Finally, and most importantly, the AGA concept means the landlord retains another person to sue: the assigning tenant. In residential leases, the landlord cannot refuse to agree to an assignment to a new tenant on the grounds that the existing tenant will not enter an AGA on the landlord's terms unless this would be reasonable in all the circumstances. In commercial leases, however, the long established obligation that consent to assignment cannot be withheld unreasonably has been abolished, as this was the price extracted by landlords' interest groups for not obstructing the Bill entirely in Parliament. It is a heavy price, for it gives commercial landlords full control over the land by allowing them to deny consent to assignment unless the tenant complies with onerous (and unreasonable) obligations.

Notes

The LTCA is a very important piece of legislation, although we must not forget that the old rules still apply to pre-1996 leases. There are few cases on the LTCA: see *BHP Petroleum v Chesterfield Properties* (2001) and *Oceanic Village Ltd v United Attraction Ltd* (2000). This is either a tribute to the clarity of its provisions or the lull before the storm. The Act does have some serious drawbacks, particularly the way in which commercial landlords may now refuse consent to assign on the basis that the tenant cannot comply with the terms of the AGA they wish to impose, even if totally unreasonable.

Question 22

(a) Lawrence is the registered proprietor of a large industrial site on the edge of Camford. In 1990, he lets Unit 1 to Alex on a 21 year lease by deed containing covenants that Alex shall not use the premises for the purpose of the manufacture of sports equipment, shall not assign or sub-let the property without Lawrence's consent and shall carry out all reasonable external and internal repairs to the property. Seven years later, Alex assigns his interest, with Lawrence's consent to Billy, a car manufacturer. Billy's business suffers in the recession and he sub-lets to Clive, a bicycle manufacturer, without Lawrence's knowledge.

(b) Unit No 2, title to which is unregistered, is let to Mildred on a 10 year lease by deed in 1995 for the purpose of establishing a pub on the site to service the estate during working hours. Mildred covenants not to open after 7 pm and to sell only beer manufactured by Lawrence in his brewery. In return, Lawrence covenants not to carry on any catering business elsewhere on the site. Unfortunately, Mildred turns into an alcoholic and must leave the premises for the sake of her health. She assigns her lease in writing to Norman, who finds that the only way to make a profit is to open until 11 pm and sell a wider range of beers. Meanwhile, Lawrence has sold the entire site to Polly, who starts to manufacture chocolate in Unit 3. Polly finds she can make quite a profit selling chocolate cakes to the site workers at lunchtime.

Polly has discovered about Clive and the roof of Unit 1 is leaking. The police are concerned about drunkenness on the estate at night and Norman is about to sue for breach of covenant.

Answer plan

The following areas should be covered:

- pre-1996 lease – LTCA does not apply;
- meaning of 'privity of estate';
- requirement of 'touching and concerning' – *Swift Investments*;
- ss 141 and 142 of the LPA 1925;
- *Spencer's* case;
- *Re King*;
- *Tulk v Moxhay*.

Answer

This question concerns the operation of the rules relating to the enforceability of leasehold covenants, both between the original parties to the lease and their respective successors in title. Importantly, because both leases in this problem were granted before 1 January 1996, the applicable law is the 'old' mix of common law and statute. The Landlord and Tenant (Covenants) Act 1995 (LTCA) has no application to the facts of this problem, except in so far as liability for a 'fixed' charge is sought to be enforced against the original tenant, in which case, the provisions of s 17 of the LTCA apply and the 'problem notice' procedure must be observed.

On the facts, both the original landlord, Lawrence, and the original tenants Alex and Mildred have assigned their leasehold estates. Obviously, the original parties are bound to each other in contract to perform the covenants contained in their lease. Thus, in this problem, Lawrence can sue Alex, Lawrence can sue Mildred and Mildred can sue Lawrence in contract on all the covenants, whether or not they concern the land. This liability continues throughout the life of the contract, that being the term of the lease, although due to the wording of s 141 of the LPA 1925, a landlord will not be able to sue the original tenant after he has parted with the land as that right is statutorily transferred to the new landlord (*Arlesford Trading Co v Servansingh* (1971)).

Of course, for practical purposes, the present landlord, Polly, will wish to enforce the leasehold covenants against the present tenants (and vice versa) and, in this respect, the issue turns on whether the benefit of the covenant (the right to sue on it) has passed to the plaintiff and the burden of the covenant (the obligation to perform it) has passed to the defendant. In simple terms, under pre-1996 law, both burden and benefit will have passed to successors in title of the original landlord and tenant so as to enable an action on the covenant if: (i) there is privity of estate between the parties; and (ii) the covenant touches and concerns the land. In the case of the landlord, these common law conditions are now replicated in slightly modified form in ss 141 and 142 of the LPA 1925.

Before we consider the particular facts in detail, it is wise to determine, as a matter of principle, whether these covenants 'touch and concern' the land. In other words, whether they are so intimately connected with the land that they are not personal to the particular covenanting parties. Only if they do 'touch and concern' can the covenants be enforceable between successors to pre-1996 leases. The requirements for determining whether a covenant does 'touch and concern' have been re-stated by the

House of Lords in *Swift Investments v Combined English Stores* (1988), viz:

(a) whether the covenant could benefit any estate owner as opposed to the particular original covenantee;

(b) whether the covenant affected the nature, quality, mode of user or value of the land; and

(c) whether the covenant was expressed to be personal.

In our problem, there are six covenants in all:

(i) The covenant by Alex that the premises shall not be used for the manufacture of sports equipment. This is a covenant restrictive of the user of premises and *prima facie* touches and concerns the land. It seems to fall within the *Swift* formula: see, for example, *Williams v Earle* where the property was restricted to domestic use only.

(ii) The covenant by Alex not to assign or sub-let without consent – clearly acceptable, as in *Goldstein v Sanders* (1915).

(iii) The covenant by Alex to undertake all reasonable repairs – clearly acceptable, as in *Martyn v Clue*.

(iv) The covenant by Mildred not to open after 7 pm. Although, at first sight, this may seem to be a merely personal covenant, it is clear that it is intended for the benefit of other units on the site. It is not for Lawrence's personal benefit and does affect the mode of user of the land within the *Swift* formula. It seems to touch and concern.

(v) The covenant by Mildred to buy beer only from Lawrence – this also touches and concerns the land and is identical to the covenant in *Clegg v Hands*.

(vi) The covenant by Lawrence not to open a catering business. Once again, this covenant affects the mode or user of land retained by Lawrence and is intended to benefit land granted by him. It is an anti-competition covenant and is also a 'touching and concerning' covenant.

In result, then, all these covenants touch and concern the land and are *capable* of passing benefit and burden, as appropriate to successors in title.

(a) Unit 1

It is necessary in respect of Unit 1 to determine a number of issues. First, which parties are within 'privity of estate', for it is only between these parties that 'touching' covenants can run under the pre-1996 leasehold rules. 'Privity of estate' exists where there is a relationship of landlord and tenant under a legal lease or, in other words, where the particular plaintiff and particular defendant are now landlord and tenant of the same legal estate. In our case, Polly is in privity of estate with Billy. There is no privity of estate between Polly and Clive because Clive is a sub-tenant. (In fact, Clive is Billy's tenant and in privity of estate with him.) So, presumptively, Polly can sue Billy.

Secondly, does Polly have the right to sue on the covenants made by Alex to Lawrence after she purchases the reversion: has the benefit run to her? The answer to this is clear. Under s 141 of the LPA 1925, the benefit of every covenant 'having reference to the subject matter' of the lease is attached to the reversion and passes with it. The requirement of 'having reference to the subject matter' is taken to be synonymous with 'touching and concerning' (see, for example, *Caerns Motor Services v Texaco* (1994)). So, Polly has the right to sue any person with whom she is in privity of estate (Billy) and who is subject to the burden of the covenant. Thirdly, to whom has the burden run? The position here is again clear, following *Spencer's* case, that 'touching' covenants are binding on a successor in title to the original tenant in favour of anyone with whom they are in privity of estate. Again, this is Billy.

So, as far as Unit 1 is concerned, Polly can sue Billy on all three covenants if they have been breached. That, of course, is a matter of construction, although it is reasonably clear that Billy has broken the covenant against sub-letting and the covenant to effect reasonable repairs. If bicycles are 'sports equipment' then the third covenant is also broken. We should note here that Billy is liable for breaking the covenant against the manufacture of sports equipment, even though the actual actions in breach are committed by Clive. Billy is liable throughout his term, and it is immaterial that the breach was actually committed by his own tenant. Polly will have various remedies to choose from, including an injection to restrain cycle production, money damages and perhaps even forfeiture of the lease if there is a right of re-entry.

Finally, we should also note that, even though Clive and Polly do not share privity of estate, Polly may well be able to enforce any restrictive covenants against Clive under the rule in *Tulk v Moxhay* that normally operates in disputes between freeholders (who also are not in privity of estate with each other). Under *Tulk*, restrictive covenants can be enforced against any occupier providing that person has (here, the sub-tenant) notice of the covenants (unregistered land) or is within s 23(1)(a) of the LRA (registered land) which appears to make such covenants automatically binding on a sub-tenant. Also, if Polly is able to utilise the remedy of forfeiture and thereby terminate Billy's lease because of his breaches, the sub-tenancy will also be terminated (*Shiloh Spinners v Harding* (1973)), subject to any claim for relief from forfeiture by Clive.

(b) Unit 2

As above, there is no doubt that Polly, as purchaser, has the benefit of the covenants made to Lawrence: this is the effect of s 141(1) of the LPA. Correspondingly, however, Polly also has the burden of any covenants made by Lawrence, such as the covenant not to carry on any catering business on the site. This is the effect of s 142(1) of the LPA, operating for the burden in the same way as s 141 does for the benefit. Thus, Polly can sue Mildred on the covenants not to open after 7 pm and not to sell beer other than the landlord's and Mildred's liability continues for the term of the lease even though in fact the breach is committed by Norman. If Polly does sue Mildred, this will not trigger the problem notice procedure under s 17 of the LTCA 1995 because the claim is not for a fixed charge but (presumably) for unliquidated damages for breach. Likewise, Mildred can sue Polly on the covenant to prevent breach of the covenant against catering (although, possibly, only if the breach was committed before Mildred assigned to Norman (*Greycroft*)) if as a matter of construction it has been breached. Of course, however, if possible, both the new landlord and the new tenant will wish to secure a direct remedy against the person actually acting in breach.

In this respect, there are some difficulties. For Polly to sue Norman, the burdens of the covenant must have passed to Norman. However, even though the original lease is by deed (and, hence, legal), the assignment is only in writing. It is not, therefore, correctly assigned (s 52(1) of the LPA) and cannot take effect as a legal assignment. Following *Purchase v Lichfield Brewery* (1915), this equitable assignment of a legal lease cannot pass the burdens to Norman and Norman is not liable under pre-1996 leasehold covenant rules. In essence, there is no privity of the legal estate. Of course, it is possible for Polly to seek an injunction against Norman preventing the breach of any restrictive covenants under the *Tulk* rule, provided that the equitable assignee has notice of them (in unregistered land). Both of the covenants affecting Norman's land are indeed restrictive and, given that Norman should have seen the original lease before taking an assignment of it, he will have notice of the covenants contained therein. Fortunately, then, despite the fact that these covenants cannot be enforced under the 'leasehold rules', they will be binding under *Tulk*.

The position in respect of Norman's attempt to sue Polly is not so complicated. We have seen above that Polly is affected by the burden of the covenant made by Lawrence and there is good reason to suppose that Norman may well be entitled to the benefit of it. Although the right to sue cannot exist because of lack of privity of estate, it is possible that, as a matter of contract, the benefit of the covenant will have been assigned to Norman when he purchased the lease. This is a matter of construction of the assignment from Mildred, but it is a distinct possibility that the benefit of any covenants would have been assigned to Norman personally under normal contractual principles. If that were the case, Norman could sue Polly on this covenant.

Notes

For further reference on the difficulties of pre-1996 leasehold covenant law, see Thornton (1991) 11 Legal Studies 47. A contrast with the new law is provided by Question 25.

Question 23

Assess critically the remedies available to landlords for breach of covenant by their tenants. What factors may influence a landlord when deciding which remedy to pursue?

Answer plan

The following areas need to be covered:
- forfeiture – s 146 of the LPA 1925;
- injunction;
- distress;
- action for arrears of rent;
- action for damages.

Answer

One of the great advantages of the leasehold estate is that it allows two or more persons to use and enjoy property at the same time. In the typical case, the tenant will enjoy occupation and physical use of the property even to the exclusion of the landlord, but the landlord will reap the benefits of allowing that exclusive occupation in the form of rent and profits. It is, of course, essential if this duality is to function that both parties are able to preserve the value of their respective interests in the property. This is the function of covenants in leases, which may take many forms depending on the needs and priorities of the particular landlord and tenant.

From the landlord's point of view, he will wish to ensure that the value of the property and its marketability as an income generating asset is preserved. Thus, there may be covenants restricting the user of the premises by the tenant, obliging the

131

tenant to keep the premises in repair, requiring the landlord's consent before any assignment or sub-let is undertaken and, of course, obliging the tenant to pay rent. Obviously, these covenants are designed to secure different objectives and it should come as no surprise that the landlord's remedy for breach of covenant by the tenant may well depend on the particular type of covenant that has in fact been broken. In many cases, for example, the landlord will be content to secure performance of the covenant, as with repairing covenants, or simply the payment of outstanding rent. In others, the covenant broken may be so fundamental, or the breach so serious, as to suggest to the landlord that he should end the lease, thereby ridding himself of an unreliable tenant. Indeed, the law itself recognises that certain remedies are more appropriate to achieve certain ends and there are a whole range of statutory provisions which supplement or restrict the landlord in both the choice of remedy and the manner in which he may pursue it.

By far the most powerful weapon in the armoury of the landlord in the event of a breach of covenant is the remedy of forfeiture. A successful forfeiture of the lease effectively brings the lease to an end. It is, in other words, a remedy which can result in the tenant's estate in the land being terminated and, as such, it is not surprising that the right of the landlord to forfeit the lease is strictly controlled by statute. In general terms, in order for forfeiture to be available the lease must contain a right of re-entry. This is a stipulation that the landlord is entitled to re-enter the premises should the tenant fail to observe their covenants. All professionally drafted leases will contain such a right and one will be implied in all equitable leases (*Shiloh Spinners v Harding*). Subject to what will be said below, the existence of a right of re-entry gives the landlord two potential paths to a successful forfeiture. First, the landlord may physically re-enter the property by obtaining actual possession of it. A typical example being the changing of locks. Secondly, and more frequently, a landlord may seek to exercise his right of re-entry through an action for possession in the courts. At one time, a landlord had a free choice about which path to take but this is now modified by statute, mainly to protect the tenant from an over-zealous landlord using unrestricted force. Thus, a right of re-entry under a residential lease 'while any person is lawfully residing in the premises' must take place through court action (s 2 of the Protection from Eviction Act 1977). Any attempt to physically re-enter will result in criminal liability. Likewise, even if the lease is non-residential (or otherwise outside the scope of s 2), it is only peaceful physical re-entry that is permitted and the landlord must avoid committing offenses under the Criminal Law Act 1977. In short, this means that physical re-entry is possible only when the premises are held under a business lease and are unoccupied.

That, however, is not the end of the statutory code relating to forfeiture. In all cases where the landlord is seeking to forfeit because of a breach of a covenant, other than a breach of a covenant to pay rent, the procedure specified in s 146 of the Law of Property Act (LPA) 1925 must be strictly followed. (Forfeiture because of breach of a covenant to pay rent is dealt with under separate rules.) Section 146 requires a landlord to serve a notice on the tenant specifying the breach of covenant of which complaint is made, requesting compensation, if desired, advising the tenant of their rights under the Leasehold Property (Repairs) Act 1938, if appropriate, and requesting that the covenant is remedied, if that is possible. If the covenant is capable of remedy, and this depends upon the test laid down in *Expert Clothing v Hillgate House* (1986), the landlord must give the tenant a reasonable time to make amends before proceeding to forfeit by re-entry or court action. Only if the covenant cannot be remedied (is 'irremediable'), such as where the tenant has committed a once and for all breach of a negative covenant (*Scala House v Forbes* and *Cooper v Henderson*), can the landlord proceed to forfeit with reasonable speed. Even then, however, the landlord's remedy is controlled. If the landlord decides to proceed by way of court action, it is clear that the tenant has a right to relief from forfeiture under s 146(2) of the LPA. This will be granted if the tenant has performed the covenants or the court considers that it would be just and reasonable to allow the lease to survive despite the breaches of covenant (see *Shiloh Spinners v Harding*). Likewise, it is now clear after the House of Lord's decision in *Billson v Residential Apartments* that, even if the landlord proceeds to forfeit by physical re-entry, such as changing the locks as in that case, the tenant can still apply to the court for relief under s 146(2). This 're-interpretation' of s 146 emphasises once again that forfeiture is a drastic remedy, almost a remedy of last resort.

Forfeiture for breach of the covenant to pay rent is also controlled, although the procedure varies slightly according to whether action is taken in the county court or the High Court (depending on the amount owed) and whether the inherent jurisdiction of the court (High Court), or statute (county court), is the source of a tenant's right to relief. In essence, the landlord must make a formal demand for rent, unless this is excluded by the express terms of the lease or by statute, as where more than six months is in arrear and 'distress' (see below) would be inadequate (s 210 of the Common Law Procedure Act 1852). After this, in both county court and High Court, the tenant has a statutory right to have proceedings stayed by payment of rent interests and costs up to a specified time before the hearing date, although, in the High Court, this right arises only if six months' rent is in arrears. However, the High Court has an inherent jurisdiction to grant relief for forfeiture if less than six months is owing and payment is rendered before trial and may grant relief subsequent to a possession order (or physical re-entry: *Howard v Fanshawe* (1895)), if the tenant pays within six months and probably longer in exceptional cases (*Di Palma v Victoria Square Property* (1984)). In the county court, there is a statutory right to relief if payment is made within four weeks of a possession order and the court has a discretion to grant relief up to six months after possession is obtained (s 138(3), (9A) of the County Courts Act 1984 – see, for example, *Maryland Estates v Joseph* (1998)). The rationale behind these generous provisions is, of course, that the landlord has let the premises in order to generate income and should not be entitled to bring that arrangement to an end when that income is paid.

Indeed, taking all cases of forfeiture together, it is clear that the remedy may well be the most powerful in result, but it is also the one that the courts control most closely. It will be the remedy that the landlord resorts to in cases of serious and sustained breach of covenant but in other circumstances an attempt to forfeit is likely to be met with a successful claim for relief. The Law Commission has accordingly proposed a reform of the law of forfeiture which would essentially rationalise and assimilate the procedures for forfeiture for rent and non-rent covenants and seriously restrict further forfeiture by way of physical re-entry.

The Law Commission has also proposed reform, or rather abolition, of another of the remedies available to a landlord for breach of covenant. The remedy of distress allows a landlord to seize certain of the tenant's goods present on the property and sell them for the purpose of realising the arrears of rent. It is a remedy for non-payment of rent pure and simple and cannot be used in respect of breaches of any other covenant. With the exception of tenancies controlled under the Rent Acts and similar legislation, distress is a remedy by way of self-help requiring no court process. It is, however, bounded by traditional and often confusing common law conditions. There are, for example, many classes of privileged goods that cannot be seized (for example, tools of the trade, goods in actual use) and there are common law conditions dictating when distress may be levied (for example, not on a Sunday, only between dawn and dusk). All in all, despite the increased use of distress in times of recession, the Law Commission's proposed abolition of the remedy would not cause significant hardship to landlords and would remove one more right of self-help and the attendant dangers of abuse. At the moment, its most important consequence is that distress and forfeiture are mutually exclusive. Of course, should the landlord simply be concerned with rent and not wish to go to the trouble of distress or use the threat of forfeiture (which, of course, may often produce the rent), he may bring a simple action for arrears of rent up to the maximum of six years in arrears allowed under the Limitation Act.

Finally, for covenants other than the covenant to pay rent there remain two other possible remedies. First, the landlord may sue for damages for breach of covenant which in general terms will follow the normal contractual rules and will place the landlord in the position he would have been in had the breach not been committed. The exception is damages for breach of a covenant to repair which are limited by s 18 of the Landlord and Tenant Act 1927 to damages no greater than the loss of value in the reversion. Secondly, it may be possible for a landlord to obtain an injunction to prevent continued breach of a restrictive covenant under the rules of *Tulk v Moxhay* (1848). In reality, this is just an example of the general rule that equity may intervene to restrain conduct which is contrary to explicitly undertaken obligations. Furthermore, until recently, it was thought that the landlord could not obtain the remedy of specific performance to compel the tenant to perform a covenant to repair. This was thought to be established in *Hill v Barclay* (1811), despite *dicta* to the contrary in *SEDAC v Tanner* (1982). However, in *Rainbow Estates v Tokenhold* (1998), the judge held that specific performance of a tenant's covenant could be ordered in special circumstances, particularly where the court could supervise the order. This remains a controversial decision and it is unclear what 'special circumstances' justify this unusual step. Nevertheless, it may mark a change in the attitude of the courts when faced with persistent breaches of covenant by a tenant well capable of performing his obligations.

It is indeed true then, that there is a range of remedies available to the landlord in the event of breach of covenant by the tenant and that the choice of these remedies will depend ultimately on the type of covenant that has been breached and the purpose of the landlord in seeking to enforce it. If the landlord merely wishes to recover rent there is a range of actions. If, however, the aim is to terminate the tenancy and recover possession the remedy of forfeiture is available albeit subject to many restrictions. In essence, it will only be available to a landlord when the tenant has behaved in such disregard of the leasehold covenants that they have effectively taken themselves outside the landlord and tenant relationship.

Notes

A very general essay question. Students can improve this answer by discussing Law Commission's recommendations for the reform of remedies in respect of breach of covenant and the DETR's proposals for the limited reform of leasehold remedies in the Commonhold and Leasehold Reform Bill 2001, which is expected to receive Royal Assent in mid-2002.

Question 24

Lyn is the freehold owner of a large warehouse and a block of offices on the harbour in Cityport in an area of unregistered land.

In 1990, he leases the warehouse to Tim, an electrical goods importer, by deed for 20 years. Tim covenants to keep the premises in good repair, not to use the premises for residential occupancy, not to employ Zola (Lyn's deadly rival) in any capacity and to provide Lyn with a new television set every three years. The lease contains a right of re-entry. In 1997, Tim goes out of business and was forced to assign the lease to Albert by deed, a property developer. Unknown to Lyn, Albert begins to convert the warehouse into modern flats and employs Zola as his architect. Meanwhile, Lyn has let the offices to Dolly for use as company headquarters on the same terms as the lease to Tim plus covenants by Dolly not to assign or sub-let without Lyn's consent and not to carry on the trade of insurance brokerage, Lyn's own profession. Dolly discovers that she could have obtained a better deal in the centre of town and sub-lets to Enid, a financial consultant. Unfortunately, Enid is implicated in a city fraud and fails to pay rent to Dolly, who in turn cannot pay Lyn. Discovering this, Lyn changes all the locks on the office block late one night and refuses to let either Dolly or Enid gain entry.

Lyn now comes to you for advice and he has just learnt of the proposed residential development. He is outraged that Zola is on his property. He would also like a new television.

Answer plan

The answer should cover the following:
- enforceability of leasehold covenants in pre-1996 leases;
- touching and concerning;
- ss 141 and 142 of the LPA;
- forfeiture: s 146 of the LPA; *Billson v Residential Apartments*;
- other remedies in brief.

Answer

This question revolves around two central issues. First, the enforceability of the covenants contained in the leases made by Lyn and subsequently assigned or sub-let by the original tenants, and secondly, the remedies available to a landlord in the event of breach of covenant, particularly that of forfeiture. As the leases are granted before 1 January 1996, the Landlord and Tenant (Covenants) Act 1995 (LTCA) does not apply, save to the extent that a remedy is sought against an original tenant no longer in possession, in which case the 'problem notice' procedure of s 17 of the LTCA applies to attempts to recover a fixed charge (rent, service charge, liquidated damages).

(a) The warehouse

The first point is something that Lyn should bear in mind should all other remedies prove to be unavailable. Tim, the original tenant, will be liable throughout the term of the lease as a matter of contract. Thus, if all else fails, Tim can be sued for the breaches of the covenants, even though the acts in breach were those of Albert. The only substantive restriction on this is where the original contract (that is, the lease) limited Tim's liability expressly to the period of his possession of the demised premises: there is no evidence of this in our case. Of course, if Lyn wishes to recover unpaid rent from Tim (as original tenant), a 'problem notice' must be served on Tim within six months of the liability arising (s 17 of the LTCA 1995) and Tim would have the option of taking an overriding lease under s 19 of the LTCA. Again, there is no evidence that Lyn proposes to sue anyone for unpaid rent.

It is clear, however, that Lyn may be able to enforce the covenants against the persons more directly responsible as he and Albert, the assignee, share privity of estate. The original lease was by deed, hence legal, and the assignment is by deed. For all intents and purposes, therefore, Lyn and Albert are as landlord and tenant. This makes Lyn's position much stronger under pre-1996 law for it means that under the rule in *Spencer's* case, Albert will be subject to the burden of all covenants that touch and concern the land. In this case, there are four covenants in all and each must either be justified by previous authority as 'touching and concerning' or must pass the general test put forward by Lord Oliver in *Swift Investments v Combined English Stores* (1988), namely:

(a) whether the covenant is capable of benefiting any estate owner as opposed to the particular original covenantee;

(b) whether the covenant affects the nature, quality, mode of user or value of the land; and

(c) whether the covenant is expressed to be personal.

In this problem, the covenant to repair is of no difficulty, *Parker v Webb*, and the same is true of the covenant against residential occupancy: both clearly 'touch and concern'. There might, however, be thought to be some difficulty with the remaining two covenants and, certainly, the covenant to provide a new television set is clearly personal to Tim in his capacity as an importer of electrical goods. It is not related to use of the land as such. Although not strictly relevant, it is worth noting that the position would have been different had the lease been granted on or after 1 January 1996. In such leases, all covenants run unless they are expressed to be personal, which this is not (ss 2 and 3 of the LTCA 1995). With respect to the covenant against the employment of Zola, at first blush, this too seems to be personal. However, in *Lewin v American and Colonial Distributors*, a covenant not to allow a named individual to be connected with any business carried on upon the land was held to touch and concern as it was intended to affect the mode of user and value of the land. The covenant in our case is not quite of this kind and could be distinguished from that in the *Lewin* case. It will be a matter for argument because this covenant prevents the covenantor from employing Zola in any capacity and does not seem to be restricted to an activity carried on on the land. This covenant might be too wide and unconnected with the land for it to touch and concern.

As it is, this is a pre-1996 lease and it seems that Tim, the original tenant, is liable in respect of the television as a matter of contract law (original tenant liability) and probably not liable in respect of the employment of Zola: after all, Tim has not employed him and the covenant probably does not run to Albert, being personal. Albert, however, is subject to the repairing obligation and the restriction against residential occupancy. Obviously, it is these last two covenants that Lyn will be most concerned with and he has several remedies available – for example, damages; injunction. More than likely, however, he may well seek to forfeit the lease under his right of re-entry.

There is no doubt that, in principle, Albert is subject to forfeiture as the right of re-entry is enforceable against him. Being attached to a legal estate, it is itself a legal right and binding on Albert. However, the right of forfeiture for covenants other than to pay rent – and, here, we are dealing with breach of a covenant against residential occupation (see below for the repairing covenant) is controlled by statute, irrespective of whether forfeiture is by action in the courts or by physical re-entry. Under s 146 of the LPA, the landlord must serve a 's 146 notice' specifying the breach which is complained of, requiring compensation and requiring the tenant to remedy the breach if it is capable of remedy. Any attempted forfeiture without following this procedure is void (*Re Riggs* (1901)). It is crucial, therefore, for Lyn to serve such a notice. Furthermore, when the notice is served, Lyn cannot go on to forfeit by action or physical re-entry without giving the tenant a reasonable chance to remedy the covenant, if it is capable of remedy. It is crucial to know, for this reason, whether the covenant is indeed capable of remedy. The appropriate test for this purpose was discussed in *Expert Clothing Service and Sales v Hillgate House Ltd* (1986) and boils down to whether the harm to the landlord could be remedied. In the case of 'negative covenants', for example, as here, with the ban on residential occupancy, this is difficult as, once the action is done, the covenant is broken (*Scala House v Forbes* (1974)). If the breach of a negative covenant is 'continuing', it will be regarded as sufficient to stop the offending action and thereby avoid forfeiture. Similarly, in *Savva v Hossein*, the court held that there was no requirement that negative covenants always should be regarded as irremediable and that the *Expert Clothing* test should be applied individually to the facts of each case. This may result in a less rigid attitude to negative covenants even if the breach is not 'continuing'. Of course, under *Expert Clothing*, a positive covenant (such as to repair) can more easily be remedied by carrying out the required repairs.

Having served a s 146 notice and given a reasonable time for remedy (if appropriate), Lyn may be able to forfeit by physical re-entry, as this is not a residential property (cf s 2 of the Protection from Eviction Act 1977). However, after *Billson v Residential Apartments* (1992), also a case where work was done to property without consent, it is clear that even physical re-entry does not destroy the tenant's right to relief from forfeiture under s 146(2) of the LPA. Such relief can be granted even if a covenant is technically irremediable as the law leans against forfeitures. It is a matter for the courts' discretion in the circumstances of the case (*Shiloh Spinners v Harding* (1973)). Lyn would be wise, therefore, to seek forfeiture by action in the courts if Albert does not desist from the conversion work and pay compensation. The effect of a successful forfeiture would be to bring the lease to an end. Finally, it may be that due to the redevelopment work, the warehouse is not kept in good repair. If this is the case, Lyn might be better advised to sue for damages for breach of the repairing covenant as the procedure for forfeiture for breach of repairing obligations is complicated by the requirements of the Leasehold Property (Repairs) Act 1938. This gives the tenant added protection under s 146 of the LPA and a longer time to fulfil repairing obligations. Forfeiture for lack of repair will not be necessary if forfeiture for the non-observance of the domestic occupancy covenant is successful.

(b) The offices

The position here is similar to that above, with the exception that the breach of one covenant has been caused by the action of a sub-tenant. The obvious point is, of course, that Dolly is bound by all the covenants as a matter of contract (being the original covenantor) and, if it is true that her lease also contains a covenant to provide a television set, she must do so. This would not be subject to the s 17 of the LTCA notice procedure, as the liability is not in respect of a 'fixed' charge. It is in damages for an unliquidated sum. On the other hand, it is also clear that there is no privity of estate between Lyn and Enid. Enid is a sub-tenant and is in privity of estate only with her own landlord, Dolly. Thus, the burden of the covenants do not run to Enid under *Spencer's* case.

However, this does not mean that Lyn is left without a remedy apart from the contractual action against Dolly. In the first place, Lyn can enforce any negative covenants which touch and concern the land (as with the covenant restrictive of user) by injunction under the rule in *Tulk v Moxhay* provided that Enid has notice of them (as is most likely: *Gosling v Woolfe* (1893)).

Secondly, however, Lyn can proceed to forfeit the headlease for breach of covenant, although if forfeiting for breach of the covenant not to sub-let, the procedure outlined above has clearly not been followed. There has been no 's 146 notice'. Even if there had been, *Billson* makes it clear that relief from forfeiture can still be granted even where the landlord has forfeited by physical re-entry of the premises (changing the locks) instead of by action in the courts. Furthermore, under s 146 of the LPA a sub-tenant may apply for such relief in an action by the reversioner against the head tenant. Thus, although breach of the covenant not to sub-let may not be capable of remedy (it is a once and for all breach of a negative covenant – *Scala House*), Lyn has not followed the correct procedure of s 146 which was designed to give the tenant or sub-tenant the chance to claim relief.

Alternatively, Lyn could choose to forfeit for non-payment of rent, although again certain procedural limitations exist. For example, it is clear that unless expressly excluded by the lease, a landlord must issue a formal demand for rent if less than six months rent is owing. We do not know if Lyn has done this. Moreover, Dolly has a right to have the proceedings stayed on payment of all arrears and costs and, even after physical re-entry, the court has a discretion to grant relief from forfeiture (*Howard v Fanshawe* (1895)). In general, the court looks very carefully at attempted forfeiture for non-payment of rent as immediate payment plus costs will always remedy the situation. In this respect, threatened forfeiture is a costly way of recovering rent and Lyn would be well advised to use the normal action for rent recovery.

Notes

These last two questions concern the remedies available to a landlord in the event of breach of covenant, with particular reference to forfeiture. In this respect, *Billson* must be thoroughly understood as must the operation of s 146 of the LPA, although this may change under legislation passing through Parliament in 2002 (the Commonhold and Leasehold Reform Bill 2001). These two questions illustrate the most likely issues that can arise, although sometimes questions about the determination of tenancies can also appear, for example, by effluxion of time, notice and unity of title.

Question 25

Lucifer is the registered proprietor of a dockside warehouse. In 1995, he sub-divides the warehouse into two distinct units. The same year, he lets Plot A on a 30 year lease by deed to Tiger, an importer of soft toys. Tiger covenants not to use the premises for any manufacturing process and to provide Lucifer with three free soft toys each Christmas. Lucifer promises 'to maintain in good repair the Premises comprised within Plot A'. In 1996, Tiger assigns his lease to Kanga and she begins to make computer chips. She continues to store some soft toys, having purchased Tiger's excess stock. In 1997, Kanga allows her son, Roo, to take over the premises, acknowledging his assumption of the tenancy in a written agreement. Roo disposes of all the soft toys and begins large scale manufacture of computer chips. The same year, Lucifer assigns his reversion to Archy.

Plot B is let for 10 years in 1997 to Charlie, an importer of computer games. Charlie covenants not to use the premises for any manufacturing process and to supply Lucifer with four computer games each Christmas. Lucifer agrees an identical repairing covenant relating to Plot B as that agreed with Tiger concerning Plot A. In January 1998, Charlie is made an offer for his business and assigns his lease to Microfun Ltd. Microfun use Roo's computer chips to assemble PCs and no longer import computer games. In February 1998, Lucifer assigns his reversion to Norman.

Roo now complains to Archie that the guttering around the building is defective. Microfun Ltd also complains. Archie and Norman come to you for advice about their leasehold obligations and rights.

Answer plan

The answer needs to include a discussion of the following areas:

- pre-1996 leases and the enforceability of covenants: privity of estate, touching and concerning: ss 141 and 142 of the LPA 1925;
- legal and equitable pre-1996 leases;

- leases falling within the LTCA: automatic passing of benefit and burdens, personal covenants, no distinction between legal and equitable lease.

Answer

This problem concerns the enforceability of leasehold covenants between landlords and tenants, and their successors in title, of two separate properties. Importantly, one lease (that of Plot A) is granted before 1 January 1996 and so the covenants are governed by a mix of statute and common law. The second lease, that of Plot B, is granted in 1997 after the coming into force of the Landlord and Tenant (Covenants) Act 1995 and so falls to be dealt with under this statutory regime.

(a) Plot A

Being a lease governed by pre-LTCA principles, the enforceability of covenants is determined by common law principles overlaid by some statutory modifications. The 30 year lease granted by Lucifer (L) to Tiger (T) is executed by deed. It is therefore a legal lease which we can assume is registered under the Land Registration Act with its own title number. If it were not so registered, it would take effect only as an equitable lease (see *Brown and Root v Sun Alliance* (1996)), but this is unlikely given that the existence of a deed implies that the parties used a solicitor who would have registered the lease as a matter of course.

The lease contains three covenants. Two of them – the tenant's covenant prohibiting manufacturing and the landlord's repairing covenant are clearly proprietary: that is they 'touch and concern' the land or 'have reference to the subject matter of the lease' within the test laid down by Lord Oliver in *Swift Investments v Combined English Stores* (1988). Consequently, they have the potential to run with the land in appropriate circumstances. The third covenant – T's covenant to provide L with soft toys – is certainly personal in nature. So, for pre-1996 leases, it is impossible for the burden of this covenant to run to any assignee of the tenant: *Spencer's* case. Consequently, although Archie (the assignee of the reversion from L) may have been given the benefit of this personal covenant by contract when he purchased the reversion (because the benefit of contracts/covenants can be personally assigned), only T (the original tenant) is liable on it. No liability runs to either Kanga or Roo. It is unlikely that Archie will wish to pursue a remedy on this covenant against Tiger.

The remaining two covenants present a different picture. It is possible for the benefit and burden of these two proprietary covenants to pass to assignees of the reversion and the lease in appropriate circumstances. Taking Archie first, we are not told whether the assignment of the reversion to him is by deed or merely in writing. However, although the 'legal' status of his reversion can be maintained only if the assignment is made by deed (*Julian v Crago*) and he is subsequently registered as proprietor, this does not matter as far as the running of the covenants is concerned. By virtue of ss 141 and 142 of the LPA 1925, the benefit and burden respectively of proprietary leasehold covenants pass to an assignee of the landlord. Thus, we know that Archie may enforce the covenant against manufacture and is potentially liable on the repairing covenant. But whom may he sue, and who may sue him?

Clearly, the original tenant (T) remains liable throughout the entire term of the lease. So, Archie may well wish to sue Tiger in damages for breach of the manufacturing covenant if no other remedy is available. Archie does not have to comply with the 'problem notice' procedure of the LTCA 1995 (which applies even to pre-1996 leases) because such an action would not be an action for a fixed charge but for unliquidated damages. Obviously, however, Archie would prefer a remedy against the person committing the breach and we should note here that both Kanga and Roo's leases are binding on Archie as overriding interests (if not registered as titles) under s 70(1)(k) of the LRA if legal and s 70(1)(g) if equitable. In respect of Kanga, we are not told whether Tiger's assignment to her was by deed. This is critical as the burden of this covenant can run to Kanga only if she was in privity of estate with Archie and privity of estate depends on the existence of a legal lease (and, hence, an assignment by deed and registration if applicable): *Spencer's* case; *Julian v Crago* and *Brown and Root*. If such privity existed, Kanga can be held liable in damages to Archie for the period for which she was in possession under the lease. If the lease is equitable (that is, the assignment was in writing only), no such claim arises and Kanga cannot be liable (*Purchase v Lichfield Brewery* (1915)). Again, however, damages may not be adequate for Archie who may want the manufacturing process halted. This is difficult as it is clear that Roo is in possession of the property under an assignment from Kanga that is merely equitable, being made in writing. This means no burden passes to Roo under leasehold covenant law. Fortunately, however, Archie may be able to rely on a related doctrine. Under *Tulk v Moxhay*, a proprietary restrictive covenant (as here) can be enforced against any person in possession of the land (for example, an equitable tenant, or sub-tenant or squatter) if that person has 'notice' of the covenant. In registered land, which this is, the bindingness of the restrictive covenant on these occupiers is assured by virtue of s 23 of the LRA 1925. So, it is possible for Archie to obtain an injunction against Roo preventing the manufacture of computer chips (*Hall v Ewin*).

Finally, we must determine whether any person has the right to sue Archie on the repairing covenant – assuming that the facts disclose a breach. In principle, Tiger could have maintained a remedy providing that he has not assigned the benefit of the covenant when he assigned the lease, but not only is it implausible that Tiger would wish to sue, he almost certainly has assigned the benefit. Consequently, Kanga would have enjoyed the benefit of the repairing covenant while she was in occupation either because the lease was legal and privity of estate existed (*Spencer's* case) or because of an assignment of the contractual benefit by Tiger. Again, however, Kanga cannot obtain anything other than damages for the loss suffered by her while she was in possession and these are likely to be nominal. That leaves Roo. As we know, Roo is an equitable tenant and cannot rely on the 'privity' rules. Again, however, if Kanga has assigned the benefit of the covenant to Roo expressly, Roo may sue Archie. Had this been a simple case of assignment of a lease – albeit in writing – we could have readily implied such a personal transfer of the benefit. In our case, however, the matter is doubtful as we are told that Kanga 'acknowledges' Roo's assumption of the tenancy. All then turns on whether this acknowledgment expressly or impliedly passes the benefit of the repairing covenant. If it does, we must advise Archie that his attempt to obtain an injunction in respect of the manufacturing process may be met with a counter-plea for damages for lack of repair.

(b) Plot B

The enforceability of the three leasehold covenants in respect of Plot B raise similar issues to those considered above, save that being contained in a lease granted on or after 1 January 1996, the Landlord and Tenant (Covenants) Act 1995 is applicable. Consequently, some points of importance can be made. First, it matters not whether the leases are legal or equitable. Under the Act, the enforceability of leasehold covenants does not depend on the quality of the lease in which they are contained. So, whether the original lease and subsequent assignments are legal or equitable does not affect the enforceability of the leasehold covenants (s 28(1) of the LTCA 1995). Secondly, the Act makes no distinction between personal and proprietary covenants. Consequently, all leasehold covenants will run to assignees of the reversion and the lease irrespective of whether they 'touch and concern' or 'have reference to the subject matter of the lease' provided they are not expressed to be personal (ss 2 and 3 of the LTCA). In our case, therefore, the original tenant's covenants against manufacture and the covenant to supply computer games may well run to assignees as neither are actually expressed to be personal, even though the latter is 'personal' under the pre-1996 *Swift* test. Thirdly, by force of statute, the benefits and burdens of the leasehold covenants pass to assignees. There is no need to prove privity of estate or to plead ss 141 and 142 LPA. Both of these rules are irrelevant for LTCA leases (s 3 of the LTCA). Fourthly, the original tenant is released from liability on assignment, subject only to the possibility of being required to guarantee his assignee under an Authorised Guarantee Agreement (ss 5 and 16 of the LTCA). The original landlord is not released automatically, although can request the court to grant such release if the tenant objects on receiving a notice to that effect (ss 6 and 8 of the LTCA and *BHP Petroleum v Chesterfield Properties*).

So, with these general principles in mind, who is liable to whom and for what under the covenants for Plot B? Clearly, Charlie, the original tenant, is not liable under any of the covenants. He has assigned to Microfun Ltd and there is no suggestion that Lucifer extracted an AGA prior to such assignment. Charlie is statutorily released from liability although neither can he enforce any covenants, having gone out of possession (s 5 of the LTCA). However, as Microfun is an assignee of the tenant, and as no covenant is expressed to be personal, it is clear that Microfun is subject to the burden of both covenants (not to manufacture, to provide computer games) and enjoys the benefit of the repairing covenant. This is the effect of the LTCA irrespective of whether the lease is legal or equitable: the benefits and burdens have passed automatically (ss 3 and 28 of the LTCA). Consequently, we now need to know whom Microfun can sue, and who can sue it.

In principle, Lucifer has not escaped liability under the repairing covenant merely by assigning to Norman. For landlords, the LTCA does not provide for automatic release (s 6) and we have no suggestion here that Lucifer has served a notice requesting such release (s 8). However, unless Norman (L's assignee) is in some way unable to perform the repairing covenant or cannot pay damages, there is no reason for Microfun to sue Lucifer. This is simply because Norman, as assignee, is liable on the repairing covenant under LTCA. The burden has passed to him automatically (s 3). Similarly, Norman may also rely on the LTCA to pass to him the benefit of both the 'no manufacture' covenant and the covenant to provide computer games (s 3). Norman may seek an injunction against Microfun in respect of the former (assuming 'assembling' PCs counts as 'manufacture') and may seek damages or maybe even specific performance for breach of the latter.

Notes

This type of question is common in examinations. First, the problem requires knowledge of the pre-LTCA law. Secondly, the question may pose a different set of facts for each lease (as above) or may ask whether the answer would have been different had the LTCA applied. Nearly always, the answer would have been different. At the moment, there is little useful case law on the LTCA, so a good knowledge of its statutory provisions is essential.

CHAPTER 6

LICENCES AND PROPRIETARY ESTOPPEL

Introduction

In one sense, there is no necessary reason why the law of licences and the law of proprietary estoppel should be considered together. 'Licences' are one way in which a person may enjoy some right or privilege over the land of another and much of the dispute in this area concerns the theoretical and practical distinction between 'licences' and other types of right over land, such as leases and easements. 'Proprietary estoppel', on the other hand, is a method for the creation of certain rights and privileges over land. Viewed in this way, proprietary estoppel is a mechanism that may give rise to licences, easements, leases or any other kind of right connected with the use and ownership of land and should be considered in its own right. However, that said, it is true that many of the cases and most of the textbooks consider licences and proprietary estoppel together. This is because 'licences' seem to be a common result of the application of proprietary estoppel to a given set of facts. Whether this is theoretically justified or practically necessary is an issue that will be explored in this chapter, but, for the moment, the conventional form of exposition, which groups these matters together, will be used.

Licences then, involve a permission from the owner of land, given to another, to use that land for some purpose. This can be to do anything from attending a cinema, parking a car or occupying premises to erecting an advertising hoarding. The range of activities that can be covered by a licence are, indeed, virtually limitless and we have already explored this issue in one respect in considering the distinction between leases and licences. Crucially, however, the orthodox view of licences is that they are not proprietary in nature: in other words, they are not interests in land, but rather personal rights over land. As a consequence, the right conferred by a licence can be enforced only against the person who created it. It does not run with the land and, unlike

149

easements and restrictive covenants, cannot be enforced against a purchaser of the land over which the licence exists. The licence is a matter of contract, not property law. In the 1970s, this fundamental theoretical distinction was attacked (although it has been reaffirmed a number of times: *Lloyd v Dugdale* (2001)) and many examination questions now ask students to analyse whether the status of licences has changed over the years as the use of land has changed. In dealing with both problem and essay questions on licences, students will need to have a firm grasp of what it means to say that something is an interest in land, as well as an understanding of the law of easements and general principles of equity concerning constructive trusts. Case law is particularly important.

Proprietary estoppel is the name given to a doctrine or set of principles whereby an owner of land may be held to have conferred some right or privilege connected with the land on another person. Typically, the right or privilege conferred will arise out of the conduct of the parties, usually because of some assurance made, which is relied upon by the person claiming the right. In other words, proprietary estoppel is a mechanism whereby rights in or over land may be created informally without the need for a deed or signed writing. In this respect, it is close to the doctrine of constructive trusts considered in Chapter 3 and many cases use these doctrines interchangeably. This is not necessarily accurate although the precise ambit and differences between the two doctrines have not yet been worked out. In the law of proprietary estoppel, cases are vital as this is a judge made doctrine, so typical of a court of equity. There are parallels with promissory estoppel in the law of contract, although proprietary estoppel is a much more powerful doctrine. The former is a defence to an action on a contract, the latter is a means of acquiring rights over land belonging to another. It is a sword as well as a shield.

Question 26

To what extent have the courts recognised contractual licences as interests in land? Why is the issue important?

Answer plan

The following areas need to be covered:

- definition of an interest in land: *National Provincial Bank v Ainsworth*;
- definition of a licence: *Thomas v Sorrell*;
- types of licences and purposes of licences;
- the supposed need to bind third parties;
- judicial developments: *Errington v Errington*; *Binions v Evans*; *Re Sharpe*; *Midland Bank v Farm Pride Hatcheries*; *Ashburn Anstalt v Arnold*; *Kewal Investments v Arthur Maiden*; *Lloyd v Dugdale*;
- theoretical considerations.

Answer

A licence is classically defined in *Thomas v Sorrell* (1673) as a permission to use land belonging to another which, without such permission, would amount to a trespass. It is the consent of the estate owner to the use of their land by another. Importantly, as Vaughan CJ makes clear in *Sorrell*, the orthodox view of licences is that they 'properly passeth no interest nor alters or transfers property in any thing'; in other words, licences are not proprietary in nature but personal to the parties that created them. In effect, that they are not interests in land and therefore not within the scope of the 1925 property legislation and are incapable of binding third parties when the licensor (the grantor of the licence) passes the affected land on to a third party.

However, such an orthodox view has been subject to attack and various cases and theories have sought to explain why licences are, or should be, regarded as interests in land in the full sense. The aim is often to ensure that subsequent transferees of the burdened land are bound. Not least, this is due to the multitude of purposes that licences can serve. The law reports are replete with cases covering such matters as entry by ticket to a cinema (*Hurst v Picture Theatres Ltd* (1915)), permission to use local facilities for a conference (*Verrall v Great Yarmouth BC* (1981)), permission to erect an advertising hoarding (*Kewal Investments v Arthur Maiden*) and even permission to occupy premises for residential accommodation (*Ogwr BC v Dykes* (1989); *Gray v Taylor* (1998)). Indeed, it is in respect of this last category – so called occupation licences (but see Chapter 5) – that much of the debate has taken place, for, if it is possible to grant licences to occupy property as a residence, it is in the interests of the licensee to claim that the licence can in fact bind any transferee from the licensor.

This multipurpose use of licences is reflected in the traditional categorisation that is used to identify types of licences. All categories are noted here, although it must be borne in mind that it is really in respect of the last two that the debate about the proprietary nature of licences has taken place. First, there are 'bare licences', being the most simple form of permission to use land given voluntarily by the owner of property. Typically, such licences allow the 'licensee' to carry on some limited activity on the 'licensor's' land, as where permission is given for children to play. It is intrinsic to this type of licence that the permission may be withdrawn at any time and, because given voluntarily without consideration, does not give the licensee any claim to damages or other legal remedy. Secondly, there are those licences grouped together because they are 'coupled with an interest in the land'. In essence, these licences comprise the implied permission which a person obtains and which enables them to enjoy some right previously granted over the land, as where a person is granted the right to fish, cut turf or gather wood, as in *James Jones & Son v Earl of Tankerville* (1909). To some extent, however, the label 'licence' is misleading, for the licence is merely incidental and ancillary to the right which has actually been granted over the land. Thus, where as in the above examples the right granted may also be proprietary in nature, as with the profit of piscary (fish) and the profit of turbary (to cut turf), it is the right granted that is important and not the licence which facilitates it. So, the licence will last for as long as the profit is granted and be enforceable against whomsoever the profit is enforceable against, being merely an ingredient in the greater right. Likewise, should the grantee (and licensee) be unlawfully denied the right granted, the normal remedies will be available to prevent interference with the right, such as injunction.

As noted above, it is with the third and fourth categories of licence that the question whether they amount to an interest in land has been most commonly posed, those of contractual licences and licences arising by estoppel. Contractual licences are, in principle, little different in nature from bare licences, save that contractual licences are granted to the licensee in return for valuable consideration moving to the licensor; the purchase of a cinema ticket is a good example. Crucially, of course, such contractual licences are governed by the ordinary rules relating to remedies for breach of contract and it is now clear that either an injunction will be granted preventing the licensor from revoking the licence before its contractual date of expiry (*Wintergarden Theatres v Millennium Productions Ltd* (1948)) or even a decree of specific performance requiring the licensor to permit the activity authorised by the licence to take place (*Verrall v Great Yarmouth* (1981)). It is obvious that the effect of the availability of these remedies may, in appropriate circumstances (depending on the contract and the conduct of the parties), make the licence *de facto* irrevocable throughout the contractual time period (for example, the theatre performance). Of course, this is in reality only an issue between the original licensor and licensee, but the fact that such licences could be irrevocable during their contractual period *and* that they related to land did raise the inevitable question of their effect on third parties. Put simply, the question is asked whether, given that a contractual licence is irrevocable between the licensor and licensee throughout its contractual period, can the licensor nevertheless defeat the licence by conveying the property to a third party during that period. In such cases, the licensee may well have a good claim in contract against the licensor, but that is not the same as allowing the licensee's rights to use the land to continue against the third party for the remainder of the period.

In the event, under the influence of Lord Denning's Court of Appeal, two strands of thought developed which sought to explain why a licence could bind a third party and, perhaps, why it should be regarded as a new species of interest in land. On the one hand, in *Errington v Errington* (1952), Lord Denning regarded

153

a contractual licence as binding on a third party who received the property which was subject to the licence by a will, her husband being the original licensor. In this case, the reasoning was explicit that since the licensee could restrain revocation of the licence for its period against the licensor, there was no reason why the licence could not continue against a third party who was not a *bona fide* purchaser of a legal estate for value in the property. This assumes that licences are *capable* of binding third parties as only if they actually are does it matter whether the third party is 'equity's darling'. The reasoning for the decision is unclear, although it seems that the contractual licence was supported by 'an equity' which transformed it into a proprietary right. Unfortunately, the court in this case did not make it clear why a previous House of Lords decision (*King v David Allen & Sons, Billposting* (1916)), which had expressly decided that contractual licences could not bind third parties, could be ignored.

The second line of attack on the traditional view came with the Court of Appeal in *Binions v Evans*. In that case, a purchaser of land subject to what looked like a contractual licence, expressly agreed to take the land subject to that licence. The purchaser later sought to evict the licensee. Two judges in the Court of Appeal actually decided that no licence was involved at all: rather, the occupier had a life interest under a settlement which was protected under the Settled Land Act. Lord Denning, however, took a different view and decided that the purchaser was bound to give effect to the licence because he had purchased the property subject to it and that such licence was protected by the imposition of a constructive trust on the purchaser. In the case itself, it is not clear whether Denning MR regards these as separate or complimentary grounds for the decision but subsequent decisions (for example, *Bannister v Bannister* (1948); *Re Sharpe*) have tended to rely on the constructive trust argument as a means of protecting the licence against a third party. However, as we shall see, this does not necessarily mean that the contractual licence has become an interest in land.

This seems to have been the position, cloudy though it was, until the decision of the Court of Appeal in *Ashburn Anstalt v Arnold* (1988). In that case, Fox LJ thoroughly re-examined the question of licences as interests in land and, relying on the House of Lords in *King* and *National Provincial Bank v Ainsworth* (1965), reaffirmed the orthodox view of the law. In his view, *Errington*, in so far as it decided that a licence was an interest in land, was *per incuriam*, because of the existence of the binding authority of *King*. In any event, in Fox LJ's view, *Errington* could have been decided on at least three other grounds (the existence of an estate contract binding a non-purchaser, a *Rosset* type equitable right of ownership, or estoppel against the widow). Indeed, Fox LJ's judgment makes it clear that *as a matter of principle* licences are not interests in land and cannot bind third parties for that reason. This has now been reaffirmed by the Court of Appeal in *Lloyd v Dugdale* (2001) and effectively settles the matter. However, turning to the *Binions v Evans* argument, Fox LJ in *Ashburn* accepted that in appropriate cases a contractual licence may take effect behind a constructive trust, binding on the purchaser, if the purchaser has so conducted himself that it would be inequitable for the licence to be denied. Such a trust does not exist, however, merely because the purchaser bought the land 'subject to' the licence, but only if there was unconscionable conduct on the part of the purchaser (for example, paying a lower price as a result of the promise to respect the licence). In any event, the licence is only protected behind a *personal* constructive trust binding on this particular purchaser because of their particular conduct: it has not thereby assumed the status of an interest in land. Again, this has been confirmed by *Dugdale* where the court makes it clear that the imposition of a constructive trust on a purchaser can be justified only in exceptional circumstances where it is clear that the purchaser has, by his conduct, accepted the obligation imposed by the licence.

This position in *Ashburn* and *Dugdale* is, without doubt, a thoroughly orthodox approach to the problem and it serves to highlight the fundamental distinction between interests in land and purely personal interests which just happen to relate to property. It without doubt represents the law (although even now there are glimpses of the 'Denning' heresy: *Saeed v Plustrade* (2002)). No licences are proprietary interests in land. In fact, now that the House of Lords has in *Street v Mountford* and other cases asserted that residential occupation usually gives rise to a lease and not a licence, there is a certain symmetry to the picture. To be entirely fair to Lord Denning and the other judges following his lead, their attempt to confer proprietary status on mainly occupation licences came at a time when landowners were able to avoid granting leases. In this respect, attempts to protect occupation licences could be seen as an attempt to protect what were really leases and, after *Street*, would be regarded as such. Indeed, if one takes Lord Wilberforce's definition of an interest in land in *Ainsworth* ('before a right or interest can be admitted into the category of property, or of a right affecting property it must be definable, identifiable by third parties, capable in its nature of assumption by third parties and have some degree of permanence or stability'), it is obvious that there is some circularity in the whole issue. What these cases show us is that the distinction between licences and interests in land is a real and immovable one, but what amounts to either a 'licence' or an 'interest in land' in any given case depends ultimately on the facts of that case. The categories are boxes, which have pre-determined consequences, but what goes into those boxes is a matter of judgment.

Notes

This is a standard examination question, although it cannot be completed successfully without knowledge of case law. The distinction between the ability of a proprietary right to bind a third party and the purely personal way in which a licence may bind someone because of a purely personal constructive trust is most important.

Question 27

In 2000, Bluebell acquired registered title to a small cottage on Dartmoor, formerly part of a large farm and quite close to the old farmhouse. Being fond of animals, she acquires several horses and asks Farmer Cowslip whether she can keep them on his land. He agrees, but only if he may use the horses to hire to tourists who stay on his farm. Farmer Cowslip also provided riding holidays for tourists, using his own horses, and Bluebell agreed that, if there was insufficient space in the farmhouse, she would accommodate any extra tourists and provide them with breakfast and an evening meal if desired. Bluebell also pays Farmer Cowslip £20 per month to park her car in an old barn on the farm. She also regularly collects firewood from the fields as her only source of heating is an old wood burning stove. In 2001, Farmer Cowslip proposes marriage to Bluebell but she refuses. Farmer Cowslip takes great offence and immediately threatens to turn Bluebell's horses out, although he does continue to use them for his riding business. In anger, Bluebell refuses to accommodate any of Farmer Cowslip's tourists and evicts those that are currently in occupation. They subsequently sue Cowslip for a ruined holiday. Cowslip's response is to sell the barn and fields to Grockle Holidays plc who immediately refuse Bluebell the right to park her car or gather wood.

Bluebell comes to you for advice as her car has broken down due to standing in the cold and she cannot live in the cottage without her source of fuel. She hopes to be able to sell the cottage to her friend, Daisy, who would also like to keep horses. It also emerges that Grockle plc knew of Bluebell's activities and paid Farmer Cowslip a much reduced price for the land it has purchased. You discover subsequently that Farmer Cowslip is the major shareholder in Grockle plc.

Answer plan

The following areas need to be discussed:

- identification of rights over the land – licences or proprietary interests;
- effect of licences between the original parties – remedies;
- effect of licences on third parties;
- constructive trusts and the protection of licences;
- the creation of new licences binding on a 'third party'.

Answer

This problem concerns the creation of rights over land, the identification of the nature of those rights and the consequences which flow from subsequent dealings with the land over which those rights exist. In essence, as we are asked to advise Bluebell, it is necessary to determine: (a) whether she has any right to insist that her horses be accommodated and whether this right can be enforced against Farmer Cowslip; and whether the benefit of the right can subsequently be passed on to Daisy; (b) whether

Bluebell is under any liability in respect of the displaced tourists and the refusal to house further tourists; (c) whether Bluebell has any rights to park her car and collect wood and whether these are binding on Grockle plc; and (d) whether Grockle's conduct and the involvement of Farmer Cowslip suggest any other remedy for Bluebell.

(a) The horses

There seems little doubt that Bluebell and Farmer Cowslip have entered into a contract whereby Bluebell agrees to allow the horses to be used for Cowslip's business in return for which Cowslip allows Bluebell to keep the horses on his land. However, the nature of the rights created by this contract are the crucial factor, for that may determine their enforceability and status in respect of third parties.

The contract is purely oral and, if it to be argued that this contract confers some sort of proprietary interest on Bluebell, there are going to be difficulties in fulfilling the formality requirements of s 2 of the Law of Property (Miscellaneous Provisions) Act 1989. In fact, the only possibility of a proprietary right is that Bluebell has some lease of the land (cf *University of Reading v Johnson-Houghton* (1985)) in the form of a periodic tenancy, which would be binding on Cowslip according to its terms and could be assigned to Daisy in the normal way by deed (*Julian v Crago*). However, the nature of Bluebell's right to keep horses, and the circumstances in which it was created, militate against the granting of any proprietary interest. Indeed, it is likely that her right is in the nature of a contractual licence over Farmer Cowslip's land. Presumptively, a contractual licence is revocable during its term by the licensor, although the licensee (Bluebell) would have a claim in damages. On the other hand, however, it is clear from *Wintergarden Theatres v Millennium Productions* (1948) that if, on construction of the contract, a contractual licence was intended to be irrevocable during its period of operation, equity will intervene to restrain breach of that contract by the licensor by way of injunction or specific performance as appropriate. Whether the remedy is available to Bluebell will depend on many factors, not least her own conduct. Her willingness to continue to allow her horses to be used (that is, that she kept her side of the contract) will be important, although her apparent refusal to cater for the very tourists who would ride will count against. It will be a matter for the court. As far as Daisy is concerned, it has always been true that the benefit of a contract can be expressly assigned and there is no reason why Bluebell cannot transfer to Daisy such rights as she has against Cowslip under the contractual licence for the accommodation of her horses. We might also note that, although not in issue in this problem, the benefit of the contract could have been conferred on Daisy at the time of the contract under the Contracts (Rights of Third Parties) Act 1999.

(b) The tourists

The precise nature of Bluebell's liabilities here will depend on the exact terms of the contract she made with Farmer Cowslip. It may well be that she is in breach of contract in evicting the tourists before the end of their holiday and in refusing to accommodate future arrivals. In such a case, Farmer Cowslip will have a right to sue Bluebell in contract and recover the loss caused by the action against him by his disgruntled clients. What is quite clear, however, is that the tourists have no short term lease over their rooms in Bluebell's cottage. Under *Street v Mountford*, there is no doubt that these occupiers are lodgers and, therefore, not tenants. There is the provision of board and services within *Markou v Da Silvaesa*. The tourists may, of course, have a contractual licence to occupy the cottage, although it is difficult to see on the facts how they could be in direct contract with Bluebell. If they were, and were occupying on a contractual licence from Bluebell, *Tanner v Tanner* suggests that an injunction could be obtained to prevent eviction for the duration of the licence. However, not only is this the least likely remedy sought by the transient tourists, the *Tanner* case is fundamentally different in that it concerned a long term occupier who was denied continued occupation by the licensor in very inequitable circumstances.

(c) Car parking and collecting wood

The issue of the car parking and the collection of wood raise rather more difficult issues, both as to the nature of the rights granted and because of the involvement of a third party who purchased the land over which the rights existed.

As to the car parking, it is clear from *Newman v Jones* (1982) and *London and Blenheim Estates v Ladbroke* (1992) that it is perfectly possible to have an easement giving a right to park on a neighbour's land. However, it seems that this can occur only if the easement is to park generally and not in a defined space: exclusive possession or excessive control over the servient land cannot amount to an easement (see *Batchelor v Marlowe* (2001) and contrast *Saeed v Plustrade* (2002)). In any event, even assuming that this could be an easement, the requirements of formality needed to create a legal or equitable right have not been met and there is little possibility of an estoppel easement. All in all, this looks as if Bluebell has been granted a contractual licence to park her car which, of course, is enforceable against Cowslip as the licensor. However, it is now clear from *Ashburn Anstalt v Arnold* (1988) and *Lloyd v Dugdale* (2001) that licences as such are not interests in land and cannot therefore bind a subsequent purchaser of the land. They are not proprietary in nature. So, subject to what will be said below, at first sight it looks as if Bluebell's right to park her car cannot be enforced against Grockle.

The right to collect wood poses different problems. There is no doubt that it is possible for a person to be granted a profit *à prendre* to collect wood for the purpose of fuel, otherwise known as a profit of estovers (*AG v Reynolds* (1911)). Profits are proprietary rights and any licences attached to the profit to enter onto another's land for the purpose of exercising the profit take the character of the superior right's proprietary status (*James Jones v Earl of Tankerville* (1909)). However, it is also clear that in order for the profit to exist – and, hence, be capable of binding a third party such as Grockle – it must be created in due form. In this case, there is no deed of grant to support a legal profit and no written contract to support an equitable profit. Bluebell's only hope is, perhaps, to plead the creation of a profit by estoppel, similar to the creation of an easement by estoppel in *Celsteel v Alton* (1985). If that were the case, the profit would constitute an overriding interest against the servient land (s 70(1)(a) of the LRA 1925) and be binding automatically on Grockle plc. If, on the other hand, no estoppel profit can arise, Bluebell's only hope is to prove that it was never the intention of the parties to grant her a profit but, rather, that she has a mere licence to collect wood. Obviously, a mere licence cannot bind Grockle plc as such – not being an interest in land – but she may gain some comfort from the principle of constructive trusts considered below.

(d) Grockle and Farmer Cowslip

Although it is clear that the licence to park the car (and to collect wood if established as a licence) cannot bind Grockle as a matter of property law, there is the possibility that a purchaser of land will be bound by a personal constructive trust, imposed to give effect to such licences as exist, because of the purchaser's inequitable conduct. That even a licence can gain protection in this way is accepted in *Ashburn Anstalt v Arnold* (1988) and *Lloyd v Dugdale* (2001), for its essence is that equity imposes an obligation on the conscience of a particular purchaser. The nature of the right is not crucial. The circumstances in which such an obligation will be imposed are obviously varied and it is not enough that the purchaser simply promised to give effect to the licences (*Ashburn*, criticising *Binions v Evans*). In our case, the fact that the purchaser paid a lower price because they knew of the existence of the licences may well be important (*Dugdale*), although as we know from *Midland Bank v Green* (1981) (in another context), undervalue and knowledge that rights will be defeated do not necessarily amount to inequitable conduct (and see *Melbury v Kriedl* (1999)). It will in essence be a matter for the court. If a constructive trust is imposed, it will ensure that Grockle plc permits the continuance of the rights of Bluebell.

Finally, two further points should be noted. First, as with (a) above, Bluebell may transfer the benefit of any contract to Daisy irrespective of the nature of the rights created by the contract. That is a matter of contract law. It is not clear, however, whether the transfer of the benefit of the contractual rights to a third party will affect the court's decision to impose a constructive trust on the purchaser of the land over which those rights exists. Secondly, it may be possible to argue that there is no third party purchaser at all on the grounds that Grockle plc is just Farmer Cowslip in another guise. If that were the case, because Cowslip is the majority shareholder, no question of the enforcement of licences against third parties arise. It is more likely, however, that given the separate legal personality of companies and their owners, that Cowslip's majority shareholding will be relevant to the question of the imposition of the constructive trust on the 'third party' rather than in deciding that there was no third party at all (see *Jones v Lipman*).

Notes

This question illustrates just how easy it is for questions to raise issues concerning licences and easements. In some senses, a licence is what a person obtains if they cannot claim an easement: either because the right is not capable of being an easement at all or because the 'easement' has not been created with the necessary formality of a deed or signed writing.

Question 28

To what extent is it possible to predict the circumstances in which a plea of proprietary estoppel will be successful and the consequences thereof for the person against whom the estoppel operates?

Answer plan

The answer needs to include the following:
- the general nature of proprietary estoppel and its relationship to rules regulating the acquisition of estates and interests in land;
- the five probanda for proprietary estoppel (*Willmott v Barber*);
- the changing definition of proprietary estoppel (*Taylor Fashions v Liverpool Victoria Trustees; Mathura v Mathura*);
- its relationship to unconscionability – *Taylor v Dickens; Gillett v Holt*;
- the role of proprietary estoppel in the modern law.

Answer

Section 2 of the Law of Property (Miscellaneous Provisions) Act 1989 establishes the minimum level of formality necessary for the valid creation, acquisition or transfer of estates and interests in land. In effect, s 2 stipulates that a contract for the disposition of an interest in land must be in writing and it replaces s 40 of the Law of Property Act 1925 which permitted purely oral contracts providing these were supported by sufficient acts of part performance. Since s 2 came into force, purely oral contracts are not in general capable of giving rise to an enforceable right in land. Moreover, s 2 stipulates a *minimum* level of formality, because compliance with its provisions without more usually results in the creation of an equitable right only. Legal estates and interests on the whole require the additional formality of a deed and (for registered land) registration in the relevant section of the land register (see *Brown and Root v Sun Alliance*). It is in such a context, where statute requires a considerable degree of formality and deliberateness for the creation of rights in land, that the doctrine of proprietary estoppel should be examined.

The exact purpose or role of proprietary estoppel is a matter of some debate. On the one hand, and in similar fashion to the related doctrine of promissory estoppel, proprietary estoppel can provide a defence to an action by a landowner who seeks to enforce his strict rights against someone who has been promised some right or liberty over the land. For example, in *Mathura v Mathura*, an action for possession by a landowner was met by a successful plea of estoppel by the person in physical possession of the property. However, the role of proprietary estoppel is not limited to providing a person with a defence to an action by the paper owner of land. There is no doubt that a successful plea of proprietary estoppel can operate positively, in the sense that it can generate new property interests in favour of a claimant. As is typically stated, proprietary estoppel is both a shield and a sword (*Crabb v Arun DC* (1976)). In essence, proprietary estoppel may be seen as either a means of defeating the claim of the paper owner of land and as a method of creating rights in or over land. Moreover, it is the second aspect of proprietary estoppel that relates so closely to the formality requirements discussed above because, as we shall see, proprietary estoppel can result in the creation of proprietary rights without a deed, without any writing and without the existence of even an oral contract or formal contract. It is the creation of rights arising from the action of equity on an individual's conscience.

The doctrine of proprietary estoppel is not a creation of the modern law, although it certainly has come to the fore in recent times. In *Willmott v Barber* (1880), Fry LJ laid down what was to be regarded for many years as the five 'probanda' of proprietary estoppel or, in other words, the five conditions that needed to be established before a claimant could be awarded a right to another's land arising informally. The five conditions were that: first, the claimant should have made some mistake as to their legal rights; secondly, that the claimant must have expended some money or done some act on the faith of the mistaken belief; thirdly, that the true landowner must know of the existence of their own right and that it is inconsistent with the right claimed by the claimant; fourthly, the landowner must know of the claimant's mistaken belief as to their legal rights; and, fifthly, that the landowner should have encouraged the expenditure by the claimant, either directly or by abstaining from enforcing their legal right.

It is obvious that these five conditions are fairly strict: they limit the circumstances in which equity will intervene to award a right to the claimant and circumscribe the circumstances in which rights connected with property may be created informally. Indeed, this formulation is appropriate when the purpose of proprietary estoppel is to limit the ability of the 'true' owner of land to rely on their formal title in circumstances where it would be inequitable to do so. As such, Fry LJ's formula was relied on in the recent case of *Mathura v Mathura* (1994), and although the lack of reference to more modern authority was unusual, it was consistent with the limited role that estoppel played in that case. However, as *Orgee v Orgee* makes clear, the *Willmott* criteria are not to be applied mechanically to restrict unduly the role of estoppel.

Consequently, although the five probanda of *Willmott v Barber* undoubtedly establish a clear framework for ascertaining the likelihood of a successful plea of proprietary estoppel, it became clear that courts were prepared to accept a plea of proprietary estoppel when one or more of Fry LJ's probanda were missing (for example, *Berg Homes v Grey* (1980)). To all intents and purposes, this was because the emphasis of proprietary estoppel shifted from situations where the purpose was to prevent the true owner from relying on their strict legal rights over land, to a doctrine which asked whether the claimant had any positive right to that land. In short, the focus shifted from the landowner to the claimant, wherein the latter's actions and perceptions became much more central to the issue. Of course, there are still cases where Fry LJ's formula is used in full (*Coombes v Smith*, and *Mathura*) but these cases are the exception. Essentially, the modern position is that put forward in *Taylor Fashions v Liverpool Victoria Trustees* (1981). In that case, Oliver J made it clear that proprietary estoppel is not limited to cases where the landowner knows of their rights, or their extent, but is indeed a flexible doctrine, springing from equity which should not be unduly restricted by rigid rules.

The position after *Taylor Fashions* is that a person may be entitled to claim rights in or over land which belongs formally to another where it would be unconscionable to deny those rights. Effectively, this means that the claimant must prove an assurance – express or implied – by the landowner as to the claimant's position in relation to the land; reliance on that assurance by the claimant; and detriment by the claimant as a result of relying on the assurance. Indeed, so general and flexible are these criteria that sometimes little evidence will be needed in order to support an estoppel. In *Greasley v Cooke* (1980), for example, the Court of Appeal held that if it is clear that assurances have been made, and detriment suffered, it is permissible to assume that reliance has occurred (and see *Cho v Han* (2000)). Likewise, in *JT Developments v Quinn*, it became clear that an estoppel could arise even though there was no intention to create binding obligations, as where the parties had attempted to negotiate a contract in respect of land but failed. Numerous examples now exist of successful claims of proprietary estoppel and cases such as *Re Basham* and *Gillett v Holt* illustrate that it is an all purpose remedy resorted to as much by claimants seeking to avoid the formality requirements otherwise imposed for the creation of property rights as by judges seeking to achieve a 'just' result in the case before them.

In this regard, the case of *Lim Teng Huan v Ang Swee Chuan* (1992) before the Judicial Committee of the Privy Council represents the highest watermark so far of the doctrine. In that case, the plaintiff and defendant had entered into a contract for the sale of land which was unenforceable. Nevertheless, the defendant undertook works on the disputed land and subsequently claimed the land by estoppel. The plaintiff (suing for possession) argued that no estoppel had arisen because he had not behaved unconscionably, but had simply refused to carry out an unenforceable contract. The Privy Council held that for an estoppel to exist, all that was necessary was an assurance, reliance and detriment and that no unconscionable conduct *per se* was necessary. Furthermore, in their view, the unenforceable contract actually represented that assurance, which had been relied upon and so an estoppel did exist. Clearly, this is a remarkable decision but not unique (see similar facts in *Flowermix v Site Developments* (2000)). Not only does it divorce proprietary estoppel from its equitable roots (by divorcing it from unconscionability), it amounts to the enforcement of an otherwise unenforceable contract simply because that contract existed. Of course, estoppel often results in the creation or transfer of proprietary rights when there is no enforceable contract, but the reason why the formality rules discussed above (that is, a deed or enforceable written contract) can be ignored is precisely because it would be unconscionable to insist on them. Thus, once it is clear that there is no unconscionability, there is no reason to ignore the formal requirements for the creation of interests in land. Such a view – which urges a return to the search for unconscionability – is evident in some decisions, including *Taylor v Dickens* (1997) where it was found that it was not unconscionable for a person to change their will to deprive a claimant of a promised interest *if* there is no additional promise not to revoke the will. On the other hand, this should be contrasted with the similar *Gillett v Holt* where the Court of Appeal held that there always would be unconscionability if an assurance was withdrawn after detrimental reliance. This recent pronouncement does not deny the relevance of unconscionability, but rather defines it in such a general way that its value as an *additional* requirement for proof of estoppel must be doubted. If the *Gillett* approach becomes the norm, unconscionability will be simply a function of an assurance, reliance and detriment.

It appears, then, that proprietary estoppel is now the embodiment of the equitable jurisdiction: it allows for the creation of property rights without needing to fulfil the strict requirements of statute, in cases where it would be 'unconscionable' to do otherwise. The flexibility this permits is apparent in the way that a court may 'satisfy' the estoppel or, in other words, the flexibility a court has to grant the most appropriate remedy to the claimant. For example, if the claimant successfully establishes an assurance supported by detrimental reliance, the estoppel thereby generated may be satisfied by awarding the fee simple to the claimant (*Dillwyn v Llewellyn; Pascoe v Turner*), the grant of an easement (*Celsteel v Alton*), a life interest (one view of *Bannister v Bannister*), a right of occupation until expenditure is repaid (*Dodsworth v Dodsworth*), a complete readjustment of the parties rights over the property (*Voyce v Voyce*), a readjustment of testamentary dispositions (*Re Basham*), a licence to use the property (one view of *Inwards v Baker*), a cash sum (*Campbell v Griffin*) or, simply, dismissal of the paper owner's claim for possession (*Mathura*). In fact, the range of remedies is open ended and, importantly, does not necessarily have to result in the creation or transfer of a proprietary interest at all. In some cases, it will be the 'expectation loss' of the claimant (that is, that which they were promised). In others, it will be their 'reliance loss', being the repayment of any detriment incurred. In fact, it could be a combination of the two: *Jennings v Rice* (2002).

All in all, the conditions required for establishing an estoppel, and the court's wide discretion in satisfying a successful plea, demonstrate the highly flexible nature of this doctrine. Of course, accompanying such flexibility is a large measure of uncertainty, both for any claimant and their legal advisers. It is not surprising, therefore, that proprietary estoppel has been regarded as a panacea for all ills and certainly has been used as such by the courts (for example, *Re Basham*). Moreover, insofar as it allows the creation of rights over property by entirely informal means, it provides an easy escape route for the claimant who has failed to observe the statutory requirements for the creation of proprietary rights, as in *Lim* and *Flowermix*. That said, the existence of a doctrine which enables a court to resolve matters according to the conscience of the parties involved, rather than according to the strict forms of a statute, is a necessary adjunct to any legal system which stipulates formalities as a means to certainty. The key is, however, not to go too far. There is merit in certainty, especially in relation to transactions concerning land and policy considerations should not be forgotten when considering the informal and flexible doctrine of proprietary estoppel. This will be all the more important when electronic conveyancing introduces even stricter formality requirements for the creation or transfer of proprietary rights in registered land.

Notes

This question is interesting as it gives the good student an opportunity to explain how proprietary estoppel is related to the general formality requirements of land law. It also illustrates the wide, and still undefined, reach of estoppel. A knowledge of recent case law is most important.

Question 29

'The law of proprietary estoppel has altered fundamentally the distinction between licences and proprietary interests in land. To all intents and purposes, to make such distinctions is no longer practically necessary or theoretically justified.'

Discuss.

Answer plan

The following areas need to be discussed:
- the nature of proprietary estoppel;
- its relation to estoppel licences;
- estoppels and third parties;
- the need for theoretical clarity.

Answer

In recent years, the courts' resort to proprietary estoppel as a means of resolving disputes over property has increased dramatically. Of course, this in itself is worthy of note but not truly startling: the fact that the courts are prepared to intervene more readily where they perceive unconscionability shows that 'equity' remains a developing body of law able to meet in part the demands of a modern law of property for the 21st century. Indeed, since *Taylor Fashions v Liverpool Victoria Trustees* (1981) deconstructed the law of proprietary estoppel, by making the conditions for a successful claim less rigid, the doctrine has moved into new fields, as both *Voyce v Voyce* (1991) and *JT Developments v Quinn* illustrate. It may be that proprietary estoppel emerges as the main counterweight to the formality requirements contained in s 2 of the Law of Property (Miscellaneous Provisions) Act 1989 (see, for example, *Maloo v Standish* (2002)) and the proposed forms for electronic conveyancing found in the Land Registration Act 2002. However, the development of this doctrine supposes not only that there are clear (or relatively clear) principles which can separate the legitimate from the spurious claim, but also that the consequences of a successful invocation of proprietary estoppel are clearly understood.

It is clear from *Taylor Fashions* that an estoppel will arise in favour of a claimant if they can prove an assurance, relied upon to their detriment. It is also clear from *Crabb v Arun DC* (1976) that, once the court has decided that the equity is established, it may seek to 'satisfy' it in a way appropriate to the case before it, in essence, using its discretion. The cases of *Voyce v Voyce* (1991), *Mathura v Mathura* (1994) and *Yaxley v Gotts* (1999) where the court unscrambled the complicated property dealings of the parties and imposed a solution apparently outside of the parties' intention, show that the court's power is wide and unfettered by the actual expectations of the parties. The Court of Appeal has now confirmed this in very clear terms in *Jennings v Rice* (2002). However, none of this settles the question of the nature of proprietary estoppel *per se*; all it does is tell us that the court may use the doctrine to achieve such results as it thinks fair and reasonable in the circumstances. In particular, the question has arisen in the context of licences which on the now confirmed orthodox view (*Lloyd v Dugdale* (2001)) are not interests in land. In simple terms, if the result of the courts' deliberations are that one of the parties has a licence over the other's land, generated or protected by estoppel, does this amount to an 'interest in land'? Or, to put it another way, is the estoppel itself an interest in land that can bind third parties in the normal way appropriate to proprietary interests in registered or unregistered land, such that it can confer such a status on what would otherwise be a purely personal licence to use the land?

The answer to this question is by no means clear, for there is little specific guidance in the case law. This is not surprising given that the courts are more concerned with reaching practical solutions to practical problems without delving into the theoretical niceties of the nature of proprietary estoppel (for example, *Bibby v Stirling* (1998)). In general, however, two distinct trends may be distinguished. First, there is some support for the view that licences generated by estoppel, or protected by estoppel, are themselves interests in land. This seems to be another way of saying that an estoppel *per se* has a proprietary character. Support for this view may derive from *Ives v High* and from *Inwards v Baker* where *dicta* suggest that estoppel, once arisen, may bind a third party. A similar hint is given in *Habermann v Koeller* (1996) and, more recently, is inherent in the decision in *Lloyd v Dugdale*, where the claimant benefitted from an estoppel but it did not bind because Dugdale was not in 'actual occupation' under s 70(1)(g) of the LRA 1925 – thus implying that the estoppel *itself* is proprietary and would have bound if Dugdale had been in actual occupation. In unregistered land, this would be through the mechanism of notice (*Ives v High* (1967)) and, as noted in *Dugdale*, in registered land, through occupation giving rise to an overriding interest under s 70(1)(g). Certainly, if this view is correct, it seems that estoppel has been elevated to an interest in land *per se* and for the future this is without doubt the effect of s 116 of the Land Registration Act 2002. However, in respect of licences at least, there are difficulties. First, a distinction should be made between estoppel which creates a right between A and B and estoppel which protects a pre-existing right (created by A and B) against C. It is only the first of these scenarios that gives rise to the problems we are considering. For example, in *Ives v High*, one explanation of the case is that A and B had by their action created an easement binding on A's land and, when the land was sold to C, C so acted as to be estopped from denying the right. In effect, this has nothing to do with the transfer of existing rights to a third party because the third party is bound by estoppel because of their own actions. In other words, C is bound by their own estoppel, not that which existed between A and B. (The same could be said of *Bibby v Stirling*, where an estoppel *appears* to bind a third party without argument.) Secondly, there is only fragile evidence that an estoppel licence has ever been held binding against a third party. The acid test would be whether an estoppel generated licence has ever had this effect, because, given that we know that pure licences cannot bind third parties, any such effect must be due to the estoppel itself. The evidence is equivocal, despite *Lloyd v Dugdale*. It is true that in *Inwards v Baker*, the court indicated that the claimant should be awarded a licence to occupy which could bind third parties and the same solution was adopted in *Greasley v Cooke*. Likewise, in *Re Sharpe*, the court accepts that the estoppel (the 'equity') can bind a trustee in bankruptcy and there is implied support in *Locabail UK v Bayfield* (1999). However, it is also true that both *Inwards* and *Cooke* can be justified on other grounds (that the claimant should have had a life interest under a settlement; see *Dodsworth v Dodsworth*) and, in *Williams v Staite* the matter was assumed rather than argued. The same assumption was made in *Bibby v Stirling*, though not of course in *Dugdale*.

Indeed, after the decision in *Dugdale*, it may be that a dual approach should be preferred. Thus, while *licences* are not interests in land, 'estoppels' may be. However, if the court chooses to satisfy the equity by the award of a licence to the claimant, perhaps it will not then be *enforced* against a third party, at least if the equity is crystallised *before* the third party becomes involved. Conversely, if the estoppel is satisfied as a proprietary right *before* a third party becomes involved, then there is no doubt that a third person buying the land over which the right takes effect will be bound by it: they are bound in the same way that any lease, freehold or easement would bind. Section 116 of the LRA 2002 will ensure this for the future in registered land. Of course, if the third party becomes involved before the estoppel is crystallised, it now seems that it will be regarded as proprietary, irrespective of the way the court chooses then to crystallise it.

In conclusion, then, whether proprietary estoppel has altered the fundamental distinction between personal rights and proprietary rights depends on the view one takes of the doctrine. Is an estoppel in itself a right, or is it merely a method whereby rights are created, some of which will be proprietary, some of which will be personal? The Land Registration Act 2002 confirms that estoppel gives rise to an interest in land from the moment the equity arises (that is, when the assurance is acted on to detriment) and not the later date when it is crystallised by the court. This will bring certainty, but will it also restrict courts in that their ability to grant rights arising by estoppel that are not (and should not) bind third parties?

Notes

This is a difficult question as it raises an issue to which the courts have not yet given a final answer: namely, the nature of proprietary estoppel. Help can be obtained from academic comment; see, in particular, Battersby [1991] Conv 36 and (1995) 58 MLR 637. *Lloyd v Dugdale* (2001) may come to be regarded as the definitive word. Even if it does not, s 116 of the LRA 2002 has settled the matter for the future for registered land.

Question 30

In 2000, Alberto, Benito and Claudio live in Nos 1, 2 and 3 Abdication Street respectively, an area of registered land. Each house has a large garden, although Alberto has concreted over his and uses it to store spare parts connected with his car repair business. Last year, Alberto asked Benito (in No 2) whether he would mind if Alberto constructed a small shed to store some more valuable equipment even though this meant siting some foundations in Benito's garden. Benito readily agreed and helped Alberto construct the shed. A little later, before the shed is complete, Alberto promised that Benito could store some of his (Benito's) own goods in the shed. Benito also asked if Alberto would mind if his wife's mother, Tosca, parked her cycle in the shed.

Alberto readily agreed, not realising that Tosca drove a very large motorcycle which would occupy considerable space. Meanwhile, Claudio has been negotiating with Benito over the purchase of some land at the back of Abdication Street owned by Benito. Benito is unwilling to sell, but permits Claudio to occupy the land pending the negotiation of a long lease. Benito asks Claudio to pay him £300 per month as 'a down payment' for the lease, but, when Claudio comes to pay, Benito tells him to keep his money as Benito has decided to sell and will give him a full price later. Claudio subsequently seeks planning permission from the local council to build a pizza parlour on his new land and gets Alberto's and Benito's guarantee that they will not oppose planning permission. However, just as he is about to instruct a local builder, Benito informs him that he has sold the property to Bigburger Inc.

Alberto is distraught at the prospect of a large takeaway restaurant behind his house and manages to sell to Hank. Hank has just discovered Tosca's motorcycle in the shed and has removed it, along with Benito's property. In retaliation, Benito is about to knock down that part of the shed that stands on his land. Claudio wants to know whether he has any rights which can be enforced against Bigburger Inc.

Discuss.

Answer plan

The answer needs to include a discussion of the following areas:

- what rights, if any, are created by the actions of the parties: proprietary estoppel;
- what are the nature of those rights: how is the equity satisfied;
- how, if at all, do those rights affect subsequent purchasers of the land.

Answer

This problem essentially revolves around two central issues, although their application to the particular facts of the individual circumstances of Alberto, Benito and Claudio may vary. First, it is necessary to determine the nature and extent of any interests created by the actions of the brothers in favour of each other. Secondly, and depending on the answer to the first question, whether any or all of those interests are rights binding on the subsequent purchasers of the plots, Hank and Bigburger Inc.

(a) Alberto and the shed; Benito and the storage; Tosca and her motorcycle

As a preliminary matter, it is apparent from the facts of the problem that none of the arrangements of the parties have been recorded in writing. This immediately raises the problem that unless the activities fall within one of the recognised exceptions to the formality requirements found in s 2 of the Law of Property (Miscellaneous Provisions) Act 1989, then such interests as may have arisen will be void. Further, although it is not absolutely certain (see *Street v Mountford* (1985)) there is little evidence that any of these arrangements – particularly those relating to storage in Alberto's shed – were intended to or do amount to a lease. If that were the case, if the lease were three years or less, the absence of writing would be immaterial (s 54(2) of the LPA 1925) and it would be binding on Hank according to its terms as a legal lease and an overriding interest under s 70(1)(k) of the LRA 1925.

The absence of writing means that Alberto, Benito and Tosca may all have to rely on proprietary estoppel if they are to claim rights. It is then another matter whether these rights will be binding on subsequent third parties. Alternatively, these rights could arise from contract and be in the nature of contractual licences and, so, not presumptively binding any third party (*Ashburn Anstalt v Arnold* (1988); *Lloyd v Dugdale* (2001)).

(i) The shed

Clearly, Benito the owner of the land over which the shed will intrude has agreed that Alberto can build that shed in the full knowledge that use of his own land will thereby be diminished. In such circumstances, Alberto will have a reasonable chance of establishing that Benito is bound by proprietary estoppel from demolishing the shed. In the language of *Taylor Fashions v Liverpool Victoria Trustees* (1981), Benito made an assurance to Alberto (albeit in response to Alberto's request) that the shed could be built, which was relied upon by Alberto to his detriment. The fact that Benito assisted in the building can only reinforce this presumption. In such circumstances, following cases such as *Crabb v Arun DC* (1976) and *Ives v High* (and subject to what will be said below in respect of Benito's claim of storage), it is unlikely that Benito will be able to renege on his promise and destroy the shed. Equity will intervene by way of an injunction.

What is not clear, however, is what will happen if either or both of the properties are sold. There is authority that the *benefit* of the estoppel cannot be transferred to a successor in title (*Fryer v Brook* (1984)) because it is merely personal to the promisee, although this appears to have been contradicted by Lord Denning in *Ives v High* and indeed, it is difficult to see why the alleged personal nature of an estoppel (even *if* this were true) should stop the *benefit* passing to another (and see, also, the analysis in *Bibby v Stirling* (1998)). In our case, then, it is unclear whether the estoppel that exists in favour of Alberto can be passed on to Hank when he purchases the land. However, Hank might argue that the benefit of the right has been expressly assigned to him under the contract of sale (that is, as a personal transfer of a personal right). Likewise, if Benito were to sell his house (although there is no evidence here), it is unclear whether the estoppel binding on him could be made to bind a subsequent purchaser. The matter is considered in more detail below.

(ii) The storage of Benito's goods

The position here is somewhat complicated. On one view of the facts, Alberto has simply agreed that Benito can store his goods in his shed. This may have been done as a personal favour – in which case Benito has a bare licence – or it may have been done as a counterpart to Benito's promise and assistance with the shed – in which case it may be a contractual licence. If it is a bare licence, it seems that it is revocable at will by Alberto (*Thomas v Sorrell* (1673)), although, if it is contractual, it may be irrevocable by Alberto according to its terms (*Wintergarden Theatres v Millennium Productions Ltd* (1948)). However, in either case, it is clear that a contractual licence as such cannot be binding on a third party (Hank) (*Ashburn Anstalt v Arnold* (1988); *Lloyd v Dugdale* (2001)).

An alternative view is, however, that there has been some form of estoppel generated in Benito's favour by Alberto's conduct in relation to the storage. It would be necessary to establish that there was an assurance reliance and detriment (*Taylor Fashions*), although it might well be difficult on the facts of the case as there appears to be little in the way of detriment suffered by Benito in reliance on the promise (and such detriment is crucial: *Orgee v Orgee* (1997)). However, if the estoppel is made out, Benito could go on to argue either: first, that the estoppel should be satisfied by the granting of an easement of storage in his favour. This would be binding on Hank, a subsequent purchaser, as an overriding interest under s 70(1)(a) following the judgment in *Celsteel v Alton* and *Thatcher v Douglas*. We know, however, from the law of easements, that a right to storage may be incapable of being an easement because it amounts to exclusive possession of the servient tenement (*Copeland v Greenhalf; Grigsby v Melville; Batchelor v Marlowe*); secondly, therefore, Benito could argue that the estoppel itself is capable of binding a third party, irrespective of whether it generates an easement or a licence (*Lloyd v Dugdale*). If this is the case – that an estoppel is an interest in land – it might be binding on the purchaser Hank as an overriding interest, possibly under the catch all s 70(1)(g) of the LRA 1925.

(iii) The shed and the storage

In the above analysis, we have assumed that the shed building and the storage were separate events. It might be possible to argue that they are so interconnected that, at least for Alberto and Benito, they must be taken together. Hence, by analogy with *Ives v High*, it could be argued that, if Alberto wants the benefit of the shed, he must be subject to the burden of the storage of Benito's goods, although *Thamesmead Town v Allotey* (1998) suggests that this type of reciprocal benefit/burden is not truly *mutual* benefit and burden. This would, of course, prevent either of the original parties from reneging on their agreement. Whether the 'burden' of Alberto's obligations could be passed to Hank is another matter. There is no evidence that Hank purchased Alberto's land with express knowledge of Benito's rights (or in an inequitable manner), so as to subject him to a personal constructive trust within *Ashburn Anstalt v Arnold* (1988) and *Lloyd v Dugdale* (2001). Alternatively, however, if Hank seeks to make use of the shed, it is just possible that the court would stipulate that if he wished to take the benefit, then he must be subject to the burden. The problem with this is, however, that we could apply it to every subsequent purchaser of the two plots with the effect that purely personal rights could evolve into proprietary obligations. This is not an attractive solution.

(iv) The motorcycle

The position over Tosca's motorcycle is very similar to the position above in respect of Benito's goods and it may well be difficult for Benito to establish anything other than a bare or contractual licence to support the parking/storage. Moreover, if we were to approach this issue on a benefit/burden analysis, it may well prove decisive that the 'benefit' is to be conferred on someone other than the person who is subject to the burden of the shed: viz, the benefit is Tosca's but the burden of submitting to the shed falls on Benito. This makes it highly unlikely that Hank would be bound by this obligation when he purchases Alberto's land (*Allotey*). The right is essentially personal and the analogy with benefit and burden is not appropriate.

(b) Claudio and the plot of land and Bigburger Inc

The first matter is to determine the nature of Claudio's interest, if any, in the plot of land that Benito has sold, and then to see whether this interest is binding on the purchaser, Bigburger Inc.

Clearly, Claudio and Benito start off by negotiating the terms of a lease, as that is the clear intention of the parties following Benito's initial refusal to sell the land. Equally clearly, there is no doubt that Claudio and Benito fail to reach agreement on the terms of the long lease. On the other hand, Claudio is let into occupation by Benito on the grounds that he can occupy pending successful conclusion of negotiations and provided that he pays £300. At first sight, this may appear to raise the possibility of a periodic tenancy. If this could be established then Claudio would have an overriding interest against the purchaser Bigburger (s 70(1)(k) of the LRA 1925), who would be bound by the terms of the lease. Unfortunately for Claudio, however, it appears from *Javad v Aqil* that occupation and payment of rent (and there was none here, merely offered) will not give rise to a periodic tenancy if the occupation can be attributed to negotiations pending the grant of a 'real' lease. This is Claudio's position and he will be a tenant at will which, even if it is binding on Bigburger Inc, can be terminated. Circumstances then take a different turn. Benito makes it clear that he will now sell to Claudio and Claudio, acting in reliance on this, begins to make plans for his small restaurant. Benito even re-enforces this by promising not to oppose a planning application. This may, then, raise a proprietary estoppel in Claudio's favour, providing he can establish assurance, reliance and detriment in the normal way. On the facts, Benito will argue that he simply made an offer to sell which he has now withdrawn (see, for example, *Ravenscroft v Gardner* (2001)), whereas Claudio will argue that he has relied on the promise to such an extent as to raise an estoppel in his favour. The answer is one of judgment, but, certainly, Claudio does not appear to have suffered the same degree of detriment as the promisees in other cases such as *Re Basham*, *Pascoe v Turner* and *Inwards v Baker* and, although the cases of *Lim Teng Huan v Chuan* and *Flowermix v Site Development* offer some support, it may be that the estoppel cannot be made out as the promise is legitimately withdrawn (*Canty v Broad; Taylor v Dickens;* but contrast *Gillett v Holt* and *Jennings v Rice*). However, were it to be accepted that Claudio had an estoppel in his favour, there is every chance that this could be binding against Bigburger. Either the court will satisfy the equity with the award of a proprietary right (for example, the freehold; *Pascoe*) which could be binding on the purchaser as an overriding interest under s 70(1)(g) of the LRA 1925, Claudio being in actual occupation; or, the estoppel itself can be regarded as an interest in land which will bind Bigburger in the same way, or, in the most extreme case, the court could nullify the sale to Bigburger and order a sale to Claudio.

Notes

This is similar to Question 28, being the practical application of the problems there raised.

CHAPTER 7

EASEMENTS

Introduction

Easements comprise those rights which one landowner may exercise over the land of their neighbour. Common examples are the right of way, the right of light and the right of support. It is essential to the understanding of the law of easements that the student appreciates that every easement has two aspects: one landowner will enjoy the benefit of an easement and another will be subject to its burden. This is just another way of saying that easements exist over a servient tenement for the benefit of a dominant tenement. It is important to remember the dual nature of an easement as this will make problems concerning the transmission of easements to third parties easier to understand. It is often said that easements can either be 'positive' or 'negative' in character. The former are those which allow the dominant tenement owner (the person who has the benefit) to do some thing on the servient land, such as enjoy a right of way, while the latter prevent the servient tenement owner (the person subject to the burden) from doing some thing on their own land, such as building new premises. However, it is obvious that most easements have a positive and negative aspect, depending on how you look at it, and the distinction is not of great practical use. Its one advantage is that it illustrates that many so called negative easements are similar to restrictive covenants and perhaps their subject matter would be more appropriate to the legal regime of the latter rather than the former.

Checklist

Questions on the law of easements can come in either problem or essay form and the student should be aware of the following issues:

- the nature of easements;
- the creation of easements;
- the distinction between legal and equitable easements;

- the transmissibility of easements to third parties, both benefit and burden;
- reform of the law of easements.

Question 31

Is there any consistent policy evident in the rights that the courts have recognised as easements?

Answer plan

The answer should discuss the following areas:
- *Re Ellenborough Park*;
- positive and negative easements;
- relationship to restrictive covenants;
- public policy.

Answer

An easement is essentially a right of property that is enjoyed or exercised over land belonging to another. In one sense, the law of easements can be regarded as the private law equivalent to public planning law as where an easement prevents the owner of land from doing something on his own property. For example, if land is subject to an easement of light, this effectively prevents the owner of that land from building so as to obstruct that light. However, easements are not only negative in nature. Many easements authorise a neighbour to use the land subject to the easement in a way that would otherwise be a trespass. Thus, a right of way enables the owner of the easement to walk across his neighbour's land. Indeed, this distinction between 'negative' and 'positive' easements is often said to be one of the most important factors in the law of easements since case law establishes that the law should be wary of accepting new negative easements, as in *Phipps v Pears* where it was alleged (and rejected) that the servient owner was under a negative easement preventing him from demolishing his premises. In fact, it is inherent in the nature of all easements that they comprise both a positive and a negative aspect, for what the dominant owner is allowed to do, the servient owner must suffer. In this sense, irrespective of whether the easement is positive or negative, all easements comprise a benefit and a burden. The land subject to the easement (the servient tenement) bears the burden of that easement whilst the owner of the land entitled to enjoy the easement (the dominant tenement) has the benefit of it. It is important to remember this duality when considering questions of the transmissibility of the benefits and burdens of easements to subsequent purchasers of the dominant or servient land.

The traditional starting point for a discussion about the essential characteristics of an easement is the judgment in *Re Ellenborough Park* (1956). This gives us a four fold test. First, there must be a dominant and a servient tenement. Secondly, an easement must accommodate, that is benefit, the dominant tenement. Thirdly, the dominant and servient tenement owners must be owned or occupied by different persons and, fourthly, the easement must be capable of being the subject matter of a grant. If the alleged right satisfies these conditions, it is most likely to be recognised as an easement irrespective of the name given to it by the parties that created it. The only small caveat to this is that occasionally certain rights which fulfil these criteria are not accepted as easements on grounds of public policy. It is rare, however, for an alleged easement to be disallowed on this ground explicitly and it is more likely that a judge will prefer to base his decision of lack of fulfilment of one of the flexible *Re Ellenborough* criteria.

The essential duality of an easement is evident from the first condition. It is crucial that if an easement is to exist there must be a dominant and servient tenement. The easement must burden land but it must also benefit land and in technical terms the easement cannot exist in gross (*Hawkins v Rutter* (1892)). The easement runs with the land, both the benefit and the burden.

The second condition established by *Ellenborough* is that the easement, or rather the alleged easement, must confer a benefit on the dominant tenement: it must accommodate it. Easements are proprietary rights and therefore confer benefits on land, not persons (*Manson v Shrewsbury Railway*). Rather like covenants that touch and concern the land, easements must benefit the user of land, the value of land or the mode of occupation of land. This particular requirement can be manifested in several ways. Thus, the servient tenement must be sufficiently proximate to the dominant tenement to be able to confer the benefit on it (*Bailey v Stevens*). However, the most widely cited example of an alleged easement that was disallowed as not conferring a benefit on the dominant tenement was the personal advantage in *Hill v Tupper* where the owner of a canal granted the plaintiff the right to put pleasure boats on the canal. This was deemed not to be sufficiently connected with the land so as to amount to an easement. It is not, however, authority for the proposition that mere commercial advantages cannot be easements. *Moody v Steggles* makes it clear that an easement which benefits a trade or occupation carried on on the land, such as a public house, is permitted, as where a pub sign is hung on adjacent property. Of course, the distinction here is sometimes difficult to draw and with such flexible criteria consistency cannot be guaranteed. On the other hand, this criterion does give judges a certain amount of hidden discretion to exclude those rights which for matters of policy should not fall within the ambit of easements. In *Hill*, for example, it may well have been against the public interest for a particular individual to have exclusive rights to a waterway. The same cannot be said for the easement in *Moody*.

As indicated above, an easement has a dual aspect. It confers both a benefit and a burden. It is essentially a right in another's land. For that reason, the third *Ellenborough* condition is that the dominant and servient tenements must not be both owned and occupied by the same person (*Roe v Siddons*). Indeed, should the dominant and servient tenements come into the ownership and possession of the same person, any easement over the servient land will thereby be extinguished. In effect, this means that a man cannot have an easement against himself, although due to the operation of the rule in *Wheeldon v Burrows* an easement may be created in such a situation when part of the merged land is sold off. The rule is, however, that the dominant and servient tenement must not be both owned and occupied by the same person and so there is nothing to stop a tenant having an easement against their landlord as in *Wright v Macadam* (1949) (and vice versa).

Finally, no right may amount to an easement unless it is capable of forming the subject matter of a grant or, in other words, an easement must be capable of being expressly conveyed by deed. This appears to be an all engrossing condition, itself having several different manifestations. First, there is the obvious point that an easement cannot exist unless there is a capable grantor, that is somebody legally competent to create an easement, and a capable grantee. So, for example, no easement can exist where purportedly granted or received by a limited company having no power to grant or receive easements under its articles of association. Secondly, it is clear that all rights that are capable of forming the subject matter of a grant must be sufficiently definite. In the case of an easement, therefore, the right must be capable of clear description and precise definition. So, for example, in *Re Aldred* (1610), a right to a good view could not exist as an easement. Similarly, there is no easement of privacy (*Browne v Flower* (1911)) and no easement to receive light generally as opposed to a right to receive light through a defined window. It is, however, with the final element of this condition that consistency gives way to flexibility and, to some extent, judicial discretion. Only those interests actually lay in grant that are capable of lying in grant or, in other words, that the right must be within the general nature of rights recognised as easements or be rights by close analogy thereto. This does not mean, of course, that new easements for new times cannot exist. Thus, there has been an easement to use a letterbox in *Goldberg v Edwards* (1950), an easement to use an airfield in *Re Bolton Paul* and an easement facilitating use of a supermarket in *London and Blenheim Estates v Ladbroke* (1992).

In essence, this last condition means that the courts will strike down alleged easements which do not appear to the particular judge to be within the class of rights that should be recognised as such. Of course, some general principles have developed and it is often said that no new easement will be recognised that requires the servient owner to spend money (*Phipps v Pears* (1965)). Again, according to *Phipps*, the law will look unfavourably on claims to an easement which give the dominant tenement owner the right to prevent the servient tenement owner from doing something on his land. These so called negative easements are more properly to be regarded as within the sphere of restrictive covenants. It is also said that no right will be recognised as an easement which gives the dominant tenement owner the right to use exclusively the servient tenement. So, in *Copeland v Greenhalf* (1952), no easement could exist to store tools of the trade on the servient land and, in *Grigsby v Melville* (1974), a right of storage in a cellar could not be accepted and in *Hannina v Morland*, use of a neighbour's flat roof was too extensive to be an easement. Similarly, the right to park in a defined space in a carpark cannot be an easement (nor if it amounts to storage of cars: *Batchelor v Marlowe*) although as *Newman v Jones* and *London and Blenheim Estates v Ladbroke* make clear, there can be an easement to park generally on a piece of land. The position here is, however, somewhat policy orientated. For, as *Macadam* shows, the particular facts of a case may require the granting of an easement so as to facilitate commodious living. In that case, the tenant successfully claimed an easement of storage of coal in a small part of the landlord's coal shed. There is no real distinction that can be sensibly drawn between this and *Copeland* and *Melville*, other than to say that the court in *Macadam* believed that the tenant deserved the right claimed. Such flexibility is inherent in the *Ellenborough* conditions and it would be unfortunate if the development of the law of easements was hindered by too exacting and rigorously applied conditions.

At present, the *Re Ellenborough* rules provide an outline outside of which a judge usually will not go but inside of which he may recognise an easement or not according to the circumstances of the case, the needs of the property and, indeed, the behaviour of the parties. In this sense of course, the law is uncertain as it becomes difficult to predict whether a new right will be regarded as an easement. However, to some extent, many issues which formerly would have fallen within the range of easements are now dealt with under the law of restrictive covenants and local planning regulations. Of course, the easement has one great advantage. Not only is it proprietary like the restrictive covenant (so, therefore, capable of binding third parties), it may, unlike the restrictive covenant, be legal and bind those third parties automatically in unregistered land and as an overriding interest in registered land. The powerful effects of easements on servient lands and on successors in title to those lands means that care has to be taken when considering any proposed reform in the definition of these rights.

Notes

This has to be one of the most textbook based questions any examiner can ask in any subject. It is straightforward and easy to score a 'safe' mark. Any attempt at criticism will be rewarded as most students repeat verbatim the same answer, as above. It is difficult not to.

Question 32

Apart from easements established by long user, by what methods can easements be created? Is there any significant difference between legal and equitable easements?

Answer plan

The answer needs to include a discussion of the following:
- legal and equitable easements;
- distinction between grant and reservation;
- express creation;
- implied creation; necessity (*Wheeldon v Burrows*); s 62 of the LPA 1925 (*Long v Gowlett*; common intention (*Stafford v Lee*; *Peckham v Ellison*).

Answer

Easements are, essentially, a species of right that one landowner enjoys over the land of another. They are proprietary in the sense that they attach to the land rather than to the owners of the land. Moreover, like restrictive covenants, easements have a dual aspect. They both confer a benefit on one piece of land to be enjoyed by the owners for the time being thereof and they impose a burden on land which must be accepted by the owners for the time being of the servient land. It is intrinsic in this duality that the benefit and the burden of an easement can be transmitted independently. Thus, it is quite possible for the benefit of an easement to be passed onto several owners of the dominant tenement even though ownership of the servient tenement remains in the hands of the person who granted the easement. Likewise, it may be only the servient land that is transferred, or both. Indeed, the ability of easements to bind third parties is one reason, perhaps the most important, why it is necessary to have clear rules governing both the creation of easements and the conditions which must be fulfilled before an easement can be regarded as legal or equitable.

All easements are either created expressly, impliedly or by long user under the law of prescription. However, this tells us nothing about whether the easement will be legal or equitable and we must start, therefore, with a consideration of these requirements. In general terms, an easement can qualify as a legal interest only if it is held as an adjunct to a fee simple absolute in possession or as an adjunct to a term of years absolute (s 1 of the LPA 1925). More important in practice, however, is the rule that easements are only legal if they are created by statute, by deed, or by the process of prescription (long user). All other easements must be equitable. We are not concerned, here, with the creation of easements by prescription, and the creation of easements by statute speaks for itself, as where a local or private Act of Parliament gives certain rights to the person for whose benefit the Act was passed. The requirement of a deed for a legal easement is also reasonably straightforward, as this ensures that its existence is easily discoverable by a prospective purchaser of the servient land.

However, although all other easements must be equitable, that does not mean that equity requires no formality at all. Thus, under s 2 of the Law of Property (Miscellaneous Provisions) Act 1989, a contract for the creation of an interest in land (for example, an easement) must be in writing containing all the terms and signed by both parties. So, rather as is the case with equitable leases, if the parties have a written agreement to create an easement which can be regarded as specifically enforceable under *Walsh v Lonsdale* (1882), equity will treat an equitable easement as existing. However, it is no longer true that mere oral promises or agreements can create equitable easements, save only where the easement is created by proprietary estoppel, as in *Ives v High*

(1967) and, possibly, *Bibby v Stirling* (1998). These then, are the formality requirements under the current law, although they will be modified to permit electronic documents in due course. What then are the consequences of an easement being legal or equitable according to these principles?

For the most part, the consequences concern the effect of the easement on third parties, particularly purchasers of the servient land. In fact, the position is relatively straightforward. In unregistered land, all legal easements will bind any subsequent owner or occupier of the servient land under the general rule that legal interests bind the whole world. In registered land, the legal easement may well have been noted on the servient tenement title at the time of its creation and will be binding for that reason. Moreover, under s 70(1)(a) of the LRA 1925, legal easements not entered at the time of creation (for example, because they pre-date the registration of title) are overriding interests and so automatically bind all subsequent transferees. This is as it should be, because most legal easements will be evident to a potential purchaser and he should take his land aware of their existence. Of course, the same is not always true of equitable easements and, so, the conditions under which purchasers of the servient land can be bound are different. In unregistered land, most equitable easements are Class D(iii) land charges and they must be registered as such in order to bind a subsequent purchaser. If they are not registered, they will be void (*Midland Bank v Green* (1981)). The exception to this seems to be equitable estoppel easements which according to Lord Denning in *Ives* are not within Class D(iii) land charges because that category includes only those equitable easements which could once have been legal but are rendered equitable by the 1925 legislation. Estoppel easements are, of course, purely equitable and, according to *Ives*, bind a purchaser through the doctrine of notice. In registered land, equitable easements are minor interests and must be registered as such. Again however, certain equitable easements (including estoppel easements) may be exempt from this requirement and may, in fact, take effect as overriding interests under s 70(1)(a). This is the effect of *Celsteel v Alton* (1985) (confirmed in *Thatcher v Douglas* (1996)), which decided that equitable easements openly exercised and enjoyed were not excluded from s 70(1)(a). This has been criticised by many commentators, although the status of equitable estoppel easements as overriding interests might be justifiable on policy grounds: viz, that its 'owner' may not know that he enjoys the benefit of it and so cannot be expected to register. In any event, equitable easements will cease to be overriding under the LRA 2002. These rules then are reasonably clear and they determine when an easement will be legal or equitable and the consequences that flow from that distinction. What we must now discuss are the circumstances in which easements can be created, or, rather, the practical methods by which they come into existence.

Generally speaking, and putting prescription on one side, the creation of easements is either by express or implied grant or express or implied reservation. A grant is where the owner of the servient tenement grants an easement to the owner of what will become the dominant tenement. A reservation is the opposite. It is where the transferor of land reserves to themselves an easement over the land they are transferring. In very broad terms, it is easier to grant easements to somebody else than it is to reserve easements to oneself because of the rule that a man cannot generally derogate from his grant.

Turning first to reservation. If A sells land to B, A may expressly reserve to himself an easement over the land sold. The easement will be legal if it is reserved in a deed and it will be equitable if it is reserved in a written document. Likewise, however, it is clear that an easement of necessity and are arising by common intention can be impliedly reserved by the vendor. Thus, if A sells land to B, but the only access to the land retained by A is over the land sold to B, an implied reserved easement of necessity will exist in A's favour, as in *Pinnington v Galland* (see *Peckham v Ellison* (1998) for a reserved easement by common intention). However, in order for an easement of necessity to be reserved in this fashion, it must be true that the land retained by the vendor would be unusable without the easement claimed and no easement will be allowed where it is merely inconvenient to use another route, as in *Re Dodd*. It should be noted that impliedly reserved easements may also be legal or equitable. The easement is implied into a sale by A to B in favour of A. If, therefore, the sale is by deed the easement is implied into a deed and is legal. If the sale is by written document for valuable consideration, the easement is implied into that document and will be equitable. In other words, the easement carries the character of the document into which it is implied.

Turning now to easements by grant, as where one landowner (A) expressly grants an easement to his neighbour B, either by deed or in writing, or where A sells some land to B and as part of that sale grants B an easement over the land retained by himself. In the first case, of course, the easement is expressly granted and will be legal or equitable according to the form it takes. In the second case, the easement may well be expressly granted, as part of the sale. However, it is this second scenario, the sale of land by A to B that most often gives rise to implied grant. In fact, implied grant can take one of four forms, although, in all cases, the principle is the same: that an easement is implied into the grant of land by A to B so that the land sold becomes the dominant tenement and the land retained becomes the servient tenement. As with reservation, if the easement is implied into a deed, the easement will be legal and, if it is implied into a written transfer, it will be equitable. First, it is clear that easements may be impliedly granted by way of necessity. So, if the land granted cannot be used except by, say, access over the land retained by the vendor, an easement of necessity will exist. As in *Wong v Beaumont*, an easement of ventilation by necessity was held to exist when the land granted was intended to be used as a restaurant but could not be so used without a ventilation shaft over the land retained by the vendor. Generally speaking, it is easier to claim an implied grant of an easement of necessity than it is an implied reservation but, as *Re MRA Engineering* (1987) shows, a real necessity must exist, not merely a more convenient use of the land.

Secondly, easements may be impliedly granted under the rule in *Wheeldon v Burrows*. As we know, no easement can exist where the dominant and the servient tenement are owned and occupied by the same person. However, it often happens that a landowner will use one part of his land for the benefit of another, as where a landowner walks across a field to get to his house. These are sometimes known as quasi-easements because they would be easements had the land been in separate ownership or possession. So, if it should happen that the owner of the entire plot of land should sell the quasi-dominant part of his land, in the previous example, the house, or, in other words, the land benefited by the right, the rule in *Wheeldon v Burrows* (1879) stipulates that the vendor will have impliedly granted that right to a purchaser. This rule, which is based upon the idea that a person cannot derogate from their grant, can be expressly excluded and, of course, he cannot grant as easements any rights which are incapable of being easements. Furthermore, it appears from *Wheeldon* itself, that the rights that are impliedly granted must have been used by the vendor at the time of the grant for the benefit of the part sold (for example, the path must be being used), and the easement must be continuous and apparent and/or necessary for the reasonable enjoyment of the part granted. (It is most likely that the second and third conditions are alternatives and they were so treated in *Wheeldon*.) Providing, however, that these conditions are fulfilled, the purchaser of that part of the common owner's land which is the dominant part will acquire those easements impliedly granted in the conveyance of the land. Again, the right may be legal if the conveyance of the land was by deed or equitable as in *Borman v Griffith* (1930), where the grant of the land was under an equitable lease. Furthermore, if the common landowner grants the dominant part to X and, at the same time, grants the servient part to Y, it is clear that the rule in *Wheeldon* operates to give X an easement over Y's land, as in *Swansborough v Coventry* (1832). Although the rule in *Wheeldon* does not apply to reservations of easements (confirmed in *Ellison*), it is obvious that any owner of land who intends to sell that land in parts may well find his own land bound by easements he has impliedly granted. It is, in fact, a very powerful means of creating easements.

Thirdly, easements may be impliedly granted under s 62 of the LPA 1925. At the outset, however, it should be noted that s 62 only applies to conveyances which are defined in the Law of Property Act as transfers by deed. Thus, s 62 can operate only to create legal easements because it only operates when there has been a transfer of land by deed or its registered land equivalent, the registered disposition. Section 62 is a very wide ranging statutory provision and it has many purposes beyond the creation of easements. Moreover, it is clear that it is not limited to rights which are continuous or apparent or reasonably necessary as in *Wheeldon*. The only requirement is that the right is capable of being an easement. The factual situation of s 62 is, however, quite different from *Wheeldon*. If a landowner has two or more plots of land and, then, conveys by deed one of those plots to a purchaser, the purchaser will be granted by s 62 all of those rights that were previously enjoyed with the land. This is straightforward enough, but s 62 will convert into easements all of those rights enjoyed for the use of the land sold, even though prior to sale they were merely precarious, in the sense of being exercised by permission only. According to *Sovmots Investments v Secretary of State for the Environment* (1979) (following *Long v Gowlett* (1923)), it is essential for the operation of s 62 that the land owned by the vendor was in prior diversity of occupation before the sale. Practically, this means that, before the land is sold to the person acquiring the easement, it must have been used by either a tenant or a licensee of the vendor who enjoyed rights over that land. If, then, the land is conveyed to that person (or possibly any other person) by deed, that person will be impliedly granted the rights previously enjoyed. So, in *Goldberg v Edwards*, a licensee enjoyed a right over her landlord's land and when a new tenancy by deed was granted to her, that licence was transformed into an easement (see, also, *Wright v Macadam; Hillman v Rodgers* and *Hair v Gillman* (2000)). This has potentially devastating consequences for the landowner, although s 62 can be avoided by an express contrary stipulation. The requirement of prior diversity of occupation does of course limit the effects of its operation, but a landowner must be careful. Of all of the cases of implied grant, it is the most far removed from the intention of the parties.

Finally, the fourth method by which easements may be impliedly granted again arises in situations where the owner of land sells or leases part of it to another and is taken to have impliedly conveyed with that sale or lease an easement for the benefit of the part conveyed, to the detriment of the part retained. In this case, however, the easement is said to arise from the 'common intention' of the parties to the transaction. An example is provided by *Stafford v Lee* (1992), where the plaintiff claimed an easement of way over the defendant's land for the purpose of transporting materials for the construction of a house on the plaintiff's land. Both parcels of land had once been in the possession of the defendant's predecessor in title and the plaintiff had purchased his plot from the predecessor with the clear purpose of building a house upon it. The Court of Appeal held that an easement of common intention could be implied into the original sale by deed of the land to the plaintiff which, being legal, now bound the defendant. Importantly, an easement by necessity could not be implied for there were other routes to the plaintiff's property, albeit inconvenient and unsuitable for the carrying of construction materials. This case makes it clear that easements arising through common intention are quite distinct from easements of necessity, for, in this case, the only requirements are that there was in fact a common intention to use land in a certain way and that an easement is required to give effect to that purpose. Of course, the plaintiff in such cases bears a heavy burden of proof, having to explain why, if there was such a clear common intention, the easement was not expressly inserted into the conveyance in the first place. Consequently, the creation of easements by this method will be relatively rare, although they may be both impliedly granted (*Stafford*) and reserved (*Peckham*) although 'reservation' will be very difficult to establish (*Chaffe v Kingley*).

Notes

Although a long question, it is relatively simple. Most textbooks deal with this issue thoroughly. It is essential to grasp the distinction between a 'grant' and a 'reservation' of an easement. Note also that in due course, the formalities for the creation of an easement will change under s 93 of the LRA 2002, after the entry into force of which, an easement may not exit unless it is entered on the register.

Question 33

In 1990, Matilda, the owner of three adjacent terraced houses, title to which were registered, decided to realise some capital and resolved to sell two of her properties whilst remaining in the third. In the conveyance of No 10 to Aaron, Matilda promised to allow Aaron to park his 10 foot yacht in her garden, in return for which Aaron allowed Matilda to site a satellite dish on his roof. Matilda also agreed orally that Aaron could hang a small sign advertising his boat building business (which was based on the river some four miles away) on her end wall. When negotiating a sale of No 12 to Jacob, he insisted that he be given the right to temporarily store some building materials in Matilda's garden (next to the yacht) should he run out of space in his builder's yard opposite. This was agreed in the conveyance.

Matilda has just sold her house (No 11) to Ben who is unhappy with the elaborate sign that Aaron had erected and with the yacht taking up most of his garden. Aaron, however, has just retired and sold his business, the yacht and house to Sarah who is threatening to remove the satellite dish unless the yacht and the sign are allowed to stay. Meanwhile, Jacob has been storing materials on a permanent basis in the garden of No 11 and Ben decides to remove them.

Discuss.

Answer plan

The following areas need to be included:

- the nature of easements;
- creation of easements;
- legal and equitable easements and third parties.

Answer

This problem concerns the acquisition of easements and their effects on persons who subsequently come into possession of the servient and dominant land. In essence, there are two separate problems here, as the relationship of Matilda's property to each of the premises she has sold should be considered independently. Of course, in all cases, it is first necessary to determine whether the alleged right is capable of existing as an easement, then whether any easement that does exist is legal or equitable and then, finally, its effect on a purchaser of the dominant or servient tenement as the case may.

(a) Matilda and Aaron, and the subsequent sales of both houses

In this situation, there are three rights which it is alleged may amount to easements: the erection of the satellite dish in favour of Matilda's property, and the parking of the yacht and erection of the sign on Matilda's property in favour of Aaron's property. Can these interests amount to easements for, if they cannot, they amount only to personal licences between the original parties which cannot bind on successors in title (*Ashburn Anstalt v Arnold* (1988); *Lloyd v Dugdale* (2001)). Clearly, in respect of all rights, there is a capable grantor and grantee, there are two properties which could be the dominant and servient tenements and both

193

tenements are not owned or occupied by the same person. Thus far, there is no difficulty with the requirements for a valid easement laid down in *Re Ellenborough Park* (1956). However, some difficulty may exist in the need to show that the alleged rights benefit the dominant tenement *qua* tenement and whether they fall within the general nature of rights capable of being created as easements. This issue, and the nature of any right satisfying the *Ellenborough* formula, will be considered in respect of each right.

(i) The erection of the satellite dish is perhaps the least contentious

There seems little doubt that such a right is of benefit to the dominant tenement in much the same way as the easement to run telephone lines over neighbouring land was accepted in *Lancashire and Cheshire Telephone Exchange Co v Manchester Overseers*. It is clear that there is no necessary reason to deny the existence of new easements, provided they do not contradict the *Ellenborough* principles. There is no expenditure required of the servient owner and no exclusive occupation of his premises and the right is sufficiently definite. It would seem to be able to qualify as an easement.

Assuming that to be correct, the facts of this problem make it quite clear that the right was expressly reserved by Matilda when she sold the house to Aaron. There is, then no difficulty over its creation and, because it is expressly reserved in a conveyance (that is, a transfer by deed), this is a legal easement. What happens when the servient land is sold to Sarah? Being registered land, it is quite likely that the burden of the easement would have been registered against Aaron's title (Rule 41 of the Land Registration Rules) when he became registered proprietor. In any event, even if it were not, legal easements in registered land are overriding interests under s 70(1)(a) of the LRA 1925. In either case, therefore, Sarah is bound to give effect to the easement allowing erection of the satellite dish. It should be noted finally that, when Matilda conveys the dominant tenement to Ben, the benefit of the easement is transferred to Ben under the general rule that a benefit of an easement becomes annexed to each and every part of the legal estate and passes with it.

(ii) Can Aaron (and then Sarah) claim an easement of parking of the yacht?

This particular claim raises difficulties for the owners of the alleged dominant tenement. There is no doubt that an easement of parking does exist (*London and Blenheim Estates v Ladbroke* (1992)). However, it is also clear that easements in general must not amount to exclusive user of the servient land (*Copeland v Greenhalf* (1952)) and, for this reason, it is highly unlikely that a right to park in a defined space can be an easement (see the uncertainty in *Saeed v Plustrade* (2002)). Certainly, a right to store many cars cannot: *Batchelor v Marlowe*. The easement of parking in *Newman v Jones* was in respect of a general area of land and not a regular spot. Likewise, in *Grigsby v Melville*, a right of storage in a cellar was thought to connote exclusive use such as to oust an easement and the case where storage was permitted (*Wright v Macadam*) should be seen in the context of a dispute between a powerful landlord and a badly treated tenant. Unfortunately, therefore, it seems that this right amounts only to a personal permission between Aaron and Matilda: in other words, a contractual licence. So, even if the benefit of this contract has passed to Sarah, the burden of it is incapable of binding a successor in title of the alleged servient tenement (*Ashburn Anstalt v Arnold*; *Lloyd v Dugdale*, despite the contrary view in *Plustrade*). Ben will not be bound.

(iii) The sign

Once again, this presents certain problems. There is no doubt that erecting a sign on a neighbour's property can amount to an easement, as in *Moody v Steggles* (1879). It matters not that this is to advertise some commercial activity on the land, so long as the activity is intimately connected with the land and not a 'pure' commercial venture, as in *Hill v Tupper* (1863). Moreover, there is, it would seem, no objection in principle to a grant of an easement to a landowner on the occasion of a conveyance of property X (the house), where the easement is to benefit property Y (the boat yard). After all, easements can be created by deed between landowners irrespective of any sale, as where a freeholder grants a right of way to his neighbour.

However, every easement must accommodate the dominant tenement and, in this case, when the land was sold to Aaron, the business is carried on on property some four miles away. It is well known that, while the dominant and servient tenement need not be adjacent, there must be proximity between them (*Pugh v Savage* (1970)). This will be a question of fact in each case. Yet, even if the right is capable of existing as an easement, there is a further problem. How has it been created? This is not a case of implied grant (there is no necessity, scant evidence of common intention, no claim under s 62 and no quasi-easement within *Wheeldon v Burrows*) and, in any event, the aim seems to have been to create the easement expressly. Also, we are told that the intended right is not expressly included in the conveyance to Aaron and it cannot, therefore, be legal: not being by deed (more accurately, not by registered disposition as this is registered land). Of course, easements can be expressly granted by other means, but then they will be only equitable and, once more, there are formality problems. In order to be equitable, it is clear that the easement would have to have been granted by a valid contract which, if specifically enforceable, equity would treat as an equitable easement (*Walsh v Lonsdale*). The 'contract' in this case is not in writing as required by s 2 of the Law of Property (Miscellaneous Provisions) Act 1989 and there is no possibility of an equitable easement by this route. The only hope is that Aaron can claim an easement by proprietary estoppel, in similar circumstances to that in *Ives v High* (1967) and *Bibby v Stirling* (1998). Clearly, there seems to have been a promise made and we are told that Aaron erects an elaborate (and hence expensive?) sign. This may be detrimental reliance. Further, it is no objection to the existence of an estoppel that it did indeed arise out of a failed explicit bargain (*Voyce v Voyce* (1991) and *Flowermix v Site Development,* although *Canty v Broad* is critical of this). If an estoppel is established, a purely oral equitable easement may exist. In such circumstances, Sarah will have obtained the benefit of the easement under the normal rule that it is annexed to the land and Ben, the purchaser of the servient tenement, may well be bound by the estoppel easement because of the decision in *Celsteel v Alton*. Albeit subject to much criticism, this case tells us that an equitable easement arising out of an estoppel may amount to an overriding interest under s 70(1)(a) of the LRA 1925. It has been followed in *Thatcher v Douglas*. As such, it binds the purchaser, Ben, automatically.

(b) Matilda, Jacob, the building materials and Ben

Once again, the initial question to be answered is whether the right to store is capable of being an easement. As noted above, it is an essential characteristic of an easement that it does not amount to exclusive use of the servient tenement (*Hannina v Morland*). Thus, in *Copeland v Greenhalf* (1952); *Grigsby v Melville* (1974) and *Batchelor v Marlowe* (2001) a right of storage was not admitted into the category of easements. However, we are told here that the right expressly granted was a right to store temporarily when the need should arise. This may be completely different as there are many easements (for example, a right to use a lavatory; *Miller v Emcer Products* (1956)) which when being exercised by the dominant tenement owner on the servient land exclude any other use by the servient owner. One view is that the right of temporary storage is analogous to the right to park generally on a piece of land and, in any event, a right to store trade produce has been accepted as an easement in *AG of Southern Nigeria v John Holt and Co* (1915). Thus, it is a matter for argument whether this can exist as an easement. Of course, if it does, it seems that Jacob is going beyond its explicit terms and, of course, this can be restrained by injunction. Finally, if the easement does exist, it is clear that it has been expressly created by the conveyance (that is, by deed/registered disposition) and is legal. As with the legal easements considered above, this will bind Ben, the purchaser of the servient tenement whether as being registered against his title or as an overriding interest under s 70(1)(a) of the LRA 1925.

Question 34

Elizabeth is the owner of a large farm in Huntshire, title to which is unregistered. Last year, she built a small bungalow on her lower field for her retirement and asked her daughter, Anne, to look after it in the meantime. Anne moved in with her boyfriend, Mark. The only access to the bungalow is along a dirt track over the farm proper or by boat along the river Garter which flows through the property. Last week, Anne and Mark had a serious row and Anne has moved out. Elizabeth, who was never fond of her daughter's boyfriend, agreed with Mark in writing that he can occupy the premises for five years at £800 per month and an initial sum of £2,000. However, before any rent is paid, Mark meets another woman and moves in with her. Fortunately, soon after, Elizabeth is able to sell the bungalow to John by registered disposition for a large profit. Two months later, she decides to retire to Jamaica and sells the rest of the farm to Norman.

John has just resurfaced the dust road in order to obtain access for his car. Norman, seeing the chance for a small profit, has asked John for £1,000 to use the new road. John seeks your advice as to whether he should pay.

Answer plan

The following areas need to be discussed:

- the creation of easements by implied grant; s 62 of the LPA 1925: *Hillman v Rodgers*; *Hair v Gillman*;
- equitable or legal?;
- affect on third parties of new easement.

Answer

This question involves complicated issues about the creation of easements and their effect on third parties. In general, the position is simple enough. Legal easements must be created by deed, prescription or statute and equitable easements by written document under s 2 of the Law of Property (Miscellaneous Provisions) Act 1989 or by the law of proprietary estoppel (*Ives v High* (1967)). It is, of course, essential to determine whether any easement is legal or equitable for this may determine its ability to bind a purchaser of the servient land. However, in this problem, there is the further complication that there appears to be no express grant of the alleged easement. Such sales of the land as there are make no mention of any rights of way. Thus, we are thrown back on the creation of easements by implied grant: either by necessity, common intention under s 62 of the LPA 1925 or the rule in *Wheeldon v Burrows* (1879). However, whatever method, if any, is appropriate to this case, one important feature needs to be kept in mind. Under implied grant, the easement is said to be implied into a sale of the dominant tenement. That is, it is as if the grantor – who usually retains the servient tenement – did include the easement in the transfer document. Thus, it necessarily follows that, if an easement is impliedly granted, it takes its legal or equitable character from the grant into which it is implied. So, implied grant can give rise to legal and equitable easements depending on the quality of the transfer to the owner of what becomes the dominant land.

Clearly, then, John, the purchaser of the bungalow will wish to assert an easement of way over the road which passes over the farm of which it was formerly a part. The only way to determine whether the easement exists is consider the position of the three occupants in turn: Anne and Mark, Mark and then John. Moreover, if such an easement exists, it falls to be determined whether the easement binds Norman, the purchaser of the allegedly servient land and, even if it does, what the precise scope of the easement is.

(a) Anne and Mark

When Anne and Mark occupy the bungalow, it is clear that they do so at the invitation of the owner, Elizabeth. There is no express grant of an easement to them. Moreover, it appears from the facts that they do not occupy the premises by virtue of a grant of any estate. There is no sale of it to them and there is no lease of it to them. They appear to be licensees occupying with the consent of the owner under a family arrangement wherein there is no intention to create legal relations (*Street v Mountford* (1985) and *Heslop v Burns* (1974)). There is, therefore, no grant into which an easement can be implied. In any event, in order to create an easement where none already exists, there must exist a dominant tenement that is itself proprietary in nature. A licence is not proprietary and no easement can be created on the occasion of a grant of a licence to occupy rather than a lease (*Ashburn Anstalt v Arnold; Lloyd v Dugdale* (2001)).

(b) Mark

When Anne leaves the property, the status of the remaining occupant, Mark would appear to change. As we are told, Elizabeth, the owner, agrees by writing that Mark can occupy the premises. This is clearly an attempt to create a lease in Mark's favour, although the lease is not legal, not having been created by deed. Neither can it qualify as a legal periodic tenancy because no rent has been paid and, in any event, a premium (or 'fine') has been taken (s 52(2) of the LPA). This is, in effect, an equitable lease under a specifically enforceable contract within *Walsh v Lonsdale* (1882). This has one immediate consequence in that s 62 of the LPA cannot be used to establish the implied grant of an easement. Section 62 applies to 'conveyances' which, under s 205(1)(ii) of the LPA, does not include a contract to grant an estate (*Hillman v Rodgers* (1998)). So, there is no scope for the implied creation of an easement by this method. This leaves us with two viable alternatives: creation by *Wheeldon v Burrows* (which can apply to contracts, *Borman v Griffith* (1930)) or by virtue of necessity. There is nothing exceptional to suggest use of common intention (*Peckham v Ellison* (1998)).

As to the rule in *Wheeldon*, this applies where an owner grants part of their land and, because of the rule that a person cannot derogate from their grant, is taken to impliedly grant easements necessary for the proper enjoyment of that land. In the normal case, these impliedly granted easements were rights which the owner themselves exercised for the benefit of the plot sold, being a burden on the plot retained. In our case, this would be if Elizabeth had used the path to get to the bungalow and then granted an estate to Mark. In our case, however, the vendor was not exercising such quasi-easements before partition: it is a case where the person to whom the land was sold was exercising those rights. It is doubtful whether *Wheeldon* can apply in these circumstances because the rule appears to be that, as well as the easements being necessary for the reasonable enjoyment of the property (and/or continuous and apparent), they must 'have been and are at the time of the grant used by the owner of the entirety for the benefit of the part granted'. This does seem to rule out implied grant by *Wheeldon* unless we can say that, prior to the sale, Mark was exercising the alleged easement on behalf of the owner of the entirety. Perhaps this is possible on the facts given that Mark seems to have been a 'housesitter'. If it is, then an impliedly granted equitable easement will result and this will be binding on Norman, the purchaser of the servient tenement, only if it is registered as a Class D(iii) land charge. There is no evidence that it has been so registered and so would be void against Norman (*Midland Bank v Green*).

Assuming then that there is no new novel application of *Wheeldon* so as to support an easement, has one arisen by necessity? There is no doubt that an easement of way can arise though necessity, as in *Pinnington v Galland*, but, as *MRA Engineering Ltd v Trimster Co Ltd* (1987) confirms, an easement of way can be implied only where the land cannot be used at all, and not simply where it would be convenient to imply an easement. Moreover, in the Privy Council decision of *Manjang v Drammah* (1990), Lord Oliver relied on the Scottish decision in *Menzies v Breadalbane* as authority for the proposition that if access to land was available by water, this could negate an easement of way over *terra firma*. There is some doubt, then, over whether an easement of way by necessity could exist. Even if it did, it is impliedly granted to Mark in an equitable lease and is itself equitable. It would be void against Norman for lack of registration as a Class D(iii) land charge.

(c) John

If John is to claim an easement, it seems that, once again, it will be by virtue of an implied grant. In his case, he has been sold the bungalow by registered disposition and so has acquired legal title in the normal way. Being a conveyance of the legal estate, John can claim the benefit of s 62 of the LPA 1925.

Under s 62, a purchaser of a legal estate in the land will be impliedly granted, as easements, all those rights previously enjoyed with the property that are capable of being easements, providing there is no express provision in the conveyance to the contrary and providing that there was diversity of occupation between the alleged dominant and alleged servient tenement prior to the grant (*Sovmots Investments Ltd v Secretary of State for the Environment* (1979)). In this case, there clearly was diversity of occupation (Elizabeth and Mark) and there is no contrary intention. Of course, this case is somewhat different from the usual situation where the person to whom the land is granted was the very person enjoying the right prior to that grant. However, the words of s 62 seem wide enough to cover the situation as here where the grantee (John) acquires land but the right that is translated into an easement was in fact exercised by somebody else (Anne and Mark) and this is now supported by the decision in *Hillman v Rodgers*, applying s 62 in just such circumstances. The point of s 62 is, indeed, that rights benefiting the granted land are not personal but proprietary. If, then, an easement is impliedly granted under s 62, the easement will necessarily be legal (*Hair v Gillman*). Consequently, Norman, the purchaser of the servient land will be bound by it as legal easements in registered land are overriding interests (s 70(1)(a) of the LRA 1925).

Question 35

Lowlife Properties Ltd is the registered proprietor of a large industrial estate in the centre of Littleton which it has been using as a company headquarters. Last year it decided to split the estate into smaller properties and sell them off. The estate was split into three Units, with Lowlife keeping Unit 3. Prior to the sale, the employees of Lowlife habitually ate their lunch on the grass outside what is now Unit 2 and parked their cars and walked across the forecourt of what is now Unit 1 to get to work. Likewise, all the water pipes for the estate cross the land of Unit 3, as does an overgrown path, the only access by foot. Last month, Unit 1 was sold to Kirk, a hairdresser, by registered disposition. Unit 2 was let to Scot, a fashion designer, on a seven year lease by deed, containing a covenant not to assign or sub-let without the landlord's consent.

Initially, Scot objected to the noise created by Lowlife's employees at lunchtime, although he agreed to drop his objections when Lowlife agreed to lower the rent. Kirk does not like the employees looking in at the people in his salon as they walk to work, so he fences off the parking area. However, most of Kirk's customers come by foot and he has tidied up the footpath. Lowlife is expanding fast and threatens to cut off the water supply if its new employees cannot park their cars. It has blocked off the path in retaliation. Scot's business has now floundered and he eventually obtains Lowlife's consent to assign to McCoy, who manages to negotiate a lower price because of the lunchtime gatherings. Lowlife now plan to sell to Megacorp who seek your advice as to the problems they may encounter.

Answer plan

The answer needs to include a discussion of the following:

- nature of easements;
- creation of easements: *Wheeldon v Burrows*;
- inequitable conduct and constructive trusts: *Lloyd v Dugdale* (2001).

Answer

In this case, the issues facing Megacorp, the potential purchaser from the original owner of the entire estate, are two fold. In the first place, they may be subject to binding easements in favour of the plots granted to Kirk and Scot (and assigned to McCoy) and, secondly, they may well wish to claim the rights once enjoyed by Lowlife on behalf of their employees.

(a) The water supply and the footpath

These are rights which will be claimed as easements by both Scot (and then McCoy) in respect of Unit 2 and Kirk in respect of Unit 1. The first issue to address is whether these rights are capable of existing as easements, within the formula established in *Re Ellenborough Park* (1956). There seems to be little difficulty here: rights of way, whether limited to foot or not, are among the most common easements and a right to receive water through a pipe running on the servient land was accepted in *Goodhart v Hyett* (1883).

However, what is not so straightforward is establishing how these easements are created, for there is no evidence here of an express grant. In fact, this appears to be an instance of the operation of the rule in *Wheeldon v Burrows* (1879), whereby the owner of land will be taken to have impliedly granted to a purchaser of part of it, all those rights capable of existing as easements, which the owner enjoyed for the benefit of the land sold and exercised over the land retained. The requirements of such an implied creation seem to be that there must have been user by the common owner at the time of the grant, and the rights claimed must be reasonably necessary for the proper enjoyment of the land granted and/or continuous and apparent. In respect of the right to water supply, there is no difficulty with these conditions as (presumably) the water serviced all parts of the estate before sub-division, the reasonable necessity is obvious (as in *Millman v Ellis* (1996)) and, if required, continuous and apparent user will be deemed from the existence of water pipes. It is debatable, however, whether the same is true of the footpath. It is reasonably necessary, being the only access by foot, but, being 'overgrown', there may be some argument that it was neither in use at the date of the grant nor, if required, continuous and apparent. This is simply a matter for argument, although if the path is well defined, albeit overgrown, it will probably satisfy both conditions. The conclusion is, therefore, that both these easements have been impliedly granted to the purchasers Kirk and Scot in the leases of Units 1 and 2 against the property retained by Lowlife. As both grants were themselves legal, the easement implied into them will be legal. As such, they will be binding on Megacorp as overriding interests under s 70(1)(a) of the LRA 1925. Likewise, the benefit will be passed to McCoy, successor in title, to one of the dominant tenements, as an adjunct of his estate.

(b) The right to park and walk

As above, there is no difficulty with a right of way existing as an easement and, indeed, in *London and Suburban Land and Building Co v Carey* (1991), it was made clear that, in principle (although not on the facts of that case), a right to park on an access way for the purpose of unloading could be an adjunct to the right of way (and see the right to use a layby in *Millman v Ellis* (1996)). However, there has been considerable controversy over whether a right to park can, of itself, amount to an easement, not least because it seems to amount to exclusive user of the premises to the exclusion of the servient owner (see *Copeland v Greenhalf*; *Batchelor v Marlowe*; *Saeed v Plustrade*). In *Newman v Jones* (1982), an easement of parking was permitted, but only if the right was exercised generally and not in respect of the same defined place (see, also, *Sweet & Maxwell Ltd v Michael-Michaels Advertising* (1965)). This has now been confirmed by the Court of Appeal in *London and Blenheim Estates v Ladbroke* (1992). Megacorp should be advised that only the claim to general parking may be upheld, so long as it does not amount to storage (*Batchelor*).

There is, however, a more pressing problem than this, for it is difficult to see how the easement has been created. The easement is alleged to exist in respect of the plot retained by the original vendor, Lowlife. Thus, if at all, it must have been by way of reservation when it sold the alleged servient tenement. There is no express reservation, no evidence of exceptional circumstances so as to justify reservation by common intention, so s 62 cannot apply (it applies to grants only) and neither can *Wheeldon v Burrows*, which itself was a claim to an implied reservation of easement which failed (see also *Chaffe v Kingley*). The only real possibility is that Lowlife – and then Megacorp – could claim a reserved easement of necessity. Unfortunately, it is trite law that reserved easements of necessity (and those of common intention) are rare, not least because it was within the power of the vendor to expressly reserve such a right. The only situations where there is a real possibility of success is when the retained land would be unusable without the impliedly reserved easement. This is clearly not the case here. Likewise, although, in *Peckham v Ellison* (1998), the plaintiffs were held to enjoy the benefit of an impliedly reserved easement by way of common intention, the court described such a process as exceptional and as such a claim was denied in *Chaffe*. In our case, it cannot truly be said the parties had an unfulfilled common intention as to the reservation of an easement (as they clearly did in *Peckham*) and it is unlikely that this ground could succeed. So, if Lowlife have no easement, there is nothing to pass to Megacorp and they will have to renegotiate with the adjoining landowners.

(c) Lunchtime activities

Once again, there are serious difficulties if it is alleged that an easement was reserved for Lowlife when the land was let to Scot. As above, there is no express reservation and clearly no ground for a claim of necessity and nothing to suggest common intention. In any event, it is highly unlikely that such a right could exist as an easement. It is not something which benefits the dominant tenement as such, being related to a right of recreation (*Re Ellenborough Park*).

However, just because this right cannot exist as an easement is not the end of the matter. It seems from the facts of the problem that, after he had acquired his estate in the land, Scot agreed to allow the lunchtime activities to continue and received consideration for it. In other words, there seems to have been a contract between Lowlife and Scot so as to create a contractual licence to use the area at lunchtime. This right, which is purely personal between the parties, nevertheless can be enforced against Scot while he is in possession as an original party to the contract. However, licences are not interests in land and cannot in principle bind successors in title (*Ashburn Anstalt v Arnold* (1988); *Lloyd v Dugdale* (2001)). As a matter of property law, then, the obligation to allow the activity cannot be passed to McCoy when he buys the lease. Yet, it may well be that McCoy is bound to give effect to the licence because of his conduct at the time of the assignment. The lease cannot be assigned without Lowlife's consent and presumably Lowlife negotiated with McCoy and Scot about whether to agree. Indeed, we are told that McCoy obtains the lease for a reduced price because of the lunchtime activities. This does suggest that McCoy will be bound to give effect to the contractual licence because it would be inequitable for him to deny it. A constructive trust will be imposed upon him personally – not as a matter of property law – to give effect to the licence (*Binions v Evans*; *Ashburn Anstalt v Arnold*; *Lloyd v Dugdale*). It should be noted, finally, that, because this licence arose out of a contract between Scot and Lowlife, the benefit of the contract (that is, the right for employees to use the land of Unit 2) can be expressly assigned under normal contractual principles. Thus, Megacorp should ensure that this right is transferred to them explicitly.

Notes

The above problems put into practice the issues considered at the beginning of this chapter. Usually, the questions will mix issues of the nature of easements, their creation and transmissibility to third parties. In this respect, creation and transmissibility must be distinguished, even though factually they may appear to arise in similar circumstances as with *Wheeldon* and s 62 of the LPA 1925 and as was evident in *Hillman v Rodgers* (1998) and *Hair v Gillman* (2000).

CHAPTER 8

FREEHOLD COVENANTS

Introduction

In Chapter 5 on leases, we examined the law surrounding the operation of leasehold covenants. However, it is not only landlord and tenant that may wish to enter into promises affecting the mode of user of their property. Freeholders may also wish to control the use which neighbours may make of their land, as where owners of residential property may wish to preserve the non-business character of their area, or the owners of an industrial estate may wish to limit the type of activity carried on there. Obviously, freeholders do not stand in a relationship of landlord and tenant with each other and the rules of leasehold covenants are inapplicable. Consequently, a set of principles have developed – mainly in connection with restrictive covenants – which govern the running of covenants between freeholders. Like leasehold covenants (and easements), each freehold covenant comprises a 'benefit' and a 'burden'. It is always necessary, when considering problems in this particular area, to remember that before a plaintiff can sue a defendant on a particular covenant, the benefit must have passed to the plaintiff and the burden must have passed to the defendant. Indeed, it can quite easily happen that the benefit of a covenant has passed, but the burden has not, or vice versa. So it is imperative when dealing with these issues to consider the issue of the benefit of a covenant separately from questions relating to the burden.

Checklist

Students must be familiar with the general principles of covenants: such as the meaning of 'touching and concerning'; the requirements for the transmission of the benefit of covenants both at law and in equity; the requirements for the transmission of the burden in equity; and the requirements of registration under the systems of registered and unregistered land. In addition, some questions may ask whether the strictness of these rules –

particularly in relation to the burden of a covenant – can be circumvented in any way, for example, by use of the principle of benefit and burden in *Halsall v Brizell* (1957). Finally, we should note that the rules discussed below apply whenever there is neither privity of estate or contract between the plaintiff and defendant. This is usually in disputes between freeholders, but may also occur between a landlord and a tenant on an equitable lease granted before 1 January 1996. For leases granted on or after 1 January 1996, the Landlord and Tenant (Covenants) Act (LTCA) 1995 simplifies the position of equitable tenants and makes reliance on these 'freehold' covenant rules less likely. However, they may still be relevant in disputes between landlords and sub-tenants (between whom there is no privity of estate), as the provisions of LTCA 1995 do not significantly affect this matter.

Question 36

Consider whether the rules relating to the running of freehold covenants adequately ensure that successors in title can enforce the benefits obtained by an original covenantee.

Answer plan

The answer needs to discuss the following:
- the meaning of 'benefit' and the original covenantee – s 56 of the LPA;
- 'successors in title' – s 78 of the LPA;
- benefit at common law – s 78 of the LPA;
- benefit in equity: annexation: *Federated Homes v Mill Lodge*; *Whitgift Homes v Stocks* (2001);
- assignment;
- building schemes.

Answer

Nowhere is it more true than in the law of real property that no man is an island. The use by one person of his or her land can seriously affect the quality of enjoyment, the mode of user, or the occupation of their neighbour. This is obvious and it should come as no surprise that the law of real property has developed rules and principles that allow one landowner to control the use to which his neighbour may put their own land. This can be achieved through the law of easements or through the law of covenants in leases. It can, however, also be achieved where the neighbouring landowners are freeholders. The law relating to freehold covenants applies in all of those circumstances where no privity of estate exists between the parties, that is, where the plaintiff and defendant do not stand in the relationship of landlord and tenant. However, like covenants in leases, covenants between freeholders also have a dual aspect. Thus, each covenant will confer a benefit and a corresponding burden. Indeed, it is a curiosity of the law of real property that rules relating to the transmission of the benefit of a freehold covenant, that is, to somebody who buys the land from the original covenantee (the person to whom the covenant was made) are entirely independent from the rules relating to the transmission of the burdens of the covenant, that is, to a person who buys land from the original covenantor (the person who made the promise). It is quite possible, therefore, for the benefit of a covenant to run to a successor in title of the original covenantee but for the burden of that covenant to have been destroyed or to bind only the original covenantor, and vice versa.

This particular question raises issues concerning the transmission of the benefit of freehold covenants or, more accurately, whether a successor in title to land of the original covenantee gains the right to enforce covenants made for the benefit of land when he acquires that land. In very general terms, and putting aside for the moment situations where there has been an express assignment of contractual rights (see below), the benefit of a covenant will pass provided that the covenant 'touches and concerns' the land of the original covenantee when it was made. This is simply another way of saying that property law is concerned with the transmission of proprietary rights, not personal advantages. It also ensures that title to land is not cluttered up by obligations that are merely transient, uncertain or personal in nature. So, as with covenants in pre-1996 leases, it is essential to determine whether the covenant 'touches and concerns' according to the flexible guidelines put forward by

Lord Oliver in *Swift Investments v Combined English Stores* (1988). Assuming, however, that the freehold covenant does 'touch and concern' the land, then it is possible that the right to sue on the covenant may pass either 'at law' or 'in equity' to a successor to the original covenantee. As we shall see, the methods by which this benefit may actually pass in law or in equity are very similar, the requirements of equity being slightly less demanding. If a plaintiff had the choice of suing on the benefit of the covenant at law or in equity (which occurs frequently), much would depend on which remedy the plaintiff required. A suit at law usually would result in the award of damages, whereas in equity the discretionary remedies of injunction to prevent breach of a restrictive covenant or order of specific performance to compel performance of a positive covenant would be available. Bearing this in mind, the position at law will be considered initially and consideration of the position in equity will follow. Ultimately, once the 'touching and concerning' requirement has been met, it seems that three further conditions must be satisfied if the benefit is to run to the successor in law.

First, the persons seeking to enforce the covenant must own some legal estate in the land. Prior to the enactment of s 78 of the LPA 1925, the person seeking to enforce the covenant at law had to own the same legal estate as the original covenantee. So, if the original covenantee was a freeholder, the successor had to be a freeholder. Section 78 has, however, made it clear that the successor need only have some legal estate, such as where the original covenantee being a freeholder lets the land to a successor on a lease by deed. This has clearly made the transmission of the benefit at law slightly simpler. Secondly, it is clear that the covenant must benefit the land of the original covenantee. In most cases, it will be enough that the covenant touches and concerns the land because, from this, the fact of benefit will be presumed (*Whitgift Homes v Stocks* (2001)). However, in theory, it is open to somebody disputing the fact that the benefit has run at law to claim that the land of the original covenantee never could have benefited from the particular covenant made and therefore cannot pass to a successor in title: see *Wrotham Park Estate v Parkside Homes* (1974). Thirdly, and most importantly of all, the covenant must have been annexed to the land in order for the benefit to run with the land. In this respect, the decision in *Federated Homes v*

Mill Lodge Properties Ltd (1980) has made the position much simpler. According to the Court of Appeal decision in that case, now fully confirmed in *Whitgift Homes v Stocks* (2001), the benefit of every covenant whether positive or negative and whether in law or in equity will be annexed to the land and, indeed, to every part of it, providing the land is identified in the covenant or can be identified by extrinsic evidence (*Whitgift*). It is true, however, that later cases (*Roake v Chadha* (1983)) have made it clear that this statutory annexation can be excluded by clear contrary intention. Nevertheless, the decision in *Federated Homes* has clearly provided successors in title to original covenantees with a safe and certain method of claiming that they are entitled to the benefit of a covenant. We should note, however, that the decision in *Federated Homes* has been subject to much criticism. For example, it has been correctly pointed out that s 78 does not precisely say what the Court of Appeal allege and that it is a decision favouring certainty at the expense of individuality. Nevertheless, as noted above, it has been confirmed by a strong Court of Appeal in *Whitgift Homes v Stocks* and, until overruled by the House of Lords (which seems most unlikely), this decision will govern the running of the benefit of covenants both at law and in equity.

Indeed, if we now turn to the position in equity, we will see that *Federated Homes* has had an impact here also. Once again, assuming that the covenant touches and concerns the land, the person seeking to enforce the covenant must have some estate or interest in the land although of course this may now only be equitable. If that is established, it seems that there are three methods that the benefit may transfer in equity. The first of these is under the rule of statutory annexation that we have just considered in relation to covenants at law. As noted then, *Federated Homes* applies with equal vigour to the annexation of covenants in equity, so a covenant will be statutorily annexed to each and every part of the land providing it is clear what land is intended to be benefited. Indeed, the efficacy of the *Federated Homes* principle is such that the other two methods of transferring the benefit in equity may now be largely redundant, except perhaps in the limited circumstances of express contrary intention (*Roake*) or when the advantages of a building scheme are required.

The building scheme is the second method by which the benefit may be transferred. This is a rule based upon common intention and practicality. It allows a common vendor (such as a property developer) to transfer the benefit of the covenants received by him from every purchaser of a plot of land to every other purchaser of a plot of land. It is an attempt to create mutually enforceable obligations. Of course, there is nothing unique in this because under the normal rules, the benefits of the covenants made by early purchasers will be automatically transmitted to later purchasers who buy part of the retained land. However, the advantage of a building scheme is that it allows the benefit of later purchasers' covenants to be given to earlier purchasers even though the time of later purchases is out of synchronisation. The requirements for a valid building scheme were laid down in *Elliston v Reacher* (1900). There must be a common vendor, the land must be laid out in definable plots, the benefits must be intended to be mutually enforceable, and these must be the conditions upon which all purchasers buy. These are, however, not inflexible and later cases such as *Re Dolphins Conveyance* (1970) and *Baxter v Four Oaks* (1965) illustrate that the benefit will run under a building scheme even though all of the requirements have not been met. Importantly, however, no building scheme can exist unless it is clear what land is subject to the scheme (*Whitgift Homes v Stocks*). It is essential to such a scheme that the owners of land know the full reach of the mutuality of their obligations. It should be noted also that a building scheme does not affect the running of the burden of covenants and if the obligations are to be truly mutually enforceable the normal steps for transmitting the burden of restrictive covenants must be followed. Usually, this will mean registration of the covenants against the title of all purchasers.

Finally, the third method of transmitting the benefit of covenants is the assignment. It is trite law that the benefit of a contract (that is, a covenant) may be expressly assigned. So, for example, if a purchaser of the covenantee's land is expressly assigned the benefit of that covenant, he or she will be able to enforce it. However, this method does have some disadvantages. It seems that this is a method of transferring the benefit personally. So, following *Re Pinewood* (1958), where there has been an assignment of the covenant to the first successor of the original covenantee, a chain of assignments is required if the benefit is to be assigned to subsequent assignees. Assignment is a personal not a proprietary method of transfer. Of course, after *Federated Homes*, such a method is largely redundant and, in all cases of the transmission of the benefit in equity, the plaintiff (that is, the successor in title) is at the mercy of the court when seeking a remedy. Equitable remedies are discretionary and it is quite possible that a person who is in principle entitled to enforce covenants may not gain the remedy of injunction or specific performance if they do not come to the court with 'clean hands'.

It should be apparent from the above that it is relatively straightforward to transmit the benefit of a covenant both at law and in equity. The decision in *Federated Homes* has made this even more likely and the only real limit (except possibly for personal assignment) seems to be that the covenant must touch and concern the land. Of course, having the benefit of a covenant is useless unless there is somebody who is subject to the burden. In this respect, the rule that the burden of restrictive covenants only may run, and then only in equity, is a real limitation on the practical enforcement of covenants. It means that in all cases where the original covenantor has parted with their land, only restrictive covenants will be relevant and then only that the rules of equity will be in play. As we have seen, these give rise to only a discretionary remedy and the successor in title to the original covenantee will have to establish a *bona fide* claim if they are to succeed.

Notes

A long but straightforward question. Essentially book work. All doubts about *Federated Homes* have been removed by *Whitgift Homes*.

Question 37

In what circumstances may the burden of a freehold covenant pass to a successor in title of the original covenantor?

Answer plan

The answer needs to include the following:

- the original covenantor;
- successors in title and s 79 of the LPA;
- requirements of registration.

Answer

It is a general principle of English law that, while the benefit of a contract can be assigned to a third party, the burden of a contract cannot. In the law of real property, this can cause serious difficulties, for it means that when an owner of land makes a promise by covenant to do or not to do something on his land (in other words, imposing a burden on that land), then any successor in title to that original covenantor may well be able to acquire the land free of the burden placed upon it. Obviously, this is of great advantage to the successor to the original covenantor, but it is of no use to those persons who enjoy the benefit of the covenant, for they may see the benefits which they so carefully extracted destroyed on the first sale of the burdened land. Fortunately, the law of real property has mitigated the harshness of the contractual rule by providing that, in some circumstances, burdens attached to land by way of covenant may assume a proprietary nature and may be passed on to any person who subsequently acquires that land.

As is well known, the position is relatively straightforward if the covenantee and their successors and the covenantor and their successors stand in the relationship of landlord and tenant. Then, for pre-1996 leases, the matter is governed by *Spencer's* case and the doctrine of privity of estate and, for leases granted on or after 1 January 1996, the Landlord and Tenant (Covenants) Act 1995 has imposed a statutory scheme. If, however, the covenant was made between freeholders or concerns persons not otherwise in privity of estate under a pre-1996 lease, such as a landlord and a sub-tenant (including a sub-tenant under a lease granted on or after 1 January 1996), the rules commonly known as the rules of freehold covenants come into play. Not surprisingly, the rules allowing the transmission of burdens in non-leasehold cases are quite strict, as it is a general policy requirement that title to land should not be unduly cluttered. In essence, the starting point for a discussion of the transmission of the burden of freehold covenants must be the decision in *Tulk v Moxhay* (1848). In that case, concerning a restrictive covenant not to build in Leicester Square, it was decided that if a covenant touched and concerned the land it could, as a matter of conscience and equity, be binding on any purchaser of the land burdened by the covenant who had notice of its existence. Although the principles have developed considerably since *Tulk*, the limits put on the doctrine by that case still exist. Thus, it is clear that burdens of covenants may only run in equity and, as an equitable doctrine, there are all of the attendant problems associated with equitable rights, including the fact that remedies are discretionary. Moreover, despite some attempts to argue the contrary, it is clear that only the burden of restrictive or negative covenants may run in equity (*Rhone v Stephens* (1994)).

The conditions for the transmission of the burden of a covenant are as follows. First, the covenant must touch and concern the land and therefore pass the test in *Swift Investments v Combined English Stores* (1988). Secondly, the covenant must be negative in nature and this is a question of substance not a question of form, normally resolved by asking whether the owner of the burdened land is required to expend money. Thirdly, the doctrine takes effect in equity only thus opening up the possibility that the equitable interests (that is, the negative covenants) may be defeated by a sale to a purchaser of a legal estate for value. Of course, in many cases, these hurdles are not formidable and, in most cases, the restrictive covenant will satisfy these initial tests. If it does, there are further matters which must be satisfied before a burden will run to a successor in title. First, and most importantly of all, the covenant must have been made for the benefit of land owned by the covenantee. In other words, the burden cannot run unless it is a burden that benefits the land of the covenantee. Like easements, there must be a dominant and servient tenement. In effect, this means that not only must the original covenantee have owned land at the time the covenant was created but also that the particular covenant must have been capable of benefiting that land (*Whitgift Homes v Stocks*). This is a question of fact although the onus is on the person seeking to deny the covenant to prove that the land of the covenantee was not in fact benefited (*Wrotham Park Estates v Parkside Homes*) and may often be presumed from the fact that the covenant touches and concerns (*Whitgift*). The meaning of benefit is crucial in these circumstances and, according to *Re Gadd's Transfer* (1966), it has several components: for example, does it affect the value or mode of use of the land. Next, it is necessary to establish that the burden of the covenant is annexed to the land. Express words of annexation can, of course, be used. So, for example, a covenant expressed to be for X and his heirs and successors in title would effectively annex the covenant to the land. However, such longwindedness is no longer needed because of s 79 of the LPA. This provision effectively incorporates words of annexation into every deed of covenant. The net effect is that the burden of restrictive covenants will be automatically annexed to the land unless the deed of covenant expressly contains a provision to the contrary. The position is effectively the same as that achieved for the benefit of the covenant under s 78 of the LPA, as interpreted in *Federated Homes v Mill Lodge* (1980).

Assuming these conditions are established, the covenant now has a proprietary nature. This means that the burden of the covenant can, in principle, bind successors in title to the original covenantor's land. However, as we have noted above, these restrictive covenants take effect in equity and, like all equitable rights, they are capable of being defeated by a sale to a purchaser of a legal estate for value. Before 1925, as *Tulk* itself makes clear, a purchaser of the covenantor's land would only be bound by restrictive covenants, even if they had passed the above tests if he purchased that land with notice of the covenants. Now, of course, notice has been replaced by registration, both in registered and unregistered land. Thus, in order for a proprietary restrictive covenant to bind a purchaser, it must be registered in the relevant way. In registered land, the covenant must be protected by an entry as a minor interest on the register, usually by way of notice. In unregistered land, the restrictive covenant is classified as a Class D(ii) land charge and must be registered accordingly. It should be noted, however, that the requirement of registration is needed only to bind purchasers of the legal estate. Thus, because these covenants are already proprietary, if the covenantor's land comes into the possession of somebody who is not a purchaser of a legal estate (such as a squatter or an equitable tenant or a person receiving the property by way of gift), then a restrictive covenant will be binding, whether registered or not.

These then are the conditions upon which the burden of a restrictive covenant may be binding. As is obvious, the rules are quite strict, applying only to restrictive covenants and only operating in equity, thereby making covenants subject to a requirement of registration. Obviously, the burden of positive covenants cannot run and of course this can cause hardship. For this reason, there are a number of avoidance devices that may be used. None of these are entirely satisfactory and, in particular, the concept of 'mutual benefit and burden' has been restricted by case law (*Thamesmead Town v Allotey* (1998)). Consequently, it is only if the dusty Law Commission proposals for reform are adopted (and this seems unlikely) that the situation will change substantially.

Question 38

Victor was the freehold owner, registered with absolute title, of five shops in the Kings Road, Oxtown. No 1 sold electrical goods, No 2 general household goods, No 3 was a pet shop and Nos 4 and 5 were empty. Two years ago, Victor sold No 4 to Eve, who covenanted that she would not carry on any trade other than a dressmaker at No 4. Just after, he sold No 5 to Polly who covenanted 'with Victor and the owners for the time being of the shops in Kings Road' that she would use No 5 for no other purpose than the breeding and wholesale of pedigree budgerigars and would erect and maintain a fence to protect her neighbours in the event of an escape. Last week, Victor let No 1 to Albert on a four year lease in writing, who immediately sub-let to Bill. At the same time, he sold No 2 to Claude by registered disposition who turned the premises into a garden centre. Victor has since discovered that his original tenant of No 3 left the property some months ago and it is now occupied by Desmond, a squatter, who is selling second hand clothes and electrical goods.

In the course of her dressmaking, Eve has invented a new sewing machine and has begun a small scale manufacturing and retail outlet from her premises. Meanwhile, Polly found that bird breeding was not profitable and has turned to rabbit breeding. Unfortunately, this gets out of hand and the Kings Road is overrun with rabbits escaping from No 5. Claude's entire stock is threatened.

Advise the occupants of the Kings Road as to their respective rights and obligations.

Answer plan

The answer needs to include the following areas:
- position of the original covenantors and covenantees;
- running of the benefit at law and in equity;
- s 78 of the LPA and *Federated Homes*; *Whitgift Homes v Stocks*;
- s 56 of the LPA: *Amsprop Trading v Harris*;
- rights of squatters.

Answer

This question concerns the operation of covenants in situations where there is no leasehold estate between plaintiff and defendant and their respective successors in title. The problem concerns the law of 'freehold' covenants. However, as is made clear from the facts of this problem, there is no issue here of the running of the burden of the covenant: both the original covenantors (Eve and Polly) are still in occupation of the burdened land and it is against them that an action for breach of the covenants will be directed. Turning first to the nature of the these covenants, the covenant by Eve is clearly restrictive in nature and without doubt touches and concerns the land. Likewise, Polly's covenant to keep only budgerigars is restrictive and, because it affects the mode of user of the land (*Swift Investments v Combined English Stores* (1988)), it also touches and concerns. Polly's second covenant – to erect and maintain a fence – does touch and concern but it is positive in nature, requiring expenditure by the owner of the burdened land. However, the fact that one covenant is positive is not crucial in this case, as it is only successors in title that cannot be made liable on the burden of positive covenants. Here, the defendants are the original covenantors and there is nothing to prevent the benefit of a positive covenant passing to successors of the original covenantee.

First, we need to determine who the original parties to the covenants are, for they will be able to sue on the benefit of the covenant against Polly and Eve (the original covenantors), irrespective of any question of the passing of the benefit under land law rules. This would be simply a matter of contract. Clearly, Victor, the original freeholder (and now the landlord of No 1 and owner of No 3) has the benefit of all covenants by both Polly and Eve, being an original covenantee: he can sue on all the covenants at law and on those covenants in equity where he is still in possession of the land (*Chambers v Randall* (1923)). Of course, the remedy at law will be damages and they will be nominal if Victor does not possess the land at the time of any breach of covenant. In practice, he will wish to obtain an injunction for breach of both restrictive covenants and a decree of specific performance in respect of the positive covenant to build a fence. This will require him to sue in equity and, therefore, he should sue as freeholder of No 3. It is clear also, however, that Eve, the purchaser of No 4 (and an original covenantor to Victor), is actually an original covenantee of the covenants made by Polly. As we are told, Polly's covenants are made with her vendor (Victor) but also the 'owners for the time being of the shops in Kings Road'. This description includes Eve who, by then, is an owner of a shop in the King's Road, and so under s 56 of the LPA 1925, Eve is deemed to be a party to the deed of covenant. That section allows a person 'to take the benefit' of any covenant as an original party to it so long as they are in existence at the date of the covenant and the covenant is intended to benefit them as a party (*Amsprop Trading v Harris* (1996)). Thus, Eve may enforce both the positive and negative covenants against Polly in law or in equity, being an original covenantee. Of course, the reverse is not true, as the benefit of Eve's covenant has never been passed to Polly, either by deliberate assignment or under the rules to be discussed below.

We can now turn to the position of successors in title to the original covenantees, in this case, Victor. It is trite law that the benefit of a covenant may be transmitted to a successor either at law or in equity, provided that the covenant touches and concerns the land (except possibly in cases of contractual assignment). Each successor needs to be considered in turn and the nature of the covenants has been discussed above.

(a) The successors to shop No 1: Albert and Bill

It is clear that Albert and Bill will be able to claim the benefit of these covenants only in equity. Albert's estate in the land is under a four year lease in writing – not by deed – and so it must amount to an equitable lease (*Walsh v Lonsdale*). Albert has only an equitable estate and thus his tenant Bill can be in no better position. So, both have equitable interests and we need to consider whether the benefit of the covenant has passed in equity (*Mellon v Sinclair*).

Clearly, all covenants touch and concern the land and both Albert and Bill have some interest in the land entitling them to sue. We may note here that neither of them need have the same interest in the land as the original covenantee (Victor), so long as they have some interest within s 78 of the LPA 1925. Moreover, the covenants will be presumed to benefit the land (*Whitgift Homes v Stocks*) and, in any event, seem to be within the meaning of benefit put forward in *Re Gadd*. However, has the benefit passed under one of the three ways recognised by equity: assignment, a building scheme or annexation? There is no evidence of the first and the second is clearly inappropriate on the facts. However, after *Federated Homes v Mill Lodge Properties* (1980), it is established that the effect of s 78 of the LPA 1925 is to attach the benefit of a covenant automatically to the land, provided the land is readily identifiable (*Whitgift Homes v Stocks*), unless this is explicitly precluded, as in *Roake v Chadha* (1983). There is no such exclusion in this case. Moreover, it is immaterial that the present plaintiffs have an interest in only part of the land originally benefited by these covenants. Under *Federated Homes*, a covenant is attached to each and every part of the land, so long as each and every part is capable of benefiting from it. That is clearly the case here. It should also be noted that *Federated Homes* applies to positive covenants in exactly the same way as negative covenants and so no distinction can be drawn between the covenants made by Eve and those made by Polly. Thus, the benefit of all three covenants has run in principle to Albert and Bill and they can take action to restrain unlawful user of No 4 and No 5 as well as forcing Polly to build a secure fence, subject to the court's right to refuse the discretionary remedies in equity (*Gafford v Graham* (1998)). Of course, the action will be commenced by Bill, the present occupant of No 1 and, indeed, Albert will be permitted to sue in respect of his reversionary interest only if Bill does not take action.

(b) The successor to shop No 2: Claude

The position with Claude is much the same as above, except that Claude has a legal estate in the land. He may sue, therefore, either at law or in equity depending on whether he wishes damages or an injunction and specific performance. To recap: there is no doubt that Claude has an estate in the land, that the covenants touch and concern the land and that the benefit has been annexed to his part of the land under *Federated Homes*. He may enforce all three covenants against Polly and Eve respectively.

(c) The successor/occupier to shop No 3: Victor and the squatter

We have already noted above that Victor is an original covenantee and may sue on all three covenants as a matter of contract. Moreover, he is still in possession of No 3 so may sue for a legal or equitable remedy at his choosing. Yet, what of the squatter, Desmond (the person actually in occupation), for he may wish to enforce the covenants if his occupation and use of the property is being disrupted? Once again, the covenants touch and concern the land and, under *Federated Homes*, they are annexed to each and every part of it. However, it does appear that Desmond has no interest in the land which could entitle him to sue. This is not fatal. If we examine s 78 of the LPA 1925 closely, it declares that successors in title may obtain the benefit of covenants and then says that 'in connection with covenants restrictive of the user of land successors in title shall be deemed to include owners and occupiers for the time being of the land'. Clearly, this means that even a squatter, being an occupier, can obtain the benefit of a restrictive covenant if all of the other conditions are met. Thus, Desmond can sue on the covenants restricting the use of premises and so can prevent Eve from selling electrical goods and Polly from breeding rabbits.

Question 39

In 1998, Lucy, an insurance saleswoman from London, decided to purchase a country house in the village of Small Steeple. Finding a farm cottage with a paddock in a small private road, she offered to buy it from Giles, the owner of the farm of which it was part. The sale was completed by deed and contained covenants by Lucy, to contribute to the cost of the upkeep of the road, to maintain the paddock as an open space, to use the premises for residential occupation only and not to alter the external appearance of the cottage. These covenants are expressed to be made with 'the vendor and the owners for the time being of No 2 and No 3 Flower Lane, being similar properties'.

Three years later, Lucy has been made redundant and finds she can no longer afford the cottage and her house in London. She sells the property to John, a property developer, who announces that he is going to sub-divide the cottage into a flat and a workshop, adding a small studio at the back. He has no use for the field and Paul, a squatter, starts to build himself a small wooden cabin. Farmer Giles has already lost several sheep due to holes in the fence and the residents of Flower Lane wish to resurface the road.

Discuss.

Answer plan

The answer needs to include a discussion of the following:

- original covenantees; s 56 of the LPA; *Amsprop Trading v Harris*;
- nature of restrictive covenants;
- the running of the burden in equity;
- requirements of registration;
- mutual benefit and burden; *Thamesmead Town v Allotey*.

Answer

In this problem, a landowner has entered into various covenants in respect of her land for the benefit of adjoining properties.

Unfortunately, when the land subject to those covenants was sold to a third person – that is, someone not a party to the covenants – it appears that the covenants have been broken. Consequently, the owners of the adjoining land, who have the benefit of those covenants, will wish to enforce them against the successor in title to the original covenantor. The issue thus revolves around the transmission of the burden of covenants in cases where there is no leasehold estate.

Before we can deal with the substance of the matter in more detail, two preliminary points must be addressed. First, irrespective of all other matters, only the burden of those covenants which touch and concern the land are capable of being transmitted to purchasers from the original covenantor (*Rogers v Hosegood* (1900)). In our case, there are five covenants and it would seem that all satisfy Lord Oliver's test for 'touching and concerning' put forward in *Swift Investments v Combined English Stores* (1988). The only doubt may be over the covenant to pay for the upkeep of the private road, as this seems to be related to property other than land owned by the surrounding occupants. However, in itself this is not fatal, for the benefit is in the use of this road for surrounding properties, rather than the facility of a well made road for its own sake. For that reason, this covenant also 'touches and concerns' (see also, *Thamesmead Town v Allotey* (1998)). Secondly, it is trite law (*Austerberry v Corp of Oldham* (1885); *Rhone v Stephens* (1994)) that it is only the burden of restrictive covenants that may run, and then only in equity. It is necessary, therefore, to determine which covenants are restrictive, and this is done by examining their substance, rather than the form in which they are expressed (*Tulk v Moxhay* (1848)). In substance (and one test is whether the covenantor is required to spend money: *Hayward v Brunswick* (1881)), the covenant to contribute to the cost of the road is positive in nature. So, subject to what will be said below about avoidance devices, this covenant cannot be enforced against the purchaser John or the squatter Paul. All the other covenants are restrictive.

In essence, whether the burden of a restrictive covenant will run against a successor in title to the original covenantor will depend on two further factors, as supplemented by the requirements of the Land Registration or Land Charges Acts as appropriate. First, at the date of the covenant, the covenantee must have had land capable of benefiting from the covenant. In other words, the burden will run only if the covenant was made for the benefit of other land and that other land is in fact benefited (*London and South Western Railway v Gomm* (1882)). In our problem, there was in existence at the time of the covenant land owned by the covenantee – Farmer Giles – and it is a question of fact whether that land is benefited by these covenants, with the onus on the defendant to prove that it does not (*Whitgift Homes v Stocks*). In any event, even if it was thought that these covenants do not benefit land retained by Farmer Giles because they are 'residence' oriented (which is highly unlikely), it is clear that the covenants are also made with the owners of No 2 and No 3 Flower Lane. Although not parties to the deed, these owners are intended to be benefited by the covenants as parties and, under s 56 of the LPA, they are therefore deemed to be in the position of original covenantees (*Amsprop Trading v Harris* (1996)). Their properties are also benefited. Thus, the first criterion is satisfied.

Secondly, the burden of the restrictive covenant must be annexed to the land of the original covenantor. Fortunately, this condition is easily satisfied, as s 79 of the LPA effectively annexes the burden of all restrictive covenants unless a contrary intention is expressed in the deed of creation. There is no contrary intention here and so all four restrictive covenants are annexed.

Presumably, then, the burden of these covenants is capable of running with the land. However, it is inherent in the *Tulk* rules that such covenants – being equitable – in practice will bind only a purchaser of a legal estate who has notice of them. Notice has, of course, been replaced by registration. Thus, if this is registered land, these covenants need to be registered as minor interests to bind John, as he is a purchaser of a legal estate. If they are not, they are void against him and all future successors. Likewise, in unregistered land, the covenants must be registered as Class D(ii) land charges to bind a purchaser of a legal estate. In short, only if this requirement is satisfied is John bound in practice by these restrictive covenants. The squatter, however, is in a different position. A squatter is not a purchaser of a legal estate in the land and, therefore, it is immaterial whether the covenants are registered or not (*Re Nisbet and Potts Contract* (1905)). So long as the restrictive covenants fulfil all other requirements, they become proprietary in nature and will bind. The squatter cannot plead lack of registration, because he is not a purchaser and he at least will not be able to build on the paddock.

Finally, we should note that there is one way in which John might be forced to pay for the upkeep of the road, even though this is a positive covenant entered into by his predecessor in title. Under *Halsall v Brizell*, if a person wishes to take the benefit of certain rights, he can be compelled to honour his obligation to contribute to the cost of their provision. This is the principle of mutual benefit and burden: for example, he who takes the benefit of a private road must take the burden of the obligation to pay for its upkeep. The validity of this principle has been affirmed in *Thamesmead Town v Allotey* (1998), where it was held that an obligation to contribute to the upkeep of certain common facilities (the burden) was enforceable as the counterpart of enjoying those facilities (the benefit), provided that the person liable actually chose to take advantage of the benefit in practice. So, if John chooses to use the road, he can be made liable for a share of the cost of its maintenance.

Notes

This question demonstrates that the passing of the 'burden' of a restrictive covenant is reasonably easily achieved although the requirements of registration are vital.

Question 40

The Easy Home Housing Company have just completed the redevelopment of a large inner city estate in Liverham. It is their intention to ensure that the entire estate should be for residential occupation only and they propose to impose restrictive covenants on all purchasers to ensure this. They also wish to impose an obligation on all purchasers to keep the properties in good repair, so as to preserve the character of the neighbourhood. Advise them of the various methods by which this can be achieved, if at all.

Answer plan

The following areas need to be discussed:

- original covenantees and original covenantors;
- passing the benefit under s 56 of the LPA and *Federated Homes*;
- passing the benefit under a building scheme; *Whitgift Homes v Stocks*;
- passing the burden – negative covenants and requirements of registration;
- mechanisms to pass positive burdens and their effectiveness.

Answer

This question invites consideration of the law relating to the transmissibility of covenants between freeholders. Of course, if the Easy Home Company had wished to retain the freehold of this large estate and lease out the properties to tenants on long leases, then the objectives of ensuring only residential occupation and ensuring full repair of the properties could have been achieved with relative ease under the law of leasehold covenants. In those circumstances, the Landlord and Tenant (Covenants) Act 1995 would have enabled both positive and negative covenants to flow to, and be binding on, successors in title. Of course, it would have meant that Easy Home became responsible for enforcement of the covenants, but at least the objectives could have been achieved.

Clearly, it is the wish of the development company to ensure two things: first, that each purchaser from them is placed under the burden of a covenant against non-residential user and the burden of a positive obligation to repair; and, secondly, that each purchaser obtains the right to enforce every other purchaser's covenant. There is, in other words, a need to ensure mutuality of obligation between all the purchasers of properties on the estate. In considering these questions, however, it is wise to deal separately with the benefit of the covenants and then the burden.

(a) The benefit

In this problem, there is both a positive and a negative covenant, although, as regards transmission of the benefit to successors in title from the original covenantee, there is little distinction between the two types of covenant. However, since it is the stated objective to ensure that there is mutuality of obligation amongst the prospective purchasers of the properties, it is clear that we are really concerned with transmission of the benefit in equity. The reason is, quite simply, that the burdens of covenants (at least restrictive ones) can be transmitted in equity only.

Clearly, there is no difficulty with the requirement that the covenants must touch and concern the land (*Rogers v Hosegood*) or that the covenants do in fact benefit the land (*Re Earl of Leicester*). Likewise, each intending purchaser will have an estate in the land benefited and the original covenantee will have land capable of benefiting at the time the covenant was made (although note the problem of the last sale, considered below). The difficulty is, however, with the remaining requirement, namely, that the benefit must be transmitted by one of the methods recognised by equity. The position is not straightforward for one simple reason. The developer owns all the land prior to any sale. On sale to the first purchaser, that purchaser will make the required covenants for the benefit of the land retained by the developer. In fact, under the *Federated Homes v Mill Lodge Properties* (1980) interpretation of s 78 of the LPA, as confirmed in *Whitgift Homes v Stocks*, the benefit of the covenant will be annexed to each and every part of the retained land. So, when the second purchaser comes along, and buys a piece of the retained land, they will clearly obtain the benefit of the first purchaser's covenants. Their own covenants will, of course, then go to benefit the retained land in the same way as those of the first purchaser. The difficulty is however, that on this analysis, it is impossible for the first purchaser to gain the benefit of the second purchaser's covenants and, indeed, for the second purchaser to gain the benefit of the third's and so on. In fact, although later purchasers always get the benefit of earlier purchaser's covenants, previous purchasers never get the benefit of those who buy later because, when the subsequent purchasers actually buy the land, the previous purchasers have already bought their plots which are, consequently, no longer part of the developer's retained land. This problem, which is essentially one of timing, can be solved in two ways.

First, when subsequent purchasers purchase their property, they can expressly include all previous purchasers as original covenantees. This will put those previous purchasers in the same position as the developer. Moreover, it is not necessary to list all such persons, or even make them parties to the deed. Section 56 of the LPA 1925 allows the benefit of a covenant to be passed to a third party as an original covenantee provided they were intended to benefit as a party and were in existence and the time the covenant was made (*Amsprop Trading v Harris* (1996)). There may be some difficulty with the last purchaser from the developer, as after that purchase the original covenantee (the developer) will have no interest in the land and this is required for transfer of the benefit in equity. However, this problem can be avoided by ensuring that one of the previous purchasers who does have land capable of benefiting is actually made a party to the deed. Of course, this is a cumbersome method of achieving the desired effect, but it would ensure that the benefit of every purchaser's covenant – negative and positive – was transmitted to every other purchaser.

A much simpler way to achieve the same effect is to ensure that the transfer of benefit takes place under a building scheme. This is a rule of limited effect that allows a common vendor (for example, Easy Homes) to achieve the mutuality of benefit desired without having to worry about timing, or lack of land for the final sale or even the use of s 56 of the LPA 1925. Under *Elliston v Reacher* (1900), if there is a common vendor, an allotted plan for the building site wherein the land is laid out in lots, a well defined area (see *Whitgift*) and an intention that each purchaser shall be under the same obligation, then the benefit of all covenants can be given to all purchasers without more and irrespective of the time they purchase their own individual plot. Indeed, as later cases show, it may even be possible to omit some of the *Elliston* conditions, as where there is no allotted plan (*Baxter v Four Oaks Properties* (1965)) and where, as in *Re Dolphin's Conveyance* (1970), there is no common vendor. The advice to Easy Homes is, then, to follow this reliable and accepted method of ensuring mutuality of benefit and, in this connection, to ensure that the land which is to be subject to a building scheme is clearly identified so that all purchasers know the extent of their mutual rights (*Whitgift*).

(b) The burden

This is not inherently difficult, rather, it is that the present state of the law allows the burden to flow in only limited circumstances. Thus, it is only the burden of restrictive covenants that can pass to successors in title of the original covenantor (*Austerberry v Corporation of Oldham; Rhone v Stephens*). To ensure this, the covenant must touch and concern the land, the covenantees must at the time of the covenant have had land capable of benefiting from the covenant and the burden must be attached to the land. The first two requirements are clearly satisfied, as each purchaser will make a covenant with the developer as they purchase the land. (On sale of the last plot, the developer is treated as having land because of the special rules relating to a building scheme.) Moreover, annexation of the covenant will occur automatically under s 79 of the LPA and there will be no problem of this effect being deliberately excluded. Of course, if the covenants are to bind successors in title from the original purchasers/covenantors, they must be registered as either minor interests in registered land or Class D(ii) land charges in unregistered land. The developer must ensure this takes place as otherwise the covenants will be unenforceable after the first sale of each burdened plot.

As to the positive covenant to repair, there is little the developer can do. Of course, as suggested at the outset, he could decide to let the property as a leasehold development and rely on the rules relating to leasehold covenants. In fact, even if the purchasers were later to enfranchise their leaseholds the covenants would still be binding. However, this is not usually the object of a developer who does not wish to become a managing landlord. Neither is there any scope for the doctrine of mutual benefit and burden under *Halsall v Brizell* (1957) and *Thamesmead Town v Allotey* (1998). That principle applies only in cases where there is some shared utility or service, such as a road or sewer. It would be possible for each original covenantor/purchaser (who, of course, is under the obligation to repair as matter of contract) to extract a covenant to repair from any purchaser from them, thus creating a chain of covenants. Of course, however, this 'chain of indemnity' is only as strong as its weakest link and depends on the ability and desire of the original covenantor to impose such an obligation on a successor. A final chance – at least if this were registered land – would be for each purchaser of a plot to permit the entry of a restriction against their title, requiring any future purchaser from them to enter a direct covenant with the remaining owners to pay for the upkeep of the fence. Such a covenant would then be a condition of purchasing the land. This would work, but it is cumbersome and might well deter prospective purchasers from buying from Easy Homes in the first place.

In essence then, it is reasonably straightforward for Easy Homes to achieve the desired effect of giving each purchaser a right to sue on these covenants. The burden is, however, more problematical and it is only the burden of the restrictive covenant that could be guaranteed to run, a rule that has been confirmed in *Rhone v Stephens*.

Question 41

Choco Ltd, a biscuit manufacturer, own large premises on an industrial estate just outside London. Title is unregistered. In 1994, they decide to sell off parts of their property in order to meet mounting company debts. Plot 1 is sold to Martin, who covenants not to carry on any trade or business in confectionary on the site and to require his staff to use the catering facilities established by Choco Ltd on the estate. Later that year, Choco Ltd sells Unit 2 to Norman on a seven year lease in writing. Norman makes identical covenants as to those made by Martin and immediately sub-lets the property to Oswald by a lease in writing on the same terms. Oswald has since inherited a fortune and makes a gift of the premises to his nephew Herod, a major jelly baby manufacturer. Subsequently, Martin sells his property to Penny who begins to make seaside rock and opens a small cafeteria for her staff. Meanwhile, Choco Ltd has sold its remaining property to General Foods Inc who immediately contemplate litigation. Unfortunately, Norman has disappeared and it transpires that none of these covenants were registered.

How would your answer differ if the covenants had been registered?

Answer plan

The answer needs to include the following areas:

- covenants that touch and concern the land;
- running of benefit and burden;
- lack of privity of estate in a pre-1996 lease;
- requirements of registration and effect: purchasers and others.

Answer

It is clear that in this problem there are difficulties concerning both the transfer of the benefit and the transfer of the burden to successors in title of the original parties in respect of covenants affecting freehold land. In order to consider this problem in detail, it is first necessary to determine the nature of these two covenants – the covenant not to carry on any confectionary business and the covenant to ensure that staff working on the burdened land eat at the covenantee's cafeteria. The first point is whether these covenants touch and concern the land. There is no difficulty with the covenant restrictive of user, as this is a type of covenant often employed to control the use of land (*Re Gadd* (1966)). On the other hand, there is a serious doubt whether the covenant to use the cafeteria of the covenantee does touch and concern the land. It is doubtful whether it affects the value or mode of user of the land (*Swift Investments v Combined English Stores* (1988)) and appears to be only personal in nature. If this is the case, then this particular covenant can bind only the original parties, being Martin and Norman. It is a matter of contract. In addition, if, as a matter of construction, Oswald's covenant with Norman in the sub-lease was intended to be made with Choco Ltd (the head landlord) under s 56 of the LPA 1925, Oswald will be bound in contract with Choco as well as Norman (s 56 applies even to covenants that do not touch and concern). That apart, this covenant binds no successor in title, being personal in nature. So, Penny cannot be sued on this covenant even if it were negative and fulfilled all the other conditions relating to the transmission of the burden of freehold covenants (or leasehold covenants in a pre-1996 lease). Likewise, its benefit cannot be transferred automatically to

General Foods under property law principles when they buy the original covenantee's land. Of course, however, the benefit of it can be expressly assigned as a matter of contract, under the rule that contractual benefits can be assigned personally.

That leaves us, then, with the restrictive covenant against certain types of user. First, does the benefit of this run in equity to General Foods. (Note the position at law is not relevant as the burden of the covenant can only be transmitted in equity and thus the plaintiff must sue in equity.) For the benefit to run in equity, the plaintiff must have some estate in the land within s 78 of the LPA 1925 and the covenant must have benefited land of the original covenantee. The fact of benefit will be presumed (*Whitgift Homes v Stocks*) unless the contrary is shown. In any event, there is clear benefit within the definition of *Re Gadd* because the covenant affects the mode of user of the land. There is no difficulty with either of these conditions. In addition, however, the benefit of the covenant must have been transmitted in a method accepted by equity. In this case, there is clearly no building scheme and no evidence of an express assignment of the benefit. We must, therefore, rely on annexation. Clearly, there has been no express annexation but this is much less important after the decision of *Federated Homes v Mill Lodge Properties* (1980) which makes it clear that this covenant will be statutorily annexed under s 78 of the LPA unless the covenant contains a contrary intention, which this does not. In fact, the covenant is attached to each and every part of the land, so it is not only General Foods that can enforce the covenant, but also Norman and Herod, the first of where purchased an estate in part of the benefited land before Martin's covenant and the second is an occupier of that land entitled to the benefit of a restrictive covenant within s 78 of the LPA 1925. However, it is likely that only General Foods will wish to enforce this covenant and Norman (if he could be found) will be prevented from doing so unless Herod refuses to act.

Secondly, what of the burden of this covenant, for it appears that it has been broken in respect of both Unit 1 and Unit 2? Turning first to Unit 1, can this restrictive covenant bind Penny? It seems clear that the conditions required to give the burden of this covenant a proprietary nature have been satisfied. On the one hand, at the time of the covenant, there was land owned by the covenantee (Choco Ltd) which was capable of benefiting from the covenant, as required by *London and South Western Railway v Gomm* (1882). Similarly, the burden of the covenant appears to have been annexed to the land under s 79 of the LPA 1925: there is no contrary intention expressed. So, the covenant is proprietary within the rules of *Tulk v Moxhay* (1848). However, this means only that the covenant is *capable* of binding a successor in title to the original covenantor, not that it actually does so. In order for it to bind a purchaser of a *legal* estate in the land – which presumably Penny is – it must be registered as a Class D(ii) land charge in unregistered land. We are told that it is not and so even this covenant is not binding on her, nor can it be binding on any subsequent purchasers having been statutorily voided by the LCA. Obviously, however, if the covenant had been registered, the position would have been the reverse.

Thirdly, what of the successors in title to Unit 2, being Norman and now Herod (via a gift of Oswald's lease)? The position concerning whether the covenant is proprietary is, not surprisingly, the same as with Unit 1: the covenant was made for the benefit of land of the covenantee and it is annexed to that land. However, it also is unregistered. Yet, in this case it is not necessarily the case that the covenant is void for lack of registration. Under s 4 of the LCA 1972, a Class D(ii) land charge is void for lack of registration against a purchaser for money or money's worth of a legal estate in the land. When Norman acquires the land, he acquires it by virtue of a lease in writing – not by deed – so he purchases only an equitable estate. Moreover, Herod does not even purchase the land, for he obtains the land by gift. Consequently, both Norman and Herod are bound by the covenant even though it may not be registered. Of course, had registration occurred, this would make the covenant safe against any future purchaser of a legal estate but it is not necessary on these facts.

Finally, for the sake of completeness, it should be noted that Norman could enforce all covenants against Oswald, his tenant under privity of contract. Likewise, Choco Ltd and then General Foods, can proceed to forfeit Norman's lease for breach of covenant if the lease contained a right of re-entry. Subject to the normal safeguards surrounding forfeiture, this would terminate Herod's occupation also and would result in *de facto* enforcement of the covenant against user (*Pennell v Payne*).

Notes

This shows that questions can mix both the benefit and burden. It also makes it clear that lack of registration is not always fatal to a claim – it depends on the status of the transferee.

CHAPTER 9

THE LAW OF MORTGAGES

Introduction

There is no doubt that, for the ordinary person, the purchase of a house is their most direct contact with the law of real property. For this event most people require a mortgage and the subsequent repayment of the mortgage becomes one of their most pressing economic concerns. However, the use of the mortgage as a device to *acquire* property is a relatively modern development. In fact, for so long as people have been capable of owning land (or more precisely, an interest in it), the mortgage has been a way of converting a fixed economic asset (the land) into a flexible economic asset (its monetary value). The mortgage is, in essence, a way of realising and releasing the capital value of the land. Fundamentally, therefore, a mortgage is a security for a loan. This rather bland statement hides a multitude of consequences, not least the idea that a mortgage – being a proprietary right – is subject to controls not otherwise found in 'ordinary' loan contracts. Indeed, one of the most frequent examination questions asks the student to assess the extent to which a mortgage really is a right in property or just another species of contract.

Checklist

In order to deal with mortgage issues, three reasonably distinct areas have to be addressed. First, how are mortgages created, both legal and equitable, and are there any specific reasons for choosing a particular method? Secondly, what are the rights of a mortgagor (the borrower) under a mortgage and in particular what is the nature and extent of the 'equity of redemption'? Thirdly, what are the rights of the mortgagee (the lender) under a mortgage and what remedies may be suitably employed in the event of a defaulting mortgagor? These questions largely depend on the application of traditional equitable principles as supplemented by statute where appropriate. A good knowledge of case law is invaluable.

Question 42

Analyse the methods by which legal and equitable mortgages may be created after 1925. What was the purpose of the 1925 reforms?

Answer plan

The following areas need to be discussed:
- definition of a mortgage: *Santley v Wilde*;
- the use of the charge;
- ss 85 and 86 of the LPA 1925;
- s 53(1)(c) of the LPA 1925;
- *Walsh v Lonsdale*; s 2 of the Law of Property (Miscellaneous Provisions Act) 1989;
- proprietary estoppel;
- purposes of reform: protection of the borrower, the mortgage as a charge;
- ease of creation.

Answer

All land has an economic value and a mortgage is one of the most effective ways by which an owner may realise it. Although today the mortgage is most commonly employed to enable the purchase of land in the first place, the true nature of a mortgage is that it is a lender's security for money lent to the borrower. Of course, the mortgage is much more than a simple contract of loan, for the mortgagee will acquire an interest in the land over which the mortgage operates. In technical terms, a mortgage is a conveyance of an estate in the land to the mortgagee, with a provision that the mortgagee's interest shall lapse upon repayment of the loan plus interest and costs. It is one of the most important aspects of the mortgage that the lender obtains not only a right to have the money repaid but also a proprietary interest in the land charged as security for that loan. However, as well as being a powerful form of security for a lender, a mortgage also has advantages for the borrower or mortgagor. It is a general principle of the law of property that 'once a mortgage always a mortgage' which effectively means that the borrower has a right of full access to his property once the loan secured on it has been repaid. In other words, that the proprietary nature of the mortgage lasts only for so long as the debt remains outstanding. Thus, the mortgagee's remedies (which can be proprietary or contractual in nature) only endure so long as the borrower owes money.

Before 1925, if an owner of a legal or equitable interest in land sought to raise money on security of that land, the borrower's interest in the property was usually conveyed in full to the lender. If a fee simple was mortgaged, a fee simple was transferred and so on. In his turn, the mortgagee promised to re-convey the estate on repayment of principal, interest and costs. Moreover, originally, not only did the mortgagee have the actual estate of the borrower vested in them, the contract also made provision for the lender to retain that interest if the borrower failed to repay the loan on the date stipulated in the contract. This date, known as the legal date of redemption, became crucial and the consequences for the borrower of missing payment on that date were severe. The borrower lost their estate entirely. Fortunately, equity was soon to intervene. Adopting the policy position of 'once a mortgage always a mortgage' equity developed the 'equity of redemption' and its counterpart the 'equitable right to redeem'. Essentially, this meant that the borrower was entitled to a re-conveyance of their property should they pay the full charges due under the mortgage, even though the legal date for payment had passed. In fact, this was equity's way of ensuring that a mortgage really was security over the land and not an easy method by which a creditor could obtain the property of someone in debt. Likewise, equity took the view that if a mortgagee went into possession of the property in pursuance of the right they had been granted (which, of course, they were perfectly entitled to do), they should be called to account strictly for any rent and profits that could have been earned by the land. These rents and profits were held for the borrower and could then reduce the mortgage debt. This effectively meant the end of possession as a remedy except in cases of last resort. This then was the background to the changes made by the Law of Property Act (LPA) 1925 to the methods by which mortgages could be created.

The general principle underlying the 1925 property reforms is that, as far as possible, the owner of land should retain the fullest interest possible in their own property even when seeking a mortgage of it. Hence, since 1926, freeholds can no longer be mortgaged by a conveyance of the fee simple to the mortgagee and the mortgagee is limited to receiving some lesser right in the land. With obvious and necessary modifications, this principle also applies to mortgages of leaseholds.

The position of legal mortgages of freeholds is now as follows. Under s 85(1) of the LPA 1925, there are two methods only of creating a legal mortgage of a freehold. First, the borrower may demise a term of years absolute to the lender and no mortgage may take effect by absolute conveyance of the legal estate (s 85(2)). In effect, this is the granting of a long lease to the mortgagee with a provision for cesser on redemption (that is, that the term of years shall cease when the loan is repaid). In the typical case, the term granted is usually long, such as 3,000 years. The demised term will also fix a contractual date for redemption, being the legal right to redeem and that is usually six months after the date of the mortgage or later if the mortgage is payable by instalment. However, as was the case before 1926, the mortgagor has an equitable right to redeem on the payment of the loan at any time after this legal date has passed. The clear effect of these provisions is that the mortgagor retains his legal fee simple and the mortgage is more clearly regarded as the security for a loan, although all of the pre-1926 rights of the mortgagee are preserved and, of course, the mortgagee still has *some* proprietary interest in the land by virtue of their term of years. Moreover, this 'new' approach has one major practical advantage. Since 1925, it is now possible for the mortgagor to create further legal mortgages of their land, in order to raise further sums. So, because the mortgagor retains the legal fee simple, it is perfectly possible to grant another mortgage for another term to a second lender, as where the first mortgage was for a relatively small sum. The second term granted will necessarily be longer than the first, so as to give the second mortgagee a notional legal interest in the property distinct from that of the first mortgagee. The net effect of these provisions is that the mortgagor always retains final legal title to their property, irrespective of the number of mortgages created and, of course, that every mortgagee gains some legal estate in the land. This has enhanced the basic principle of 'once a mortgage always a mortgage'.

The second method of creating a mortgage of a legal freehold after 1925 is the charge by deed expressed to be by way of legal mortgage. This is an invention of s 87 of the LPA 1925: the legal charge is simply a statutory form of mortgage that is easier and less expensive to execute than a formal demise of a term of years. In fact, the legal charge is the main method of mortgaging legal estates currently in use. Under s 87, this charge must be made by deed and it must be expressed to be by way of legal mortgage but, that done, it is clear that a legal chargee (a lender) gets exactly the same protection, powers and remedies as if they had been given a term of 3,000 years in the normal way (s 87 of the LPA; *Regent Oil Company v Gregory* (1966)). For all practical purposes, therefore, the legal charge is as effective as a mortgage by way of demise of term of years. It is, however, cheaper, shorter and more efficient and the Land Registration Act 2002 provides that it should become the only way of mortgaging a legal estate in registered land. This is likely to take effect early in 2003.

As far as leaseholds are concerned, the methods of creating a legal mortgage are substantially similar to that of a freehold. Before 1925, the leaseholder (the tenant) would assign his lease to the mortgagee just as the freeholder would transfer their fee simple. Now, however, by virtue of s 86 of the LPA 1925, a legal mortgage of a leasehold can be created by two methods only. The first is the charge by deed expressed to be by way of legal mortgage. This is effectively the same as in the case of freeholds. The second is by a sub-lease for a term of years to the mortgagee. This sub-lease will necessarily be shorter than the term of years that the leaseholder actually has and, in practice, the mortgagee's term will be 10 days shorter than the original leaseholders. This is to ensure that the leaseholder can grant subsequent legal mortgages of his leasehold by creating a term longer than the first mortgagee's but shorter than his own. Once again, any attempt to avoid these provisions by assigning a lease will operate only as a sub-lease for a term shorter than that of the tenant (*Grangeside Securities v Collingwood Securities Ltd* (1964)).

Turning now to equitable mortgages, these can be split conveniently into two categories. First, it may well be that the borrower only has an equitable interest and it necessarily follows that any mortgage of that equitable interest will itself be equitable. The Law of Property Act has not affected this matter to any great extent and mortgages of equitable interests (such as a beneficiary's rights under a trust) are still carried into effect by a conveyance of the whole equitable interest to the mortgagee. This will, of course, be accompanied by a provision for re-transfer when the loan is repaid (*William Brandt v Dunlop Rubber* (1905)). As far as formality requirements are concerned, there is no need to use a deed, but because this mortgage will amount to a disposition of a subsisting equitable interest (that is, that of the mortgagor) it must comply with s 53(1)(c) of the Law of Property Act. This requires the mortgage of the equitable interest to be in writing, on penalty of voidness.

The second issue is the creation of the informal mortgage or, in other words, a mortgage that does not comply with the formality requirements necessary for the creation of a legal mortgage. As with many other equitable interests in land, an informal mortgage commences life as a contract to create a legal mortgage which, if capable of specific performance, will be treated as an equitable mortgage along the same lines as equitable leases in *Walsh v Lonsdale*. It is vital, however, for this informal mortgage that the contract be in writing under s 2 of the LPA 1989 (*United Bank of Kuwait v Sahib* (1995)). It must also, of course, be capable of specific performance, although that requirement is usually met in the case of contracts concerning land. If the requirements of a written contract and specific performance are met, the contract to grant the mortgage will be treated in itself as an equitable mortgage – *Parker v Housefield* – although usually the money will have to have been advanced before equity will intervene. Prior to 1989 Act, it was also possible to create an equitable mortgage by deposit of title deeds with the lender. The deposit of the borrower's deeds was treated as both evidence of the contract and performance of that contract under the then s 40 of the LPA (*Re Wallis* (1974)). This was a very informal but relatively efficient way of creating a mortgage. After 1989, contracts need to be in writing and this cannot be presumed from the deposit of title deeds (*Sahib*). As such, it is clear that this method of creating equitable mortgages by deposit is now defunct. However, it may well be possible to treat the deposit of title deeds as a form of proprietary estoppel. As we know from *Taylor Fashions v Liverpool Victoria Trustees*, if one person promises an interest in land to another and that is relied upon to their detriment, equity will enforce the promise and give effect to the claim of the promisee. Thus, if a lender has actually advanced money on the basis of a promise (represented by the deposit of title deeds), it is possible that the mortgage will be enforced under estoppel despite the absence of any formality providing there is evidence of unconscionability. Of course, equitable mortgages do suffer from the vulnerability of all equitable rights in land, viz, the prospect of being lost if the land is sold to a purchaser of a legal estate. Finally, mention must also be made of the equitable charge, a completely informal way of securing a loan over property. This requires no special form of words, only an intention to charge property with a debt (*National Provincial and Union Bank of England v Charnley* (1924)). Such a method is extremely precarious and is rarely used in either commercial or residential mortgages.

It is apparent then, that the 1925 legislation introduced a significant change in the way that mortgages could be created. Relying on the principle of 'once a mortgage always a mortgage', legal estates could be mortgaged only by giving the lender some subsidiary right in the land, not a transfer of the borrower's entire interest. Not only does this simplify the process of mortgage creation, it emphasises the nature of mortgage as a security. In addition, it also allows the borrower to create successive legal mortgages which gives protection and security to those successive mortgagees as well as bringing certainty for the mortgagor.

Notes

This is as straightforward a question as it is possible to get on mortgages. Good use of case law will re-enforce knowledge of the statutory provisions. In due course, a mortgage over registered land will not actually exist until it is entered on the register, although this will not take effect until s 93 of the LRA 2002 comes into force. When this happens, we will need to re-think the way we discuss 'the creation of mortgages'.

Question 43

To what extent do the rights of a mortgagor under a legal mortgage provide sufficient protection for the borrower?

Answer plan

The following areas need to be discussed:

- the nature of the mortgagor's rights – the legal right to redeem; the equitable right to redeem and the equity of redemption;
- the doctrine of clogs and fetters – options; collateral advantages; oppressive terms; unconscionable conduct; *Jones v Morgan* (2001).

Answer

The mortgage is one of the most versatile and unique of property law concepts. It is, on the one hand, a simple contract of loan between lender and borrower and, on the other, it creates a valuable and powerful proprietary right in land. It is a concept governed by contract law and property law and the different philosophies of each can sometimes cause confusion and difficulties. However, since 1925, the very way in which mortgages can be created is designed to re-enforce the essential nature of a mortgage as a security charged on land for a loan.

In the normal course of events, a legal mortgage will be created either by granting a demise of years (a lease) to the mortgagee or by the execution of a legal charge by way of mortgage. The former does, of course, confer a proprietary interest on the mortgagee and the latter is deemed by statute (s 87 of the LPA 1925) to have the same effect. This means that the mortgagor retains their interest in the land subject, of course, to the rights of the mortgagee. At the same time, as the mortgage is also a contract of loan, there are stipulations relating to the repayment of the loan and certain remedies that the mortgagee may pursue in the event of default on the loan. However, the mortgage remains at all times a loan and this means that the mortgagor does have a considerable degree of protection, both of her interest in the land and in respect of his position under the loan contract.

As a matter of contract, the mortgagor has a contractual right to redeem on the date specified in the contract. Traditionally, this was six months from the date of the mortgage but may be at any date specified by the parties and will often be later in instalment mortgages. At one time, if the mortgagor did not redeem on this date, he lost his security even though redemption could have been made at a later date. However, equity soon developed the maxim that 'once a mortgage always a mortgage' and allowed redemption of the mortgage after this date, on payment of principal, interests and costs (*Thornborough v Baker* (1675)). This became known as the equitable right to redeem and, without doubt, is a valuable part of the mortgagor's protection under a mortgage. In fact, the equitable right to redeem is just part of the wider rights that the mortgagor has under the mortgage. In equity, the mortgagor is protected by the equity of redemption. This equity of redemption represents the sum total of the mortgagor's rights in the property: in essence, the residual rights of ownership that the mortgagor has, both in virtue of his paramount legal estate in the land and the protection that equity affords him (*Re Sir Thomas Spencer Wells* (1933)). The equity of redemption is valuable in itself for it represents the mortgagor's right to the property (or its monetary equivalent) when the mortgage is discharged or the property sold. In fact, on subsequent mortgages, the second and third lenders are able and willing to grant further loans precisely because the mortgagor has this valuable right. The equity of redemption is a proprietary right in itself and may be dealt with by the mortgagor as such.

The inherent quality of the equity of redemption is demonstrated by the fact that equity will intervene to protect the mortgagor and her equity of redemption against encroachment by the mortgagee: *Jones v Morgan* (2001). As noted above, equity regards the mortgage as a loan, which can be redeemed, and not as an opportunity for the lender to acquire the mortgagor's property. This protection manifests itself in various ways.

First, it is a general principle that a mortgage cannot be made irredeemable: it is a security, not a conveyance, and the right to redeem cannot be limited *pro tanto* to certain people or certain periods of time (*Re Wells*). However, a provision postponing the date of redemption may be valid where the mortgage is not otherwise harsh and unconscionable, so long as the right to redeem is not made illusory (*Knightsbridge Estates v Byrne*; *Fairclough v Swan Breweries*). Again, a provision in a mortgage which provides that the property shall become the mortgagee's or which gives the mortgagee an option to purchase the property is void (*Samuel v Jarrah Timber; Jones v Morgan*). The rationale is, of course, that the mortgagor needs protection when negotiating for a loan, often being in a vulnerable position. Thus, an option to purchase given to the mortgagee in a separate and independent transaction can be valid, as not forming part of the mortgage itself (*Reeve v Lisle*).

Secondly, as a matter of principle, the mortgagor should be able to redeem the mortgage and have the mortgagee's rights extinguished free from any ancillary conditions in the mortgage other than the payment of principal, interests and costs. The basic principle is, again, the mortgage as a security which ends when its reason – the money – is repaid. Thus, on several occasions the courts have struck down 'collateral advantages' made in favour of a mortgagee, as where the mortgage contract stipulates that the mortgagor should fulfil some other obligation as a condition of the mortgage. An example is where the mortgagor promises to buy all his beer or supplies from the mortgagee. At one point, such collateral advantages were uniformly struck down, as being a clog on the equity of redemption (cf *Bradley v Carritt*). However, it is now clear that there is no objection to a collateral advantage which ceases when the mortgage is redeemed (*Santley v Wilde*). This is a matter of contract between the parties and, providing the terms are not unconscionable or do not in fact restrict the right to redeem, they will be valid (*Biggs v Hoddinot*). Indeed, at least with commercial mortgages made between equal parties at arms length, *Kreglinger v New Patagonia Meat and Cold Storage Company* (1914) suggests that a collateral advantage which does continue after redemption (for example, a continuing obligation to take supplies from the mortgagee) may be acceptable so long as the mortgagor's property returns to the mortgagor in the same form that it was mortgaged. Clearly, this is a flexible principle that can be used to invalidate harsh, unreasonable terms as the situation demands. On the other hand, courts are aware that the parties' business dealings should be upheld as far as possible in the absence of unconscionable conduct.

Thirdly, the court has the power to strike down any term which, in effect, destroys the equity of redemption. Thus, a high interest rate might render the mortgagor's equity of redemption valueless (*Cityland and Property (Holdings) v Dabrah* (1968)) or the terms of the mortgage might be so oppressive as to make it harsh and unconscionable, although it must be more than merely unreasonable or unfair (*Multiservice Bookbinding v Marden; Jones v Morgan*).

Fourthly, the mortgage may be struck down in whole or in part on the ground that the mortgagor's consent was obtained by undue influence. It is rare for the mortgagee himself to have exerted the undue influence, but the mortgagee can be tainted with the undue influence of the person who persuaded the mortgagor to sign (such as a co-mortgagor, a husband or lover). This will occur if the person exercising the undue influence can be said to be the agent of the mortgagee (rare) or if the mortgagee has notice of the undue influence (*Barclays Bank v O'Brien* (1992); *Royal Bank of Scotland v Etridge* (2001)). A mortgagee tainted by 'actual' undue influence (that is, the undue influence is proven on the facts) is, without more, unable to enforce the mortgage (or such provisions as are tainted), whereas in cases of 'presumed undue influence' (where the undue influence arises by presumption because of the relationship between the parties) the mortgagee will not be prevented from enforcing the mortgage unless the mortgage was to the 'manifest disadvantage' of the claimant (*National Westminster Bank v Morgan* (1985); *Royal Bank of Scotland v Etridge*). In recent years, 'undue influence' has been a favourite defence for a mortgagor resisting the possession claims of the mortgagee and recent case law (especially *Etridge* in the House of Lords) has sought to confine the plea to manageable and defensible limits.

Finally, it is also clear that mortgages, being contracts, are subject to normal contractual rules governing credit relationships and related matters. Thus, a mortgage may be set aside as an 'extortionate credit bargain' within ss 137–40 of the Consumer Credit Act 1974 or set aside as being in restraint of trade (*Esso Petroleum v Harper's Garage* (1968)) or be contrary to the Unfair Terms in Consumer Contracts Regulations 1999 (*Falco Finance v Gough* (1999)).

All in all then, the mortgagor does benefit from a considerable amount of protection, both by virtue of equity protecting the equity of redemption and by statute and general common law principles applicable to contracts *per se*. In addition to these, when the mortgagee seeks to exercise his remedies under the mortgage, statute intervenes to restrain, exclude or modify those remedies, particularly in the case of mortgages seeking to obtain possession by court order of a dwelling house (s 36 of the AJA 1970). The mortgage is, after all, only security for a loan.

Notes

This is a good question to answer if you know the doctrine of clogs and fetters. A good answer also considers the nature of a mortgage as a contract as well as a security and this is where knowledge of the law of undue influence is vital. The recent Court of Appeal decision in *Jones v Morgan* may signal wider use of the unconscionability rule.

Question 44

How extensive are the remedies available to a legal mortgagee?

Answer plan

The remedies of a legal mortgagee need to be discussed:
- action on the contract – bankruptcy;
- appointment of a receiver;
- sale;
- possession;
- foreclosure;
- degree of protection for the mortgagor varies according to the type of mortgage and the circumstances of default.

Answer

It is trite law that a mortgage is properly to be regarded as security for a loan so that, on repayment of the principal, interest and costs, the property mortgaged returns in full to the mortgagor. However, it is equally apparent that a mortgagee should have some means by which it can protect and/or enforce its security in the case of a breach of any of the terms of the mortgage by the mortgagor. In the usual case, this breach arises from non-payment of sums due under the mortgage, but the mortgagee will also be concerned to protect itself from other breaches, as where a mortgagor in possession sub-lets the property in violation of a stipulation in the mortgage. Fortunately for the mortgagee, the fact that a mortgage is both a contract of loan and springs from the grant of a proprietary right, means that the mortgagee enjoys a range of remedies should the mortgagor breach the terms of the mortgage. The particular remedy or remedies employed by the mortgagee (for they are cumulative not mutually exclusive (*Cheltenham and Gloucester BS v Grant; Alliance & Leicester v Slayford*)) will depend on the precise nature of the default of the mortgagor and the requirements of the mortgagee. As explained below, some are more suitable for recovery of unpaid interest, while others are more suitable for recovery of the entire loan and the ending of the charge, either because of non-payment of sums due or for some other default.

The first and most straightforward of the mortgagee's remedies against a defaulting mortgagor arises because the mortgage is a contract of loan between the parties. The mortgagee has an action on the express covenant given by the mortgagor for repayment of the sum due on a certain date plus interest. As soon as this date has passed, the mortgagee may sue for the sum owed and is normally entitled to a payment order for the full amount. Of course, this remedy may be of little practical use if the mortgagor has no funds other than those tied up in the secured property, but it is often an adjunct to possession proceedings against him or her. It may, however, lead to the mortgagor becoming bankrupt and this, in turn, can lead to a sale of the property at the request of the trustee in bankruptcy (*Alliance & Leicester v Slayford*). This is a useful weapon of last resort if the mortgagee is unable to secure a sale in their own right (for example, because of a *Boland* type overriding interest).

A second way of recovering the whole sum due and ending the mortgage occurs if the mortgagee should seek to exercise his power of sale. In most cases a mortgage will contain an express power of sale, although by virtue of s 101(1)(i) of the Law of Property Act 1925 a power of sale is implied into every mortgage made by deed unless a contrary intention appears. This power arises as soon as the legal (contractual) date for redemption has passed or, in the case of instalment mortgages, when one instalment is in arrears (*Twentieth Century Banking v Wilkinson* (1977)). However, under s 103 of the LPA the power only becomes exercisable when either: (a) notice requiring payment of the mortgage money has been served and the mortgagor is in three months arrears since the notice; or (b) interest under the mortgage is two months in arrears and unpaid; or (c) the mortgagor has breached some covenant in the mortgage (other than the covenant to pay) or some provision of the LPA. These provisions in effect give the mortgagee a power of sale of the property should the mortgagor be in serious default and the result is that the mortgagee receives such money as he is owed if sale proceeds permit. In fact, the sale conveys the land to the purchaser free from the mortgagee's mortgage, all subsequent mortgages (which are paid off in order, before the mortgagor) and the equity of redemption (ss 88 and 113 of the LPA) and subject only to any previous mortgages. Obviously, a sale of the mortgaged property is calamitous for the mortgagor, with often only a small percentage of the sale proceeds reaching them after all outstanding liabilities have been settled. Consequently, it is not surprising that equity steps in to mitigate the harshness of this procedure. Thus, the selling mortgagee is under a duty of care to the mortgagor to obtain the best price reasonably obtainable (*Standard Chartered Bank v Walker* (1982), and see *Medforth v Blake*), although an open sale by auction, even when prices are low satisfies this rule (*Cuckmere Brick Co v Mutual Finance*). If the mortgagee is negligent and thereby obtains a lower price than it would otherwise have obtained, it is liable to the mortgagor (*Cuckmere*) and the mortgagee cannot sell to himself or his agent (*Williams v Wellingborough Council* (1975)). However, this duty is owed to the mortgagor only and not to a person having merely an equitable interest in the property (*Parker-Tweedale v Dunbar*). Likewise, the mortgagee is not trustee of the power of sale and its motives in choosing to exercise the power of sale are irrelevant.

Usually, of course, the mortgagee will wish to sell the property in order to realise their security and to do this effectively the property must be sold with vacant possession. In practice, therefore, before sale, a mortgagee may wish to exercise its third remedy: the right of possession. Indeed, taking possession of the mortgaged property can also be used as a method of securing recovery of any outstanding interest on the loan, as where a mortgagee in possession sub-lets or runs the business over which the mortgage exists. Possession then does not necessarily mean the end of the mortgage. At the outset, however, we must be clear that the mortgagee's right to possession is exactly that. By virtue of the way in which mortgages are created, the mortgagee will have an estate in the land and an immediate right to possession of the property the moment the ink is dry on the mortgage, irrespective of any fault on the part of the mortgagor (*Four Maids v Dudley Marshall* (1957); *Ropaigeleach v Barclays Bank*), although in the normal course of events the mortgagee will not exercise its right of possession and might even promise not to seek possession unless the mortgagor defaults on the interest repayments or breaches some other term of the mortgage. In fact, there is a positive disincentive for a mortgagee to take possession, as a mortgagee in possession will be called strictly to account for any income generated by its possession (*White v City of London Brewery*). This means that the mortgagee will be taken to have received not only any actual income generated – which can go towards interest payments – but also any income that it should have received had the property been managed to the high standard expected. Any shortfall will then have to be made up by the mortgagee who may find that it actually owes money to the mortgagor. This is why most commercial mortgagees desist from seeking possession.

In the residential context possession is still an option for the mortgagee, often as a prelude to sale. Here, however, the mortgagor is protected from a zealous mortgagee. Under s 36 of the Administration of Justice Act (AJA) 1970 (as amended by s 8 of the AJA 1973), a mortgagee's application for possession of a dwelling house may be suspended, adjourned or postponed by the court, in its discretion, if it appears that the mortgagor would be able to pay within a reasonable period any sums due under the mortgage. Due to s 8 of the AJA 1973 (reversing *Halifax BS v Clark*), 'any sums due' may be treated only as those instalments missed and not, as most mortgages provide, the whole sum once one mortgage payment is missed. Likewise, the relief is available for endowment mortgages, despite the elliptical wording of the Act (*Bank of Scotland v Grimes*), although there is some doubt whether the statutory discretion is available if the mortgagor is not actually in default under the mortgage (*Western Bank v Schindler*) and, certainly, there can be no relief if the possession warrant has been executed (*Bristol and West plc v Dace*). Neither is the power available if the mortgagee takes possession under its common law right without a court order, albeit that this is rare and dangerous for a mortgagee (*Ropaigeleach v Barclays Bank*). In addition, while it is clear that the 'reasonable period' which the mortgagor is given to repay his arrears might actually be the rest of the mortgage – so as to spread the debt evenly (*Middlesborough Mortgage Corp v Cunningham*; *Cheltenham and Gloucester BS v Norgan*) there is no discretion if there is no prospect of the mortgagor making a reasonable attempt to actually repay the accumulated debt, let alone meet future repayments (*First National Bank v Syed*; *Ashley Guarantee v Zacaria*). However, the courts do show considerable sympathy to mortgagors pleading s 36 of the AJA and *Cheltenham and Gloucester BS v Norgan* suggests that the court will postpone possession if it appears that the mortgagor will be able to repay at some future time and not within an arbitrary period chosen by the court. Clearly, this is a generous interpretation of s 36 and, while it is understandable given the social utility of protecting residential occupiers, it does compromise significantly the undoubted right of the mortgagee to seek such possession (see also *Quennell v Maltby* (1979)).

The fourth of the mortgagee's remedies may also be used to recover the interest owed rather than ending the mortgage. The mortgagee's right to appoint a receiver is often expressly included in a mortgage but, in any event, such a power will be implied into every mortgage by deed (s 101 of the LPA). Any express power is exercisable according to its terms, although the statutory power becomes exercisable only in those circumstances in which the statutory power of sale becomes exercisable and is often an alternative to that remedy. The great advantage of the appointment of a receiver as opposed to the mortgagee taking possession of the property is that the receiver is deemed to be the agent of the mortgagor, not the mortgagee (*Chatsworth Properties v Effiom* (1971)), with the consequence that any negligence on the part of the receiver is not attributable to the latter.

Finally, the mortgagee has a powerful remedy in the event of major default by the mortgagor. The remedy of foreclosure, if successful, will extinguish the equity of redemption and cause the transfer of the property to the mortgagee, entirely free of any rights of the mortgagor. It is one of the peculiarities of a mortgage that this most final of remedies actually becomes exercisable as soon as the legal date for redemption set by the mortgage has passed, although once again it is common practice for mortgagees to covenant not to foreclose without notice and only in respect of specified breaches of the mortgage terms. Essentially, should the need arise, the mortgagee will begin an action in court asking for foreclosure of the mortgage unless the mortgagor repays the sums owed (principal, interest and costs) within a specified time. If the mortgagor fails to do so, the mortgagee will be given an order 'foreclosure nisi' which in effect gives the mortgagor a further period (usually six months) in which to raise the money to pay off the loan. Failing that, the foreclosure nisi will be made absolute and the mortgagor's interest in the property will be extinguished. This is the end of the matter save that, in exceptional circumstances, the court may open a foreclosure absolute and allow the mortgagor to redeem the mortgage at a later date (*Campbell v Holyland*), although this is very unlikely if the mortgagee has since sold the property to a purchaser with no notice of any previous mortgage. In view of the powerful nature of foreclosure, the court has power under s 91(2) of the LPA to order sale in lieu of a foreclosure (and in other circumstances: *Palk v Mortgage Services Funding*) and this means that any surplus funds after redemption of the mortgage will be paid to the mortgagor. Obviously, such a solution is desirable where the mortgage debt is far less than the value of the property. As noted above, the effect of a foreclosure is to vest the mortgagor's estate in the mortgagee and to extinguish the mortgage and its terms. Any mortgages made prior to the mortgage foreclosed remain unaffected as they are still binding on the land, although subsequent mortgages will be destroyed. In practice, this means that subsequent mortgagees are given an opportunity to redeem any previous mortgages if foreclosure is likely.

Clearly, then, the mortgagee has a wide range of remedies, albeit that statute provides some relief to the mortgagor. Likewise, we must not forget that a mortgagee is subject to the general rule that there must be no clog on the equity of redemption and that credit controls (in the form of the Consumer Credit Act 1974) and common law principles of undue influence and restraint of trade are applicable to mortgages as to other loan contracts. Yet, even with these limitations, the *bona fide* mortgagee who takes security over land for a loan has a considerable array of remedies in the face of a defaulting mortgagor.

Question 45

Florence is the owner of Roundabout House, a large Victorian freehold property in Toytown. The house is surrounded by a private housing project, Restful Towers, owned by Dilan and Dougal. They have sought for many years to buy Roundabout House as it would be easily converted to many smaller units. In order to secure her future, Florence decides to open as a hotel and seeks a loan from Noddy Bank, a private merchant bank, who finance the project by way of legal charge. The Bank are unsure of the financial viability of the scheme and insist on an interest rate at 8% above current market rates. They also stipulate that 'the borrower promises that the mortgagee shall have first option to purchase the property in the event of a judgment debt made by any court against the borrower'. Last year, Noddy Bank was taken over by Double D Holdings Ltd, a private company wholly owned by Dilan and Dougal. Shortly after, the managing director of Noddy Bank, having examined Florence's accounts, threatens to foreclose on the loan unless Florence renegotiates new terms. Florence reluctantly agrees and a new mortgage is drawn up, on the same terms but with an increase in the interest rate by 12% and a promise that 'the borrower will, for 10 years from the date of this agreement, purchase cleaning and other services from the owners for the time being of Restful Towers'. Six months later, Dilan and Dougal as owners of Restful Towers sue Florence for unpaid bills on the cleaning contracts and obtain a judgment debt against her. The bank now seeks to purchase Roundabout House.

Advise Florence.

Answer plan

The following areas need to be included:

- the nature of a mortgage;
- the equity of redemption – options to purchase; collateral advantages; unconscionable terms.

Answer

In this question, several issues arise as to the enforceability of the mortgage entered into by Florence, both as a whole and in respect of particular obligations undertaken by her. As a preliminary point, we must note that when Florence enters into the mortgage she is creating a proprietary right in favour of the Noddy Bank but, nevertheless, retains paramount legal title to it. In essence, Florence has an equity of redemption, this being the sum total of her rights under the mortgage as residual legal owner (*Re Sir Thomas Spencer Wells*). Moreover, as equity treats a mortgage as security for a loan, which can be redeemed on payment of all monies owed, this equity of redemption will be protected by the court in a number of ways. This is supplemented by various other common law and statutory provisions that may come to Florence's aid.

The first point is to consider whether Florence can have the first mortgage set aside on the ground that its provisions destroy or make illusory the equity of redemption or amount to such harsh and oppressive terms that equity will intervene. As far as the interest rate is concerned, there is no doubt that the court has a discretion to intervene if the rate is so high as to make the mortgage practically irredeemable or is in itself unconscionable (*Cityland and Property (Holdings) v Dabrah* (1968)). On the other hand, it is also clear that the court will not interfere if the mortgage between the parties represents a business agreement between them, even if it is unreasonable, for equity acts on the conscience, not to mend bad bargains (*Multiservice Bookbinding v Marden* (1979)). In our case, it is unlikely that the court will intervene as the interest rate is not excessively above the market rate and seems to have been imposed by Noddy Bank after a commercial assessment of the viability of Florence's venture.

There is then no assistance for her here. However, she may then wish to challenge the option to purchase which is contained in the mortgage transaction. As a matter of principle, any provision which stipulates that the property shall become that of the mortgagee is void (*Samuel v Jarrah Timber* (1904)) and this applies in equal measure to an option to purchase (*Jones v Morgan*). The rationale is that, even though the mortgagee may well promise to pay the market price, it still represents a compromise of the mortgagor's paramount right to recover their property (*Jones*). Of course, if the option is contained in a separate transaction, it may be permitted (*Fairclough v Swan Brewery* (1912)) and in this case Noddy Bank may argue that the option is triggered only when the mortgagor is in trouble, thus amounting to nothing more than an express provision entitling them to do what they would be able to do in any event under the remedy of foreclosure. Yet, Florence may meet this argument quite simply as it is clear that the option to purchase is triggered by *any* judgment debt against her (as appears to be the position in respect of the cleaning services bill), even though it bears no relation to the debt charged on her property. This option will, therefore, be struck out and it will not matter that Florence agreed once again to it on the granting of the new mortgage after the first threat to foreclose.

Turning now to the new mortgage, which Florence executes after the takeover of Noddy Bank by Double D Holdings and after the threat to foreclose. As already noted, the option to purchase contained in this mortgage will be set aside. However, are there any other grounds upon which Florence may rely for relief? First, it may well be possible for Florence to claim that the new mortgage interest rate is a clog on her equity of redemption or is unconscionable. The mortgage rate now becomes 20% above the market rate and this does suggest an attempt to deprive Florence of her property by forcing her out through inability to pay. Likewise, it may well be relevant that the new interest rate was set only after the takeover of Noddy Bank by Double D Holdings, a vehicle (cf *Jones v Lipman* (1962)) for the persons who so desire her property. These circumstances may well persuade a court to set a new rate under the principle in *Cityland and Property (Holdings)*. In addition, the facts do suggest that the new mortgage itself in its entirety was designed purely for the purpose of forcing Florence into liquidation. Although a mortgagee does have a right to foreclose if monies are owed, a court of equity will not stand by and let that be used unconscionably. In our case, the takeover of Noddy Bank, effectively by Dougal and Dilan, coupled with the insistence on a new mortgage may well allow equity to come to Florence's aid and have the mortgage set aside. In reply, the bank may well argue that the decision to call for a remortgage with its new terms was a commercial one, carried out by the managing director of the bank without reference to the 'needs' of the bank's new owners. This, of course, will be a question of fact, but even if established, there are grounds at least to have the high interest rate varied as a straightforward clog on the equity of redemption.

There is, in addition to these issues, one other point for consideration. The new mortgage stipulates a collateral advantage for Dilan and Dougal, namely that Florence must purchase cleaning services and supplies from them. It is interesting to note here that the collateral advantage is not actually stipulated in favour of the mortgagee (the bank) but for a third party. If anything, this supports the above analysis that the second mortgage was a device designed wholly to acquire Florence's property. However, in general terms, equity will allow a collateral advantage providing that it is neither harsh or oppressive nor extends beyond the moment of redemption by the mortgagor (*Santley v Wilde*; *Biggs v Hoddinot*). In fact, in some circumstances, especially where the mortgage is between commercial organisations operating at arms length, a collateral advantage will be allowed even though it does continue after the mortgage has been redeemed (*Kreglinger v New Patagonia Meat and Cold Storage Co* (1914)). In our case, there is little to suggest that the collateral advantage is harsh or unconscionable *per se*, although the terms of the contract for cleaning services, etc, will be relevant. On the other hand, the advantage is stipulated to exist for 10 years from the date of the mortgage and this may well be after the mortgage has in fact been redeemed; for example, if Florence can pay off the mortgage quite soon. To a large extent, this issue will depend on the facts of the case, although the court will look carefully at the arrangement, especially as the incurred debts under the services contract are then used in an attempt to trigger the (void) option to purchase the property.

All in all, then, Florence has a number of potential arguments which may either reduce her obligations under the mortgage or invalidate it altogether. In addition to these, there is also the possibility that the agreement may amount to an extortionate credit bargain under the Consumer Credit Act 1974, or contravene the Unfair Terms in Consumer Contracts Regulations 1999, as well as all the ways in which the court can soften the blow should the mortgagee actually proceed to exercise one of its remedies under the mortgage.

Notes

This problem puts into practice the law discussed in the previous two answers, although it does concentrate more on the rights and protection of the mortgagor. In one sense, it is an essay in disguise, though the question does ask you to advise Florence and that must be done. An even fuller answer would have gone on to consider undue influence and Consumer Credit Act protection in more detail.

Question 46

To what extent have recent decisions of the House of Lords clarified the circumstances in which a person may plead 'undue influence' as a defence to a mortgagee seeking to exercise its remedies under the mortgage?

Answer plan

The following areas are relevant:

- the consequences of undue influence if established;
- establishing undue influence – actual, presumed and the meaning/purpose of manifest disadvantage;
- fixing a mortgagee with undue influence – agency, notice;
- how does a mortgagee protect itself?;
- *Barclays Bank v O'Brien; CIBC v Pitt; National Westminster Bank v Morgan; Royal Bank of Scotland v Etridge; National Westminster Bank v Amin* (2002).

Answer

The law of undue influence may be called in aid by a mortgagor seeking to avoid the consequences of a mortgagee's exercise of one of its remedies. Often, it is pleaded as a defence to a possession action and, if successful, may prevent the mortgagee realising their security (but contrast *Alliance & Leicester v Slayford*). Obviously, the defence of undue influence may be raised in a variety of circumstances, although two particular situations are relevant here. First, a mortgagor may claim that the mortgagee (such as a bank) has exercised undue influence over them directly, with the effect that the mortgage is set aside. Such cases are now relatively rare given the regularised lending practices of most institutional mortgagees and the industry's codes of conduct. Secondly, a mortgagor (often a husband or male partner) may have sought a mortgage from an institutional lender over property that is jointly owned with another person (for example, a wife or sexual partner). Should this be the case, the other joint owner must consent to the mortgage if the lender is to have adequate security (see *William & Glyn's Bank v Boland* for the consequences of failing to secure consent). Of course, it lies in the power of the joint owner to refuse such consent, but their emotional ties to the person seeking the mortgage might well persuade them to agree, especially if it is to secure finance for their partner's business. If, then, at a later date, difficulties arise such as to give the mortgagee cause to seek possession or sale of the property, the consenting owner may well claim that her consent to the mortgage was procured by the undue influence of her partner. In other words, that there was no real consent to the mortgage at all and that it should be set aside either in its entirety or insofar as it binds them (*TSB v Camfield* (1995)). In reality then, undue influence is a plea that the mortgage should be set aside because of either the action of the mortgagee directly or more likely because of the action of the other mortgagor that in some way affects the mortgagee. It is this second aspect that has caused much controversy and which is examined below.

The rationale for the doctrine of undue influence is clear. However, it must be remembered that a vibrant mortgage market – with adequate protection for lenders – is just as important as providing protection for the homes of persons who may have been 'persuaded' to enter a mortgage that they did not really want. A balance must be struck. At one time, the law of undue influence was regarded as a panacea available to most mortgagors at the slightest hint of unfairness in the mortgage transaction. Thus, it was perfectly possible for a mortgagor to avoid the consequences of default by pleading simply that the mortgagee was in a dominant position when the mortgage was made. However, this rather liberal approach was rejected in *National Westminster Bank v Morgan* (1985). In that case, the House of Lords made it clear that two major requirements had to be met before undue influence could be established. First, the mortgagor had to show some victimisation, pressure or unfair advantage by the mortgagee or by a person whose conduct could taint the mortgagee. The equitable defence was not available simply because the bargain was unfair or unreasonable (*Banco Exterior Internacional v Thomas* (1997)). Secondly, and more controversially, the House of Lords indicated that even if the fact of undue influence could be established, a mortgage would not be set aside unless it could also be shown to be 'to the manifest disadvantage' of the mortgagor. It was not enough, in their Lordships' view, that undue influence existed, for that in itself was no reason to set aside a transaction. This is clearly a limitation on the undue influence defence, although after the full judgments of the House of Lords in *Royal Bank of Scotland v Etridge*, it is clear that the concept of manifest disadvantage does fulfil a vital function (see below).

As first explained by the House of Lords in *Barclays Bank v O'Brien* and *CIBC v Pitt*, there are three steps to establishing the defence of undue influence. First, establish the undue influence. Secondly, ask whether the mortgagee is tainted by it. Thirdly, assess whether the mortgagee has taken steps to prevent its mortgage being voided by the undue influence. As to the first step, these two cases established that undue influence could either be 'actual' or 'presumed'. Actual undue influence arose where the facts established positively the existence of undue influence by the wrongdoer over the 'victim'. In contrast, presumed undue influence arose either where the relationship between the persons was of such a nature that the presumption of undue influence arose automatically (for example, doctor/ patient, solicitor/client and parent/child: so called Class 2A cases) or where the substance of the relationship was that one person placed so much confidence in the other than the presence of undue influence should arise (so called Class 2B cases: for example, husband/wife or lover/lover). In addition, manifest disadvantage was required for all presumed cases, but not in actual cases.

The second step was that the mortgagee had to be tainted with the wrongdoer's actions. This would occur if the wrongdoer was the agent of the mortgagee or the mortgagee had 'notice' of the undue influence. Agency will, of course, be very rare as lenders do not usually appoint one borrower to act for it in securing the other owner's consent. However, cases of notice were much more likely as such notice would exist where there was a substantial risk that some form of pressure may have been exerted and the mortgagee was aware of facts that gave rise to that risk. In fact, it soon became clear that such a risk was present in very many cases and lenders soon concentrated on the third hurdle: that is, identifying those steps which a mortgagee should take to protect itself in the event that it was on notice of the risk of undue influence. In general terms, these steps boiled down to the fact that the lender should advise the potential victim to seek independent advice and that, if the giving of advice was confirmed (for example, by a solicitor in a letter to the bank), the lender could assume that its mortgage was safe.

All this seemed clear enough after *O'Brien*, but in reality there was too little clarity. In particular, assuming the mortgagee was put on notice, precisely what steps must it take to avoid being tainted by any undue influence? What constituted 'independent advice'? Could a mortgagee rely on the confirmation of a reputable solicitor that such advice had been given, even when the advice was defective (*Massey v Massey*) or not given wholly independently of the other mortgagor (*Banco Exterior Internacional v Mann*), provided that it was in fact given (*TSB Bank v Camfield* – no independent advice at all)? Did the mortgagee have to force the co-mortgagor to take advice? How could it do this? Also, what was meant by 'manifest disadvantage' and was a lender really always at risk that a transaction was procured by undue influence? These uncertainties soon led to much litigation, several appeals to the Court of Appeal and, eventually, an eight case consolidated appeal to the House of Lords. The result was a 'bright line' judgment in *Royal Bank of Scotland v Etridge*. Once again, the issue can be broken down into three questions.

First, prove undue influence by the 'wrongdoer' over the claimant.

If the evidence adduced by the claimant established actual undue influence, then this hurdle was surmounted. 'Actual' in this sense means evidence which shows, on a balance of probabilities, that the wrongdoer so acted as to render the claimant's consent to the mortgage no real consent at all. Where actual undue influence is established, there is no need to prove that the impugned transaction was to the claimant's 'manifest disadvantage', as such disadvantage only helps to prove undue influence (see below) and so by definition is not needed in 'actual' cases. If the case is not one of actual undue influence, undue influence may be presumed. However, this is an evidentiary presumption that merely shifts the burden of proof from the claimant to the wrongdoer. Successful reliance on the presumption of undue influence does not mean that undue influence exists, but rather that the burden of explaining why the impugned transaction was not caused by undue influence passes to the alleged wrongdoer. The alleged wrongdoer may still dispel any whiff of undue influence by producing evidence as to the propriety of the transaction. Consequently, when viewed in this light, there is no real merit in adopting the *O'Brien* categories of 'Class 2A' presumed undue influence cases and 'Class 2B' cases. There are some relationships, such as parent/child and doctor/patient (the old 'Class 2A' cases), which necessarily and irrebuttably establish a relationship of trust and confidence and, if the transaction called for an explanation (was 'manifestly disadvantageous'), this shifts the burden of proof to the alleged wrongdoer to explain the transaction. Failure to do so necessarily leads to a finding of undue influence. There are other cases where the claimant can demonstrate on the evidence that a relationship was one of trust and confidence (the old 'Class 2B' cases) and, if the transaction called for an explanation (was 'manifestly disadvantageous'), this then shifts the burden of proof to the alleged wrongdoer to explain the transaction. Consequently, two things are now clear. First, that the 'presumption' of undue influence is no more than a tool to explain the shift of the evidentiary burden from the claimant and so 'manifest disadvantage' is necessary as it explains why the burden should shift. Secondly, the difference between the now defunct Class 2A and Class 2B cases is simply that in the former, the fact of trust and confidence could not be disputed by the wrongdoer, whereas in the second, it could.

The second issue is whether the lender is put on inquiry (that is, does the lender have notice as to the risk of undue influence?). The House in *Etridge* adopted a robust and blunt approach to this question. Recognising that there are difficulties, that its answer is broad brush rather than precisely analytical, the solution provided by the House is that a lender will always be put on inquiry (have notice) if a person is standing as a surety for another's debts, providing that such surety is not offered as a commercial service (that is, the guarantor is not charging for the service, as would a bank or other institution). Although this is an extension of the law, it has the great merit of ensuring that lenders do not have to probe the relationship of the parties in order to assess whether they are on inquiry. They are if it is a non-commercial surety. Thus, it is not the relationship between the parties that triggers the 'notice', but rather the very nature of the transaction irrespective of the relationship. The principle therefore applies outside the wife/husband situation. If, however, the loan is made to the parties jointly for their joint purposes (that is, the claimant is not merely guaranteeing the wrongdoer's borrowing), the lender is not put on inquiry unless it is aware (or ought to have been aware) that in reality the money was for the wrongdoer's purposes alone.

Thirdly, if on inquiry, what steps should the lender take to avoid being tainted by the undue influence and risk losing its security? At first sight, it appears that the judgment in *Etridge* is not principally concerned with preventing the occurrence of undue influence over a claimant at all, but rather identifying what a lender must do to avoid being tainted by it if such influence occurs. Fortunately (although it is not accidental), the steps that a lender must now take are such that the chances of undue influence occurring will be much reduced, but it is important to appreciate that the primary purpose of these steps is to protect the lender, not to stop the undue influence. For past cases – that is, mortgages executed prior to the *Etridge* decision – the lender must take steps to ensure that the wife understands the risk she is running and should advise her to seek independent advice. For future cases – that is, mortgages executed post-*Etridge* – the lender must insist that the wife attend a private meeting with the lender at which she is told of the extent of her liability, warned of the risk she is running and urged to take independent legal advice. How this will operate in practice for past cases will still be attended with some doubt, although it seems that it is not the lender's responsibility to see that no undue influence has been exercised, nor necessary that it seeks confirmation from a solicitor that no such influence exists (as opposed to confirmation that advice has been given). This is because the solicitor will be acting for the claimant and the lender can expect the solicitor to act properly for his or her client. Consequently, if a solicitor gives inadequate advice, the lender is not affected, provided the lender does not know (or ought to have known) that no advice was received or that it was inadequate (as may have been the case in *National Westminster Bank v Amin* (2002), a post-*Etridge* case but considering a pre-*Etridge* mortgage). After all, the claimant can sue the solicitor. In reality then, the past practice of relying on solicitor's certificates will suffice, unless the lender knows or ought to have known that the claimant was not thereby properly warned of the nature of the transaction or of the risks it posed. In this sense, *National Westminster Bank v Breeds* is rightly decided, as the lender should have known that the advice given to the claimant was defective despite receiving a certificate from the advising solicitor (see also *Amin*: lender knew that the client could not speak English and that the solicitor could not speak Urdu).

For future transactions, the House lays down what will almost certainly become a code of conduct for lenders. First, the lender should check directly with the claimant for the name of the solicitor who is acting for her, advising that it will seek written confirmation that advice about the proposed transaction has been given. The claimant should be told that this is because the lender does not intend that the claimant should be able to dispute the mortgage later. The claimant should also be told that she may (but not must) use a different solicitor from that which her partner uses. The lender must await a response from the claimant before it proceeds. Secondly, the lender should provide the advising solicitor with all the necessary financial information required for the solicitor to give proper advice: for example, level of total indebtedness of the husband, copy of the application form, etc. This usually will require the consent of the other party. Thirdly, the lender must inform the solicitor of any concerns it has over the genuineness of the claimant's consent or understanding. Fourthly, the lender should obtain written confirmation that all these steps have been complied with and that appropriate advice has been given. If such steps are taken, the lender will be protected, as may well be the claimant, subject only to any defects in the role of the solicitor that the lender knew of, or ought to have known of.

We can but hope that *Etridge* will resolve the uncertainties left by *O'Brien*. Undoubtedly, it will force a change in lending practices, but this will soon be absorbed into the administrative practices of the competent lending institutions. As for the law, we now know or have had confirmed that the 'presumption' of undue influence is really a presumption that reverses the burden of proof and is not a presumption that such influence really exists. Hence, it can be met with an explanation of why the transaction is undue influence free; that 'manifest disadvantage' in the weak sense of a transaction which on its face needs explaining is still an element in 'presumed' cases because it (merely) helps prove the presumption to reverse the burden of proof; that the Class 2A and 2B dichotomy is not helpful; that a lender will always be on inquiry ('have notice') in non-commercial surety cases; that in other cases, the lender will be on inquiry only in exceptional cases because it is entitled to assume that a person knows what he or she is doing when the loan is for their own benefit; that for past cases, reliance on a solicitor's certificate will normally protect a lender; that for future cases, the steps a lender must take are greater than before, but not onerous and may both protect the lender and prevent any undue influence from arising in the first place; and finally, that a lender can never be protected when it knows, or ought to know, that the claimant has not received the guidance and counsel he or she needed to judge the appropriateness of the transaction. All we need now is to wonder whether any solicitor will actually take the risk of advising clients in these situations.

Question 47

To what extent is freedom of contract inconsistent with the traditional view of a mortgage as being the grant of a proprietary interest in land merely as a security, albeit one which deserves special protection from a court of equity?

Answer plan

The answer needs to include the following areas:
- the nature of a mortgage, but founded in contract;
- the ability of the mortgagee to impose contractual terms versus the equity of redemption;
- the mortgagee's contractual remedies modified by statute;
- mortgages as loan contracts under the Consumer Credit Act 1974.

Answer

In one very important sense, this question is misleading. A mortgage is both an interest in land and a contract. It partakes of the attributes of both and in the great majority of situations the dictates of contract and property law are complimentary, not mutually exclusive. In other words, just because a contract is at the heart of the dealings between mortgagor and mortgagee does not mean that the mortgage cannot also operate as a proprietary right. Thus, the mortgagee has remedies on the contract (for example, to sue for money due), as well as remedies arising because of his proprietary interest in the land (for example, the right to possession). Likewise, the mortgagor has obligations under the contract (for example, to repay the loan and observe other covenants) as well as rights founded in his equity of redemption, a proprietary right. However, that said, it is true that, in some situations, the nature of a mortgage as a security over land, regulated by equity, can come into conflict with the contract negotiated between the parties.

The most obvious example of this potential conflict arises because of the general rule that equity will safeguard the equity of redemption, sometimes in contradiction to the express terms of the bargain agreed between mortgagor and mortgagee. Thus, an option to purchase granted to the mortgagee in the mortgage deed will be void (*Samuel v Jarrah Timber* (1904); *Jones v Morgan*) and terms which make the mortgage irredeemable will be struck out (*Fairclough v Swan Breweries* (1912)), even if agreed by the parties. Of course, the court is astute to give effect to the bargain made between commercial parties who are deemed to be able to take care of themselves, especially if they are financing a commercial enterprise (*Knightsbridge Estates v Byrne* (1939)), but that does not allow them to change the essential nature of a mortgage. It is still a security for a loan under which the proprietary interest conveyed to the mortgagee can be recovered on the payment of interest, principal and costs (*Re Sir Thomas Spencer Wells* (1933)). In particular, this emphasis on the equity of redemption has led the court to examine any 'collateral advantages' that are stipulated in the mortgage, being benefits extracted by the mortgagee in consideration for the loan. Originally, such advantages were frowned upon, as constituting a clog on the equity of redemption, but, in recent times, a collateral advantage which is neither harsh or unconscionable nor destructive *in fact* of the equity of redemption will be permitted (*Santley v Wilde*). Indeed, if the advantage represents the true commercial bargain between the parties and is not void on the above grounds, it will be permitted as an exercise of freedom of contract, even where it continues after the mortgage has been redeemed (as in *Kreglinger v New Patagonia Meat and Cold Storage Co* (1914)).

In addition, it is not only a court of equity that will protect a mortgagor. General contractual principles may also be called in aid. Thus, the general common law doctrine of undue influence may allow a mortgagor to avoid a mortgage contract in much the same way as a party may avoid any other contract (*Barclays Bank v O'Brien; Royal Bank of Scotland v Etridge*). Again, the Consumer Credit Act applies to mortgages as with other loan contracts as does the doctrine of restraint of trade (*Esso v Harper's Garage*). All of these, and the Unfair Contract Terms in Consumer Contracts Regulations 1999 (*Falco Finance v Gough* (1999)), support the court's intervention when seeking to protect the mortgagor's proprietary right in the equity of redemption.

From the mortgagor's point of view, then, both the contractual and proprietary nature of the mortgage can give protection against a mortgagee. When we look at the mortgagee, however, it seems that both statute and general equitable principles do intervene substantially to control (that is, limit) the exercise of remedies under the mortgage contract. In this sense, the contractual nature of the mortgage does take a back seat to its essential nature as a security. Thus, although the mortgagor has a contractual (and proprietary) right to take possession of the mortgagor's property, both statute and equity restrict the full exercise of this right. In the former case, s 36 of the Administration of Justice Act 1970 (as amended by s 8 of the AJA 1973) gives the court power to set aside the claim for possession in respect of a dwelling house (but note *Ropaigeleach v Barclays Bank*), although only if the mortgagor is likely to be able to meet his commitments under the mortgage and pay off any sums due within a reasonable time (*Bank of Scotland v Grimes* (1985); *Cheltenham and Gloucester v Norgan; First National Bank v Syed*). This is supported by s 91 of the LPA (see *Palk v Mortgage Services Funding*). In the second case, the equitable rule that a mortgagee in possession must account strictly for any income that is derived or could have been derived from the property during his period of possession (*White v City of London Brewery* (1889)) means that most mortgagees of commercial premises will not seek this remedy, although they may rely on the appointment of a receiver instead. Clearly, the court's ability to restrict the right of possession is a firm indication that the nature of a mortgage as a security takes priority over the claims of the mortgagee based on his contract and the proprietary right thereby obtained.

Likewise, the power of sale available to most mortgagees is restricted by the intervention of equity, even though statute (LPA 1925) clearly contemplates this as one of the major remedies of the mortgagee. The duty of care owed to the mortgagee to obtain the best price reasonably obtainable (*Standard Chartered Bank v Walker* (1982)) and the trust imposed on any surplus from the sale (after payment of the mortgage) do act as a brake on an eager mortgagee, although, in so far as they prevent fraud on the part of a mortgagee, these principles cannot be criticised. The same is generally true of the mortgagee's power of foreclosure (see s 91 of the LPA 1925), although this right – itself stemming from the nature of a mortgage as a proprietary right – is often a weapon of last resort. Technically, such a right arises as soon as the legal date specified in the contract has passed, but in reality the mortgagee often contracts not to exercise the right until some specified breach of covenant has occurred, such as non-payment of interest. This is an example of contract modifying the proprietary nature of a mortgage.

To conclude, one must reiterate that which was stated at the start of this answer. The mortgage that springs from contract is effected by means of the creation of a proprietary right in the mortgagee, and partakes of the rules and principles of both contract and property law. It should not be thought that there is a great deal of tension between the two philosophies and even where the equity of redemption is concerned – the most well guarded of the mortgagor's rights – the commercial nature of the mortgage and its role in releasing the economic value of real property has been recognised in the law relating to the mortgagee's remedies. The same is true in such matters as undue influence (*Royal Bank of Scotland v Etridge* (2001)) and is illustrated by the fact that the court is only willing to interfere with mortgages on the basis of extortionate credit bargains under the Consumer Credit Act 1974 in exceptional circumstances, as in *Falco Finance v Gough*.

Notes

This is perhaps one of the most interesting questions that can be asked on the law of mortgages. The interaction between property and contract law does cause problems in practice, especially in commercial transactions. The question also requires some knowledge of how mortgages are created and therefore provides a good test of a student's understanding.

CHAPTER 10

MISCELLANEOUS PROBLEMS

Introduction

The issues considered in this chapter bear no obvious relation to each other and no attempt shall be made to find one. However, they do share one important practical characteristic: they are issues that feature occasionally in examinations in land law, rather than being habitual favourites of examiners. Of course, that makes them no less important, for a well answered question on say, adverse possession, is worth just as much as a well answered question on co-ownership. That said, this chapter deals with issues such as adverse possession and fixtures and chattels with no particular attempt to treat them as intrinsically connected.

Adverse possession – or squatting – is a doctrine that truly reflects the feudal origins of English land law and the common law systems based upon it. Behind the ability of a trespasser to actually acquire 'ownership' of land which on paper belongs to somebody else is the concept that, in fact, owners only own 'estates' or titles in the land, not the land itself. Thus, it is perfectly possible for some other person to gain a better title without any formal transfer of 'ownership'. The very idea of adverse possession is based upon relativity of title, not absolute ownership of land. It is now trite law that in England there is no equivalent of the civil law concept of *dominium* and, in practice, this means that one person's title to land is only as good as the absence of a person with a better title.

Checklist

Today, adverse possession is a mixture of common law rules overlain by statute. The student therefore needs to have an understanding of the doctrine of estates in English land law, a working knowledge of the Limitation Act 1980 and a feeling for the purpose behind the principle of limitation of actions. Likewise, recent decisions such as *Buckinghamshire County Council v Moran*; *Colchester Borough Council v Smith*; *Hounslow LBC v*

Minchinton; Central London Commercial Estates v Kato Kagku (1998) and *Pye v Graham* give considerable guidance on the practical application of these rules. It is vital that there is a clear understanding of the proposed reforms to adverse possession as it applies to registered land under the Land Registration Act 2002.

The rules concerning fixtures and chattels are often more important to practising conveyancers than students of land law. Essentially, the question is what, apart from the house/land itself, does a purchaser of property buy on completion of the contract of sale? Does the greenhouse also pass with the title? How about the garden statues and the wall coverings? The answers to these and related questions are to be found mainly in judicial pronouncements which, while developing a general set of principles, can vary considerably in the confused circumstances of a real case. As with adverse possession, there is no better way to understand the law of fixtures and chattels than a thorough knowledge of case law.

Question 48

To what extent is it possible to define the circumstances in which an occupier of land may make a successful claim of adverse possession against the title holder?

Answer plan

The following areas need to be discussed:
* the general purpose and role of adverse possession;
* the concept of limitation – the limitation period;
* the mechanics of establishing adverse possession;
* special circumstances – licences, future intentions;
* stopping the clock;
* the compromise of disputes.

Answer

Adverse possession, squatting or limitation of actions as it is variously called, embodies one of the most fundamental principles of English land law: namely that a person may only own an estate in the land, not the land itself. It follows from this that any person with a superior estate (better title) may assert that title so as to claim seisin of the land. The principle of limitation gives practical effect to this doctrine of the relativity of title by providing that a person may be barred from bringing any claim to recover possession of land after the period of limitation has passed. In other words, if an estate owner sleeps on their rights, those rights will be extinguished in the sense that a court will not enforce them against the person actually in possession of the land. In this sense, adverse possession operates negatively: it prevents an estate owner from suing on their rights and operates to extinguish their title. It does not, thereby, vest a title in any other person (see, however, the application to register title by the successful squatter of registered land) but, by virtue of the doctrine of relativity of title, the person in actual possession may have the best claim to the land and thereby become effective 'owner' of it.

With this general background in mind, adverse possession can be boiled down to three basic issues: first, how long is the limitation period or, to put it another way, after what period of time does a paper owner of land lose their right to sue to recover possession of it; secondly, when does that period start to run, or in other words, what actions by the actual occupant of the land can form the actual act of *adverse* possession; and thirdly, what is the effect of expiry of this period, both for the paper owner and the adverse possessor?

As far as the first issue is concerned – the period of limitation – the period after which no action can be brought to recover land depends on the circumstances of each particular claim. Thus, in the normal course of events, the period will be 12 years from the moment of adverse possession by the squatter (s 15 of the Limitation Act (LA) 1980). There are certain special cases where the period is different, as where Crown lands are involved (30 years: Sched 1 to the LA 1980) or where possession is alleged to be adverse to a remainderman, when generally speaking the period is six years from the falling in of the remainder or 12 years from the adverse possession against the life tenant, whichever is the longer (s 15 of the LA 1980).

Secondly, by far the most difficult problem in relation to adverse possession is deciding when this period shall be deemed to have begun. In other words, at what moment in time does the actual occupation of land by another person become adverse to the paper owner so as to give them 12 years from that date to enforce their paramount title? Another way of looking at this to ask what actions of a person in actual possession amount to adverse possession so as to give rise to the possibility that, after the limitation period has expired, the paper owner's title will be extinguished. The particular rules concerning this vital question are not to be found in statute. The LA 1980 does not tell use how to assess whether adverse possession has occurred, only how it works and what its consequences are. The rules are entirely judge made and thus flexible, open ended and subject to a variety of applications as the circumstances of each case permits.

Following a number of cases that illustrated the uncertainties in the law, the Court of Appeal sought to codify the principles of adverse possession in *Buckinghamshire CC v Moran*, where there was a claim of adverse possession by a squatter against the council. In deciding in favour of the squatter, the court enunciated the basic principles behind establishing adverse possession. First, the adverse possessor should have an intention to possess the land to the exclusion of the whole world, including the paper owner (*Pye v Graham*). It was stressed that this was an intention to possess adversely, so that any belief that the possession was with the permission of the paper owner necessarily vitiated this requirement. Likewise, a belief that possession might become authorised by the paper owner can mean that the adverse possessor fails to demonstrate a *sufficient* immediate intention to possess to the exclusion of all (*Pye*). However, it seems clear from *Moran* that the same act that amounts to the second part of a successful claim (actual adverse possession) may also be enough to establish an intention to possess to the exclusion of the whole world, as where the squatter fixes a padlock to a gate on a fence surrounding the paper owner's land with the object of excluding everybody (see, also, *Hounslow LBC v Minchinton* (1997)). Secondly, as indicated, the squatter must actually take adverse possession of the land as a matter of fact, either in consequence of the dispossession of the paper owner or following discontinuance by him. Dispossession occurs where the paper owner is effectively driven out by another (*Rains v Buxton*) and discontinuance where the paper owner abandons the land (*Smith v Lloyd*). In either case, the loss of possession by the paper owner must be followed by actual adverse possession by the squatter. This will be a question of fact in each case, although it is clear that the degree of physical possession required will vary with the type of land involved (for example, *Lambeth v Blackburn*: making a flat secure was sufficient). For example, it may well be easier to establish adverse possession over land which is not susceptible to developed use (*Red House Farms v Catchpole*) and there are some indications that adverse possession is easier to prove in cases of discontinuance as opposed to cases of dispossession (*Red House Farms*). Yet, as noted, it is a question of fact in each case (*Powell v McFarlane*) and there is no requirement that the adverse possession must actually inconvenience the paper owner (*Treloar v Nute*). Certainly, it seems that possession will not be taken from acts equivocal in nature or temporary in purpose, such as growing vegetables or clearing land so as to enable one's children to play (*Wallis's Cayton Holiday Camp v Shell-Mex and BP* (1975); *Techbild v Chamberlain* (1969)), but motive is irrelevant if the acts of the squatter effectively exclude the paper owner (*Minchinton; Lambeth v Blackburn*).

Moreover, it is clear that the possession must be adverse to the paper owner: it must not be with their consent or permission as that amounts to a licence to occupy and will not start the period of limitation. Prior to the decision in *Moran*, this particular requirement could easily defeat a claim for adverse possession as it was held in a number of cases (*Leigh v Jack; Shell-Mex*) that, if the squatter's use of the land was not inconsistent with the paper owner's future intended use of the land, an implied licence would be presumed in the squatter's favour authorising his use of the land and so ensuring that the possession was not adverse. This seemed to be the case whether or not the squatter knew of this future intention. Clearly, such a rule was extremely favourable to the paper owner and was subject to much criticism on the ground that it could be used in nearly every circumstance to defeat a squatter's claim. Now, however, *Moran* has made it clear that there is no presumption of a licence in favour of a squatter where possession is not inconsistent with the paper owner's planned use of the land. That is not to say, of course, that a licence cannot be implied from the actual facts of the case – as where a squatter is aware of the future plans and *agrees* to occupy pending the instigation of those plans – but it does mean that a claim to adverse possession cannot be defeated merely by the existence of some future plan in the breast of the paper owner. Nevertheless, if possession was once with permission, but then such permission ceased, it may be difficult to prove the relevant intention *if* the adverse possessor's activities on the land remained consistent with the permission, as in *Pye* (no adverse possession) but not in *Blackburn* (successful claim).

Assuming, then, that adverse possession is running against the paper owner, the law of limitation means that she has 12 years from the start date to bring an action to recover possession of the land. Of course, a successful action will stop the adverse possession and any future claim will have to begin afresh. The same is true of other acts which show an intention on the part of the adverse possessor to acknowledge the paper owner's title, as where the squatter pays rent or by written acknowledgment of title before time has expired (ss 29 and 30 of the LA). However, apart from actually initiating proceedings, it is not clear what other actions by the paper owner will be sufficient to 'stop the clock'. In *Moran*, a letter asserting title was not sufficient, although a letter evincing a definite intention to sue may well be (*Shell-Mex*). Once again, it will be a matter of construction of the relevant circumstances. What does seem reasonably clear is that once the limitation period has expired, both the paper owner's right to sue and their title are extinguished by operation of statute (s 17 of the LA). After this date, the conventional wisdom is that no acknowledgment, written or otherwise, and no payment, can revive the paper owner's title (*Nicholson v England*). This should be uncontroversial as it is simply the consequence of the existence of the limitation doctrine. However, the Court of Appeal has held in *Colchester Borough Council v Smith* (1992) that, in some circumstances, a written acknowledgment of the paper owner's title, even after the period has ended, can be enough to prevent the squatter relying on adverse possession in the face of a possession suit by that owner. This remarkable decision is now unlikely to be reversed and it seems to rest on the principle that a *bona fide* compromise of a dispute between two persons (that is, paper owner and squatter), both of whom had legal advice, should be upheld on public policy grounds, even if the 12 year period has run. In other words, a man will be bound by his contract. Unfortunately, this seemingly unobjectionable principle does not, in the context of adverse possession, recognise that it is also a policy consideration – recognised and effected by Act of Parliament no less – that sleeping on one's rights deprives a person of those rights which cannot later be revived by threatening protracted litigation with the adverse possessor. In short, the judgment in *Smith* fails to explain why 'act of the parties' can override the express provisions of an Act of Parliament.

This case aside, in recent years the law of adverse possession has taken on more clarity and certainty, mainly due to the clear exposition in *Moran* and the application in cases like *Minchinton*. Of course, each case will depend on its facts, but at least there is clarity in what those facts are supposed to prove. Indeed, unlike *Smith*, *Moran* was a case favourable to the adverse possessor, both in result and in the substance of the rules it established. That case represents a welcome restatement of the fundamental feudal principle of relativity of title and reminds us of the transient nature of 'ownership' in the law of real property in England and Wales.

Notes

This is a general question on the law of adverse possession, although a good answer will rely heavily on *Moran*, *Pye* and *Blackburn*, being the most recent thorough expositions of the subject. Further matters that could be considered are the social purpose of a doctrine of limitation and the differences between adverse possession and prescription. *Pye v Graham* is likely to be appealed to the House of Lords. The LRA 2002 will emasculate adverse possession as it applies to registered titles; see Question 4.

Question 49

In 1965, Paulus purchased an island in the middle of the River Trout and built a bridge from his adjoining land on the shore. He intended to use the island as a country retreat and throughout

1965–69 made regular fishing trips. He even built himself a cabin, cultivated a small vegetable garden and laid the foundations for a more substantial house in the future. Unfortunately, in 1970, Paulus became ill and had to leave for the clean air of Switzerland. Eventually, the vegetable garden became overgrown, the cabin ran to ruin and finally the bridge fell down, leaving the island as isolated as it was before. However, in anticipation of his departure, Paulus had managed to sell the land on the shore to his neighbour Aquinas who was enthusiastic about the prospects of establishing a salmon fishery but had no use for the island. Aquinas soon set about making enquiries of the local authority for planning permission for his fishery buildings and sought finance from several merchant banks. Again, however, things went awry and Aquinas could not raise the necessary capital. He resolved to wait until his resources grew and was content to use the land for walking and the occasional spell of private fishing. In 1975, Reginald, the local poacher, decided that the land bordering the river and the island were going to waste and he decided to move in and use the land for his own purposes. Shortly, he was rowing regularly to the island where he re-established the garden, rebuilt the cabin and began charging tourists for day fishing permits for fishing from the island's shore. This became so successful that he purchased a luxury caravan and parked it on Aquinas' land where he began to live. There he also planted a vegetable garden, cleared the land to make way for a dirt road and began keeping horses, also to hire to tourists. Eventually, he had to build a fence to keep the horses from straying. In 1978, Aquinas became concerned about the extent of Reginald's activities on his land, although he had tolerated them up to now, having no immediate hope of establishing his fishery. He confronted Reginald and the latter agreed to quit as soon as Aquinas demanded possession. However, in 1979, on hearing (falsely, as it turned out) that Aquinas had raised the money, Reginald extended the fence and placed a locked gate across the dirt road. In 1992, Aquinas eventually raises enough money for his project and seeks possession of the land. Reginald resists and when Aquinas tells him that Paulus will also issue possession proceedings he asserts title to the island as well.

Advise Reginald. The land is of registered title.

Answer plan

The answer needs to deal with the following areas:

- intention to possess;
- discontinuance, dispossession and adverse factual possession;
- acts of possession – equivocal acts;
- implied or actual licences to use;
- acts of possession – unequivocal acts.

Answer

This question requires discussion of the law of adverse possession, for this is at the root of any case that Reginald may have to resist the claims of possession of both Paulus and Aquinas. In order to establish adverse possession, it is clear from *Buckinghamshire CC v Moran* (1989) that Reginald must establish a number of matters. First, that he had an intention to possess the land; secondly, that he possessed the land following a discontinuance or dispossession of the paper owner; thirdly, that that possession was adverse to the paper owner; and, fourthly, that he has been in adverse possession for the 12 year period of limitation specified by s 15 of the Limitation Act (LA) 1980. If all this can be established, then the paper owner's title to the land will be extinguished (s 17) and Reginald will have a title based on possession that will, in these circumstances, amount to a fee simple.

(a) The island

The position in respect of the island seems relatively straightforward. There is no doubt that from 1965–70, Paulus was in possession of the island and his activities there clearly demonstrated his ownership, backed as it was by paper title. However, in 1970, Paulus is forced to leave the country and the following events tend towards the conclusion that he has abandoned or discontinued ownership. This is supported by the implication that Paulus wished to sell all his property but, unlike the land on the shore, was unable to find a buyer. He appears to have no future plans for the island such as would indicate continued interest. Indeed, there seems to be positive proof of abandonment in that the bridge falls down and is not rebuilt, as in *Red House Farms v Catchpole* (1977). Of course, Paulus may argue that he was unable – as opposed to unwilling – to continue possession of the land as his emigration is forced through ill health. However, this is unlikely to rebut the presumption of abandonment so clearly indicated by the facts we are given. In such circumstances, it seems that even very slight acts by a trespasser will be sufficient to constitute adverse possession of the property (*Wuta-Ofei v Danquah*; *Red House Farms*). Secondly, does Reginald make use of the land as if he were owner, combined with an intention to assert ownership? Remembering that this is a case of discontinuance, the re-establishing of the vegetable garden and the rebuilding of the cabin may well suffice but, even if these are regarded as equivocal (*Powell v McFarlane* (1977)), the fact that he charges tourists for fishing rights clearly manifests both an intention to possess and sufficient acts of possession. He is, in fact, treating the land as if it were his own (*Hounslow LBC v Minchinton*). In such circumstances, assuming that Paulus has done nothing in the intervening period to stop time running, the paper owner's title will be extinguished some 12 years later, around 1987 (s 17 of the LA 1980). Finally, as this is registered land, we should note that currently Reginald will be entitled to be registered as proprietor and thus, in fact, he obtains a *de jure* title by statutory conveyance (*Central London Commercial Estates v Kato Kagku* (1998)). Pending such registration he will have an overriding interest under s 70(1)(f) of the LRA 1925.

(b) The riverside property

The position in respect of the property owned by Aquinas is not so easily determined. Clearly, on the facts of the case, Aquinas has not abandoned the property. He has a clear, future use for the property and is actively seeking the money to finance it. There is no discontinuance. It is necessary, therefore, for Reginald to establish that he has dispossessed the paper owner and followed this by his own adverse possession for 12 years.

(i) The position up to 1978

It is clear that, originally, Aquinas had a clear, future intention to use the land and that, as a matter of fact, the acts of the trespasser were not inconsistent with this intention. In other words, up to

1978, Reginald's acts on the land did not preclude the later establishment of a fishery by the paper owner. Formerly (for example, *Leigh v Jack* (1879)), these facts would have justified the implication of a licence in favour of Reginald issuing from Aquinas. The effect of this licence – or permission – would have been to remove any possibility that the possession of the occupier was adverse to the paper owner. However, following *Moran*, it is clear that the existence of future intentions cannot, of itself and without more, justify the court in implying a licence in the actual possessor's favour. So far then, as a result of *Moran*, Reginald's claim is not defeated. However, it is still necessary for him to establish his own possession of the land following dispossession of the paper owner. In this respect, the acts of Reginald may be too equivocal to count. Thus, the planting of the vegetable garden (*Powell*) and the keeping of animals (*Techbild v Chamberlain*) may not be sufficient. Likewise, the building of the fence seems designed as much to keep the animals in as to keep the world at large out. This is also equivocal (*George Wimpey v Sohn*). On the other hand, the clearing of land for the driveway may amount to an act of ownership (*Williams v Usherwood*) although in *Williams* the road was paved and not left as a dirt track. The establishment of the caravan is also important, but again it does not necessarily evince an intention to exclude the world, merely to occupy the land.

(ii) The conversation in 1978

In any event, whether or not the acts of Reginald up to 1978 were such as to amount to factual possession becomes irrelevant in the light of the conversation and agreement between Aquinas and Reginald in that year. While it is true that *Moran* stipulated that no licence for the occupier to use the land can be assumed merely from the fact of the paper owner's future intentions, it did not establish that a licence cannot be expressly created or arise by implication from the actual facts of the case. In our problem, the evidence is clear and overwhelming. Aquinas confronts Reginald some time before the 12 year period has expired and Reginald agrees that he will vacate should Aquinas' plans come to fruition. There is here an implied licence – if not an express one – given to Reginald to occupy and he in turn agrees to this. At this moment, the possession, such as it was, ceases to be adverse and the clock stops. If it is to start again, there must be new acts of adverse possession and it must run for a further 12 years.

(iii) Reginald's change of heart

Eventually, we come to the actions on which Reginald may well be able to base a successful claim of adverse possession. Although Reginald knows of Aquinas' future intentions for the land and at one point agreed to respect them, the change of heart in 1979 brings a different perspective. The extension of the fence and the erection of the gate in response to the perceived imminent fulfilment of Aquinas' plan are the clearest evidence of an intention to possess the land to the exclusion of the whole world, including (indeed, especially!) the paper owner (see also *Lambeth v Blackburn*). The enclosure of the land in this way is without doubt the firmest evidence of adverse possession to date and is similar to the actions of the successful litigants in *Moran* and *Minchinton*. Reginald looks likely to succeed on this ground, providing 12 uninterrupted years have passed. It is irrelevant that Aquinas may have believed for all this time that Reginald was occupying under the former licence for, so long as the adverse possession was not secret (and that is unlikely on these facts), the trespasser cannot be defeated by the intentions of the paper owner alone nor, indeed, because of any additional motive of his own (*Minchinton*). Assuming, then, that, in 1992, 12 years have elapsed, Reginald will be entitled to be registered as proprietor and will again have an overriding interest pending application to the Registrar to be registered as proprietor.

Notes

This question asks the student to apply the general principles of limitation and most questions of this type give facts similar to those situations found in previous cases, as does this one. The decision in *Smith* does not feature in this question but being controversial it is likely to play a part in future problem questions.

Question 50

Hannibal arrived in the country from a long stay overseas in 1980 and sought your help in finding a quiet secluded property for his family as well as an office in town from which to run his optician's business. Unfortunately, Hannibal had difficulty in selling his previous house, but last month he went to view Roman Villas, an old property on the edge of town. After some doubt, he has just completed the purchase of Roman Villas from Vesuvius. Hannibal did not, however, have any difficulty in finding suitable office accommodation and, in 1981, he agreed with Pontius, the freeholder, for a seven year lease of suitable premises in a good location. He soon installed his equipment in the premises, fixing lights to the ceiling and a suitable chair to the floor and, in order to make the place more welcoming for his customers, he refitted one room with oak panelling and a large wall mounted fish tank. In 1988, on the expiry of the lease, he and Pontius agreed a further four year term. Now, in 1992, on the purchase of Roman Villas, Hannibal has decided to work from home and has removed all the equipment, including the lights and chair as well as the oak panelling and fish tank. He moves them to Roman Villas, only to find that Vesuvius has removed the greenhouse, the rose bushes, the garden ornaments, the television aerial and some antique bannisters, all of which Hannibal greatly admired when being shown around the property before contracts were exchanged.

Hannibal comes to you for advice as to whether he should sue Vesuvius for the return of items, only to find that you have been instructed by Pontius to sue him (Hannibal) for the recovery of the equipment removed from the office in town, as it seems that Pontius had arranged to let the premises to a new optician.

Discuss.

Answer plan

The following areas need to be discussed:
- fixtures and chattels;
- the relevance of the distinction – s 62 of the LPA;
- the way to make the distinction – *Holland v Hodgson*;
- tenant's fixtures.

Answer

It is a general principle of land law that what becomes attached to the land becomes part of the land (*Minshall v Lloyd* (1837)). Thus, any articles attached to the land in such a way as to indicate that they have merged with it are treated as the land itself: they are fixtures. In practice, this has important consequences. First, it means that when one person conveys land to another they will also convey all fixtures, save those which have been expressly excluded from the conveyance or can be removed by the vendor by virtue of some exceptional right (see s 62 of the LPA). Secondly, it means that should one person affix articles to land owned by another, those articles fall into the ownership of the landowner, as where a tenant affixes articles to the land they are leasing so that at the end of the lease they fall into the ownership of the landlord. In our problem, although there are two separate factual situations to consider, the essential points at issue are the same. First, whether the articles that are removed from the land by Hannibal and Vesuvius are fixtures so as to make them presumptively liable for such removal. Secondly, if they are fixtures, whether removal could be justified by exceptional circumstances.

(a) Roman Villas

The general rule in relation to Roman Villas is clear enough. All articles which, at the date of the contract, can be regarded as fixtures will belong to the new purchaser (Hannibal) on completion of the contract (s 62 of the LPA; *Phillips v Lamdin* (1949)). If Vesuvius, the vendor, is to have good title to any of the articles he has in fact removed, he must show either: (a) that he removed them before the contract was signed; or (b) they are not fixtures at all but chattels personally owned by him; or (c) that, if they are fixtures, his removal was by virtue of some exceptional right.

First, it is clear that a freehold owner may, at any time before they contract to sell, remove any item from their land as this is part of their normal rights of ownership (*Re Whaley* (1908)). However, in our case there is nothing to suggest that Vesuvius removed the items before the contract was signed and, indeed, we are told that all such items were present when Hannibal was shown around the property prior to signing the contract. In the absence of any other evidence, one can conclude that all the articles were present when the contract was signed.

Secondly, are the items fixtures or chattels, for it is only if they are fixtures that any problem arises? Chattels are personal goods, not forming part of the land and, therefore, not conveyed as such to a purchaser of it. The general test as to whether an item can be regarded as a fixture was summarised by Blackburn J in *Holland v Hodgson*. Consideration must be given to the *degree* of annexation to the land and the *purpose* of annexation to the land. It is clear, however, that the primary test is the degree of annexation and presumptively any item which rests upon its own weight is only a chattel (*Mather v Fraser* (1856)), for a fixture needs to be attached to the land in some substantial way, even though it could be removed quite easily (*Culling v Tufnal*). Yet, there is also no doubt that the answer supplied by this simple practical test can be overridden (or indeed supported) by the *purpose* of annexation. Thus, where affixing is necessary for the proper use of the article and implies nothing about its relation to the land, the item may remain a chattel (*Leigh v Taylor*) and, conversely, items intended to enhance the value of the property may be fixtures even though resting on their own weight (*D'Eyncourt v Gregory*). All in all, whether an article is a fixture or a chattel can only be decided on the facts of each case, bearing in mind the nature of the property, the use of the articles and the physical relation of them to the land itself.

Turning then to the articles removed in this case.

(i) The greenhouse

If the greenhouse is fixed to the land, it will be a fixture, as with the temporary sheds in *Webb v Frank Bevis*. However, there is clear authority that a free standing greenhouse is to be regarded as a chattel (*HE Dibble Ltd v Moore*) and a 'Dutch barn' was still a chattel even though it was founded in sockets in the land to give it more support (*Culling v Tufnal*). It is, then, reasonably clear, that Vesuvius was entitled to remove the greenhouse as a chattel providing that it was not actually affixed to the land in a permanent way or was not part of an ornamental garden designed for the betterment of the land as a whole (see below).

(ii) Garden ornaments

Prima facie, the garden ornaments are chattels as they are, in all probability, free standing and not attached to the land at all. This was at the root of the decision in *Berkley v Poulett* when a sundial and statue on plinths were held to be chattels. However, it is clear from *D'Eyncourt v Gregory* that, if garden ornaments are part of a general garden design, created to enhance the particular house, they will be regarded as fixtures which pass with the land. This is a clear example of the purpose of annexation overriding the degree of annexation (see, also, *Hamp v Bygrave* (1983)). Once again, then, presumptively these will be chattels unless the ornaments are integral to the property. They can be removed by Vesuvius.

(iii) Television aerial

This is a somewhat difficult article to consider as it is clearly designed to facilitate the use of another article (a television) which is so obviously a chattel. However, it is quite common that television aerials are attached to property (for example, on the chimney) and if this is the case, the presumption will be that it is a fixture. This is reinforced by the fact that the aerial can be detached from the television and is not an integral part of it. *Jordan v May* could be of assistance here, for there a fixed electric engine was held to be a fixture even though the batteries which powered it were held to be chattels. On the other hand, *Credit Valley Cable v Peel Condominium Corp* (1980) held a television cable to be a chattel, being for the better use of a television and not better use of the land. Perhaps the only solution is to revert to the basic *Holland* test: the degree of annexation. If this decrees that the aerial is a fixture, it is no reply that it thereby confers a personal benefit on the new owners of the land; so do ornamental statues, fixed greenhouses and permanent tapestries.

(iv) The bannisters

Once again, this will depend on an application of the *Hodgson* test, although there seems little doubt that these will be affixed to the land in what is intended to be a permanent fashion. If fireplaces can be regarded as fixtures (*Buckland v Butterfield* (1820)), surely so must bannisters. Vesuvius is not entitled to remove them any more than he would be entitled to remove the floorboards.

(v) The roses

Here, the position is clear. Roses, as with other trees, shrubs and flowers growing on the land are part of the legal definition of the land within s 205 of the LPA. Thus, they belong to the estate owner and were conveyed to Hannibal when he purchased the land. Vesuvius is not entitled to remove them.

Thus, as far as Roman Villas is concerned, it is clear that the roses and bannisters and probably the television aerial are fixtures. This means they are conveyed to Hannibal with the conveyance – s 62 of the LPA (assuming no express reservation of Vesuvius' title was made). Moreover, there are no grounds by which Vesuvius can claim an exceptional right to remove these fixtures once the purchase is completed.

(b) The office

As noted at the outset, a tenant who brings articles on to the land and then fixes them to it effectively passes title to those articles to the landlord. They cannot, therefore, be removed at the end of the lease unless some special rule so provides. In our case, there are the lights, the chair, the oak panels and the fish tank. However, before we consider whether these are fixtures or merely chattels, one important issue must be considered that may well save time.

There is a general rule that a tenant has a right to remove certain types of fixtures from the land at the end of the lease; that is, that even though in law they are fixtures and within the title of the landlord, the tenant may re-assert ownership for special reasons. One important category of such fixtures are 'trade fixtures' which may be removed by the tenant during the continuance of the lease or (probably) within a reasonable time after its end (*Poole's* case). Of course, this right is lost if the tenant does not remove trade fixtures during the term (or just after), but it is clear that the tenant does not lose the right to remove fixtures attached during one lease which then ends, if that lease is immediately followed by a new term in continuation of it (*New Zealand Government Property Corp v H and M Ltd* (1982)). This is the case here and it seems certain that the lights and the chair can be removed by Hannibal as trade fixtures when he quits. Of course, if they are not fixtures, he can remove them anyway. Indeed, the same may be true of the oak panelling and the fish tank, for we are told they are added to the property for the benefit of Hannibal's customers. However, they are not necessary for trade as such and probably must be considered outside this rule.

In these circumstances, can it be said that either the oak panelling or the fish tank are fixtures at all and merely personal chattels? This also seems unlikely, at least for the oak panelling, as there is authority that panelling (*Buckland v Butterfield* (1820)) and even tapestries (*Re Whaley* (1908), but contrast *Leigh v Taylor*) are fixtures because of the degree of annexation to the property. If this is followed, the oak panelling is a fixture and must remain. The fish tank might be different, as Hannibal could claim that it is fixed to the wall for steadying purposes, not as an attachment *per se* and, indeed, it is a curious item to regard as part of the land. Some help is given by *Viscount Hill v Bullock* where a collection of stuffed animals nailed to the wall were held to be chattels. In any event, however, even if the fish tank is a fixture, Hannibal can claim that he has a right to remove it under another exception, namely, the right of a tenant to remove ornamental fixtures during his lease so long as this can be done without damage to the building (*Martin v Roe*). Indeed, one case (*Spyer v Phillipson* (1931)) suggests that even panelling (assuming it is a fixture) may be removed under this general heading, although it will be rare that this can be done without damage to the premises.

All in all then, the chair and lights can be removed whether they are fixtures or not (the trade exception); the fish tank may not be a fixture but, if it is, could be removed under the 'ornamental/domestic' exception; and the oak panelling is probably a fixture and could be removed under the 'ornamental/domestic' exception only if there is no damage to the premises.

Notes

This is a long question, although really quite straightforward. It concentrates on the definition of a fixture and asks in what circumstances even fixtures can be removed from the land. Case law is important here, although *Holland v Hodgson* (1872) (supplemented by one or two others) is vital.

INDEX